MASTERING SPICE

MASTERING SPICE

Recipes and Techniques to Transform Your Everyday Cooking

Lior Lev Sercarz

with GENEVIEVE KO

Photographs by
THOMAS SCHAUER

CLARKSON POTTER/PUBLISHERS
New York

Published in the United States by Clarkson Potter/Publishers, an imprint of
Random House, a division of Penguin Random House LLC, New York.
clarksonpotter.com

CLARKSON POTTER is a trademark and POTTER with colophon is a registered
trademark of Penguin Random House LLC.

Library of Congress Cataloging-in-Publication Data
Names: Lev Sercarz, Lior, author. | Ko, Genevieve, author.
Title: Mastering Spice: Recipes and Techniques to Transform Your Everyday
Cooking / Lior Lev Sercarz with Genevieve Ko.
Description: First edition. | New York : Clarkson Potter/Publishers, [2019]
Identifiers: LCCN 2018060757 | ISBN 9781984823694 (hardcover)
| ISBN 9781984823717 (ebook)
Subjects: LCSH: Spices. | Cooking. | LCGFT: Cookbooks.
Classification: LCC TX406 .S469 2019 | DDC 641.6/383—dc23 LC record
available at https://lccn.loc.gov/2018060757

ISBN 978-1-9848-2369-4
Ebook ISBN 978-1-9848-2371-7

Printed in China

Book and cover design by ThoughtMatter

10 9 8 7 6 5 4 3 2 1

First Edition

To Lisa, Luca, and Lennon
for bringing joy, flavor,
taste, and fun to my life

CONTENTS

FOREWORD 8

INTRODUCTION
My Story 11
Bringing La Boîte Spice Home 16
How to Cook with This Book 21
Simplifying Home Cooking 22
  How to Be a Planner 24
  Getting Started 28
  Stocking Your Kitchen 30
  Must-Have Tools 33
Understanding Spices 34
The Philosophy and Flavors of My Recipes 42

VEGETABLES
Master Spice Blends 49
Skillet-Braised Fennel 50
Roasted Mixed Vegetables 54
Pan-Roasted Potatoes 58
Potato Gratin 62
Sweet Potato Puree 66
Cabbage and Apple Slaw with Carrots 70
Creamy Carrot Soup 74
Chunky Vegetable Soup 78

PASTA, GRAINS, AND BREAD
Master Spice Blends 85
Baked Penne 86
Stovetop Paella 90
Risotto 94
Farro with Toasted Noodles 98
Chickpea Flatbreads 102
Yogurt Challah 106

LEGUMES AND EGGS

Master Spice Blends 113
Chickpeas 114
Braised White Beans with Charred Spinach 118
Lentils 122
Baked Frittata 126
Shakshuka 130
Olive Oil Deviled Eggs 134

SEAFOOD

Master Spice Blends 141
Sugar-and-Salt-Cured Salmon 142
Poached Salmon 146
Seared Salmon 150
Roasted Whole Fish 154
Chraime: Seafood in Tomato Sauce 158
Seared Seafood with Pan Sauce 162
Steamed Mussels 166
Crab Cakes 170

MEAT

Master Spice Blends 177
Glazed Seared Chicken Breasts 178
Braised Chicken Thighs 182
Roasted Butterflied Chicken 186
Oven-Roasted Chicken Soup 190
Quick Seared Pork Chops 194
Oven-Roasted Meatballs 198
Braised Short Ribs 202
Roasted Rack of Lamb 206
Roasted Rolled Leg of Lamb 210

DESSERT-ING

Master Spice Blends 217
Olive Oil Cake 218
Brown Sugar Banana Bread 222
Fruit Crisp 226
Shortbread 230
Brownies 234
Crème Fraîche Clafoutis 238

CONDIMENTS AND MORE MASTER SPICE BLENDS

Condiments 246
More Master Spice Blends 248

SPICE GLOSSARY 253

INDEX 262

ACKNOWLEDGMENTS 271

Foreword

Eric Ripert, chef and co-owner of Le Bernardin

Simply put, Lior is a magician with spices.

When we first met in the kitchen of Le Bernardin years ago, I was immediately impressed—not only by the depth of Lior's knowledge but by the caliber and range of spices he was presenting to our team. It was clear from the beginning that Lior has a strong understanding of food, cooking, and how best to develop flavors through seasoning. His enthusiasm for travel and global cuisine dovetails naturally with his ability to source spices of the highest quality, as well as his genius in creating unique blends that echo and embody specific regions with their distinct flavors.

Beyond this, Lior is a highly skilled chef who trained in some of the best kitchens, including Daniel Boulud's, which has led to his passion for educating others on the necessity and intrinsic benefits of using spices in cooking. Every chef and home cook should learn how spices elevate food: they can bring happiness and even add intensity, texture, and color to a dish.

This book, like a modern-day spice trade route, takes readers on a culinary journey around the world. Lior's focus on simplicity and basic spice education is approachable, nuanced, and exciting, with an emphasis on the fundamental techniques. Much like our co-created Voyager Collection of spice blends, *Mastering Spice* takes you on a global adventure with seasonings. You couldn't have a better tour guide.

My Story

My goal for this cookbook is simple: I want to show you how easy it is to transform everyday dishes just by adding and changing spices. It's how I cook at home, after cooking as a professional chef for two decades. I rotate straightforward techniques that I've perfected over the years and change the spices and other add-ins for completely new dishes. Rather than swap methods for roasting vegetables or simmering beans, I simply switch the seasonings. This is a great way to learn how to cook: mastering basic techniques makes it easy to master new seasonings.

The dozens of techniques I'm going to teach you are ones that you can count on—always. They're like master recipes; they offer the foundation and process for getting the juiciest roast chicken, the creamiest risotto. In some cases, only the spices vary. In others, supporting ingredients, such as the vegetables that roast under whole fish or the liquids for soup, are swapped, added, or omitted even as the technique stays the same.

After more than twenty years as a professional chef and twelve years as the owner and master spice blender of La Boîte, I'm excited to share all I've learned about cooking with spices. Namely, that a modest investment and minimal effort can result in complex, nuanced dishes. All you have to do to end up with a restaurant-worthy meal in record time is buy a few fresh ingredients and reach into your pantry for spices.

As far back as I can remember, I've loved food. While I can't recall my toddler years in Rome, my mother assures me that I relished all the pasta. I do have memories from living in Brussels as a seven-year-old, though, setting little pots and pans on the radiator to "cook." I remember going with my grandfather to Antwerp, his hometown. He bought me a watch and a cone of fries with mayonnaise. They were the best fries—pure fluffy potato under crisp shells—and that they came from my very strict grandfather makes the memory even nicer.

I was born in northern Israel, and when my parents, sisters, and I returned in 1982 when I was ten years old, we found a horrible culinary environment—a pale shadow of what it is today. The many groups that make Israel diverse and delicious—Iraqis, Algerians, Moroccans—cooked great food, but in their homes, not in restaurants. As in America in the '80s, the conversation around good food simply wasn't happening yet. The kibbutz where I lived was a cash-free communal society—everyone contributed to the whole, including sharing kitchen duties. Everything was flavorless; food was not a celebration so much as a means of survival.

Even though we had to run to the bomb shelter every Monday and Wednesday (the alarm would go off and we'd get up and go, even if it was midnight), I still had a lot of freedom as a kid. On a kibbutz, the kids run free—we lived separately from our parents and only saw them for a few hours a day. I'd go fishing with my friends after school, and then cook our catch for dinner the way my father taught me. When sweet potatoes were in season, we'd build campfires and bury them in the smoldering logs until the skins ashed over and the flesh caramelized. When we craved ice cream or snacks, we'd pick up whatever we wanted from the store and bill our parents' accounts—it was heaven for a kid!

When I turned nineteen, I started my compulsory military service with the Israeli army. I did what was asked and, after two years, got a nice promotion to sergeant. One night, during drills, I was dropped off in the middle of the desert and had to find my way back with only the stars and moon for navigation. I remembered the route from the afternoon exercise, but still I thought, *What the hell am I doing here?*

I was afraid of disappointing my dad, because he had been a paratrooper officer and was proud that I had been chosen for elite training. It was a well-paying job with early retirement and benefits, but it wasn't for me, because I just didn't like the military. I wanted out. I didn't see it as a career. I packed my things, got on a bus, and reported to military court because you can't simply turn down a promotion. It's considered an act of disobedience. After waiting for hours, I was told how severely I should have been treated for my defiance. They could have sent me to jail, but they did something worse—I was shipped out to fight in Gaza. And that was that.

During my three years of service, I felt no fear. People threw Molotov cocktails at us; they dropped refrigerators on us from fourth-floor balconies. It was a strange reality, to say the least.

You develop a different set of values when life and death are involved. Every holiday feast becomes a big deal, even a bite of the most perfect challah is something to remember, because you start to think that tomorrow, this could all be gone.

When I left the army, I realized that I wanted to try cooking and that there was more to food than what I had known. But I wasn't sure where to begin, so I did what most Israelis do after military service and took a big overseas trip. Because my older sister had gone to South America after her time in the military, I did too. I spent a year traveling throughout the continent and cooking for fun. When I returned to Israel, I decided to try cooking professionally.

Israeli chef Gil Frank took a chance on me and gave me a job at Menta, his catering company. Frank said, "I'll hire you because no one has ruined your brain yet." He meant that I hadn't learned how to do things the wrong way at another cooking job, so he could teach me the right way. For the next three years, he did. Frank showed me how to hold a knife, dice an onion, master all the basics. He also gave me a lot of freedom and responsibility and helped me see that cooking could be a career. After three years, Frank said, "You're pretty good at this, so it's time

for me to let you go." I owe Frank a lot, especially for urging me to move on.

With Frank's encouragement, I set out for culinary school in France, because there weren't many options in Israel. Plus, a young Israeli chef I met right after he returned from French culinary school told me he loved it. After looking into cooking schools through the Cultural French Institute in Tel Aviv, I spent a week in France visiting the options. I chose the last place I visited, the Paul Bocuse Institute in Lyon, because it offered classes in baking and management as well as the standard savory cooking courses.

During the two-year program, I learned what I needed to know to succeed as a chef. It wasn't just about cooking, creating, and being inspired—the classes included accounting, purchasing, and nutrition. But I was a hardheaded twenty-five-year-old and grew bored in a classroom. I wanted to cook, not do profit-and-loss paperwork! I found a six-month externship program in Céret in the French Pyrenees, and while I thought that the unique Catalan culture and culinary traditions were very interesting, I was even more intrigued with a book given to me by a culinary school instructor. It was written by chef Olivier Roellinger about his three-Michelin-starred restaurant, Les Maisons de Bricourt in Brittany. This was where the world of spices truly opened up for me.

Even though Roellinger had a strict no-intern policy, he and his wife, Jane, reconsidered after I sent multiple letters requesting an internship. To this day, I don't know what changed their minds; all I know is that they changed my life. They not only took me on as an intern, but paid me, got me an apartment, and introduced me to a new way of understanding spices. Because the world's spice route passed through Brittany's ports, Roellinger incorporated seasonings from around the globe extensively into his cooking, marrying far-flung spices with local seafood and produce. He infamously paired locally caught lobster with a Thai curry sauce—standard fare now, but revolutionary then. The spices had come from the other side of the world but didn't take away from the local cuisine. My mind was blown. When I told Roellinger how excited I was by the spices and how he used them, he encouraged me to pursue my interest. He sent me to the local library and we began researching spices together. He never taught me how to use them; rather, he said, "I don't want you to become me. You have to find yourself."

After a few more years in France, I moved to New York City in 2002 and joined renowned chef Daniel Boulud at his Michelin-starred flagship restaurant. It was a high-volume

I want to show you how easy it is to transform everyday dishes just by adding and changing spices.

and demanding environment, where, as executive chef of the catering arm, I cooked for eight hundred events a year, and not in a restaurant kitchen. We were cooking off-site, at locations that felt more like high-end camping than a Michelin-starred kitchen—we used Sternos instead of stoves and washed our hands in coolers because we had no running water. After six years of that, I was ready for a change.

To figure out my next steps, I took a corporate gig to give me the headspace and energy I needed to start a business plan for my own restaurant. Just writing that proposal confirmed what I suspected: Restaurants aren't for me. I love prepping ingredients and the creativity, but I didn't love the chaos of service, the hours, or the lifestyle.

I wanted to stay in the food world, but I wanted to express myself differently through food. I thought about that first thrill of discovering spices with Chef Roellinger, and how amazing it would be to give other chefs the same experience. All the chefs I met in New York City and throughout the world relegated spices to Indian cuisine or used them sparingly. That seed of inspiration grew into my spice business, La Boîte.

Having a cooking background allowed me to think about spices from a chef's perspective. I created spice blends in terms of sweet, sour, hot, bitter, and savory, and focused on balancing flavors and textures; plus, I related to chefs and their need for quality, cost control, and culinary integrity. Creating a blend starts and ends with conversations. I'm not just making something and giving it to a chef. It's like dating, our process of getting to know each other. Through our conversations, I help them understand if they're using something in the wrong way, they help me understand their ideas, and together we create blends that exemplify their style. They get to take their techniques to new levels with new spice blends, and I'm able to build my business—and I'm always well fed.

When I opened La Boîte, I was a bachelor starting a new company and didn't cook at home much. But within two years, I met Lisa, the love of my life, and before we knew it, we had two sons, and I found myself cooking at home every night for my family and truly enjoying the experience. I was forced—in a good way—to cook more, and to cook more simply. I prefer less fuss, fewer ingredients, and simplified techniques. Ten years ago, I would've trimmed the edges of any rounded vegetable to achieve a perfect dice. Now I keep those curves. As long as the pieces are the same size, they cook at the same rate, and in the end, if cooked with care and the right spices, they're still delicious, uneven edges and all. I am willing to spend time cooking, but not too much time, and, of course, I need my food to taste

great. So I bring spices home from work and use them in everything. Sure, it's kind of R&D, but mainly it's because spices make cooking faster and easier. I don't have time to simmer stocks and mount sauces. Spices give dishes more complexity in minutes. A sprinkle on a salad makes it surprising; a coating on chicken turns it into a restaurant-worthy meal.

Everything I cook is influenced by my life: my early years in Europe, upbringing in Israel, training in France, and adulthood in New York, and now, of course, my work in spices influences my cooking more than anything. When I open a spice shipment at the shop, whether from North Carolina or Cambodia, I'm transported. I taste, see, and smell all the amazing things the world has to offer. When I blend a range of spices, I experience the world coming together, one great dish at a time. While many spices are closely associated with particular cuisines, they're not limited to them; that's the beauty of cooking with spices—they transcend borders and cultures. I create spice blends by balancing flavor and don't constrain myself to their traditional uses; I use curry spices in dessert and cinnamon on meat. No one spice or blend belongs to one culture or place: ras el hanout tastes amazing in a strawberry salad. If you drop the barrier of limiting spices to classic treatments, everything falls with it.

The recipes included here are from my home kitchen—I make them with my wife and kids in mind (or, rather, with my kids running circles around me while I cook!). Everything is simple enough for the inexperienced yet interesting enough for long-time cooks. While these dishes were designed as weeknight meals, they are tasty and unique enough to serve at a dinner party too. Most can be prepared in advance and all are easy, requiring only a few simple tools, supermarket ingredients, and no fancy equipment.

Familiar favorites like seared chicken breast, roasted vegetables, banana bread, and chicken soup can become totally new and exciting every time without the stress of learning a new technique. You don't need to consult ten different recipes for ten different styles of fruit crisps when, with one master fruit crisp technique, you can make Dutch apple pie, peach crisp, berry jam bars, berry and yogurt parfait, and a tropical fruit sundae (see pages 226 to 229).

Once you start regularly cooking with spices, you'll gain the confidence to mix and match the spice blends throughout this book and, eventually, create your own. Yes, there are over two hundred recipes here, but the reality is that you're getting an infinite number of delicious meals when you embrace the adventure of mastering spices.

Bringing La Boîte Spice Home

La Boîte began in 2008: I had a coffee grinder, a bowl, and a business plan that was inflated and seemingly impossible to achieve. Seamus Mullen, a great chef and even greater friend, asked me how much I really needed to open the store. Together, we whittled my original $150,000 estimate down to $30,000. With a bare-bones business structure, I was able to sign a lease on an Upper West Side basement without investors or loans. It was rough at the time, but now I don't owe anyone anything, and that freedom in itself is worth the initial struggle. The three principles that guided me were to evaluate what I really needed; grow with the business, not into it; and never say never. Impossible is only for lazy people!

When I first opened, I swore I wouldn't sell single spices. Now single spices (like cinnamon and cumin)—not blends—are a big part of the business. And who ever thought I'd write a book (let alone three)? I certainly didn't. What I did think was that I wanted to change the way people experienced spices.

What distinguishes La Boîte is that I oversee everything from start to finish. It begins with my culinary background. When I think about spices, I first ask myself, *How would I cook with this?* With that culinary consideration in mind, I then work directly with suppliers because I'm picky about the raw materials. I understand terroir, so I can taste the difference between poppy seeds grown in Australia versus ones grown in Denmark. When I look at peppercorns, I can tell their origins because of their size and shine. There's a seasonality and flavor that comes from terroir. The land itself is what makes one type of cinnamon taste different from another. Freshness is key too. I buy in small amounts so that no spice stays on the shelf for more than a couple of months. Spices may be dry to begin with, but they continue to lose moisture and, therefore, scent and flavor over time (see pages 34 to 41 for more about buying and storing spices).

If you want to understand spices, you need to know where they're from and what their story is. Spices are a pantry item, but their shelf life isn't as long as that of the can of tomatoes or cornstarch you have in your cupboard. Spices are fresh produce that has been dried, so you have to first recognize that they came from a farm where a person grew them, tended to them, harvested them, and readied them to be sold. Nothing about that part of the process has changed for hundreds of years. What makes me different than some of the big spice purveyors you might see in the supermarket is my ability to discern the culinary value of spices when choosing them. I'm not buying spices to sell for the sake of selling; I'm buying spices to help elevate the creations of passionate cooks. And that process starts by finding the highest-quality options.

The best spices come from growers who value sustainability. For example, I buy from a guy who grows the most fragrant, flavorful cardamom on a diversified farm. I asked him, "Why not grow only cardamom?" He replied that it's because he needs his chickens to fertilize the land, and that rich soil is the reason his cardamom is exceptional. I like to seek out small farms like his, ones that practice sustainable harvesting by producing their herbs and spices alongside other items, including vegetable crops and livestock like chicken, goats, and sheep.

I work directly with these unique farmers and also deal with importers. This is primarily an industry of brokers, not passionate growers and chefs. Spices are sold to brokers, who then sell to larger distributors. Most spice sellers view spices as a commodity; they are not even amateur cooks. They think only in terms of price per pound. I think of spices as a key ingredient, so I look for the best scent, taste, color, and freshness. And I seek brokers who know how to identify the same. During twelve years of trial and error, I've been able to find sellers who actually care about the spices and know something about food and cooking. I now have a network of sources I like, and get the highest-quality spices for all 120-plus of my imports. For example, I work with a broker in Indonesia who goes to an island by boat once a year to get some of the most fragrant, complex-flavored cubeb berries. The location is a bit of a mystery, but the cubeb is clearly the best in the world.

We take what we get and work hard to keep the quality high. I'm good at what I do, but I'm not a magician; if a product is a dusty powder with no scent or a bad taste, there is no way I can make it better, so I send it back. Sometimes products just differ from year to year because they are essentially seasonal fresh produce that's been dried. I use my culinary expertise to adjust to those differences. For example, in 2017, the black pepper crop globally was softer and oilier than usual because that year had been especially humid. These soft peppercorns didn't have the same crunch as most years, so I ground them more coarsely to deliver the mouthfeel expected from black pepper. Their oiliness made them sweeter, too, so I adjusted the other spices in the blends to deliver the same pepperiness my customers had come to expect. I strive for that consistency because it's important to deliver a reliable product. Nature is what it is, and I respect that deeply, so I take what nature gives me and play with toasting and grinding spices to maintain consistency in my signature blends.

That's not an option with single spices. Since nature will deliver different degrees of fragrance and flavor, I focus on finding the highest-quality single spices. That effort directly plays into the success of my custom blends too. In making my blends for chefs and food companies, we experiment with the spices the way we would any seasonal ingredients, tasting and balancing whatever unique qualities the spices give us. It's a conversation that helps the chefs and culinary clients create the perfect blend and gives me the joy of experiencing spices in different ways.

My commitment to treating spices like a chef—looking for the best ones available, understanding how they can change in the same way fresh produce does, and then taking advantage of that mutability—has allowed me to expand my company.

Since the beginning, 70 percent of my business has been selling to other professional chefs, mainly blends for savory dishes. On the sweet side, I baked cookies spiced with everything from Urfa pepper to sumac and packed them in tins customized by artists I admire, selling them in my store and online. Now the conversation is broader, and I work with pastry chefs, chocolatiers, ice cream makers, bartenders, breweries, and food companies to make over two hundred blends. The rest of my business is about selling directly to consumers online and in my store, which quickly grew out of that little basement into a small shop in the Hell's Kitchen neighborhood on Manhattan's Far West Side.

I like to believe that chefs and home cooks are interested in my spices simply because they're great, but I'm actually excited to be part of a larger movement in food. The "grandmother" food that a lot of professionals abandoned for decades is now ending up on their menus—dishes like rice and beans, stewed tripe, and even buttermilk pancakes. Chefs are digging deep to find their heritage and culture, and searching to bring authenticity, intimacy, and personality to their food. That journey often involves spices, and I'm here to help them.

I want to do the same for home cooks. We get to taste chefs' homages to their cultures in their restaurants and open ourselves to the world in that way. As home cooks, that exposure to diverse cuisines makes us more willing to use more spice, more excited to explore our own cultures through spice blends. I want to show everyone that blending is simply combining a few spices in a way that makes sense. I don't even insist that you—or anyone, really—need to use my spices. It's more important to me that people learn to embrace spices in the kitchen, to make them part of their daily routines, and to lead richer culinary lives because of them. La Boîte opened as my way of sharing spices and ideas for using them with chefs. This book is my way of doing the same for all cooks.

My goal is that you'll use this book, master what's in it, and then not need it anymore because you'll be able to make these dishes instinctively.

How to Cook
with This Book

Think of this book as your guide to really flavorful weeknight meals with minimal effort. I'm going to teach you dozens of basic techniques and then offer a handful of variations on each, amounting to hundreds of inspiring recipes. Even chefs who are just learning to play with spice blends start with a technique in mind. The better you are at cooking generally, the better you can improvise with spices. The method is what matters; it is the constant. The spice blends will change throughout, as they are the key to delivering totally different tastes simply by reaching into your pantry. Sometimes the base recipe will change forms even as the fundamental technique stays the same. For example, carrot soup turns into a sauce for pasta; a roasted chicken ends up shredded and sautéed with greens; brownies become ice cream sandwiches.

The techniques fall into two general categories: fast and slow. Now that I'm cooking at home for my young boys while also running my company, I'm fully aware that recipes need to be easy for busy home cooks. Easy can be a dish that comes together in minutes or that slowly braises for hours. For my slow dishes, I keep the preparation times short, so the dish is simple to put together even if it requires a long simmer on the stovetop or gentle oven heat. (Don't worry, you don't have to do anything except wait—though sometimes waiting, especially with delicious smells filling your home, is the hardest part.) The reward for your patience is a roast, soup, stew, or braise that you can eat all week or freeze for the future. If you get tired of the leftovers as is, you can try one of the variations that uses the already-cooked dish. As for the fast dishes, they're the sort of meals you can get on the table quickly on any weeknight or when you have surprise guests drop in for dinner.

Once you master the basic techniques, you'll be able to prep the meals even faster, and once you get the hang of using spices every day, you will be confident enough to create your own blends or mix the ones in this book without even measuring. You can start creating your own variations, letting your instincts take over and matching one leftover to other leftovers in your fridge, swapping seasonal produce in the base recipes and combining techniques and dishes to create menus for dinner parties, holidays, and midweek meals.

Simplifying Home Cooking

I was a professional chef for twenty years; now I cook mainly at home for my wife, Lisa, and our two young sons, Luca and Lennon. Even though the dishes I make are far simpler than what I used to prepare in Michelin-starred restaurant kitchens, I've adopted one key professional skill for my home cooking: planning.

This is the biggest difference between restaurant cooks and home cooks—aside from having a crew of dishwashers. Restaurant cooks plan every ingredient order, every prep step, every dish down to the minute. That's how they manage to serve your table's dishes all at the same time in a crowded dining room. In my position as the executive chef of Daniel Boulud's catering division, I took my planning to the next level. On a single summer Saturday, I'd have to do a wedding brunch for five hundred in a winery with no running water, air-conditioning, or even real stoves, then repeat the same on a beach miles away that evening. The only way I got that done? Planning.

Planning for meals at home is far easier. It may seem like a hassle at first, but adding this extra step to your cooking routine will ultimately make it easier and faster. Because I'm so busy between work and the kids' schedules on weekdays, I make large batches of food on weekends and throw half in the fridge and half in the freezer. For the first half of the week, we eat up the fridge stuff, turning the dishes into different meals each night (you'll learn a lot about that in this book). The second half of the week, we choose from the freezer—it could be a repeat of what I made earlier in the week, or something I made last month. That gives us a nice variety. If you "panic cook" from lack of planning, you end up eating the same things over and over, and that isn't inspiring or interesting in the least.

HOW TO BE A PLANNER

The minutes you spend planning can save you hours throughout the week. Here's how to begin.

1.

Make a list.

Before heading to the store, plan what you want to cook for the week and write a list to match. Because spices make up the bulk of my seasonings, most of my grocery list is fresh vegetables, dairy, eggs, and meat or seafood. Everything else—from spices to tomato paste— should already be in your pantry (see pages 30 to 31).

2.

Prep your groceries.

As soon as you get home, wash and scrub all your vegetables and transfer them to clean containers to store in the refrigerator. Rub meats and fish with spices before wrapping and chilling—not only will the meat be extra seasoned by the time you cook it, but you've saved yourself a mealtime prep step.

3.

Read the recipe.

If you're cooking from a recipe, read it all the way through—maybe even twice. Once you have an understanding of the method, pull out all the ingredients, measure them, and put them in separate bowls or containers. Grab the pans and tools you'll need. Make sure you understand what steps must happen in what order—and how much time you need to devote to each step and to the overall recipe.

4.

Count the ingredients.

Count your ingredients to see if they match the number of ingredients in the recipe. That way, if something's missing, you'll know right away and you won't have to run around looking for it in the middle of cooking.

5.

Keep clean.

Being clean and organized is very important when you're trying to work quickly. Here's my process:

- Place a bowl for trash on the counter to make cleanup faster.
- Set a wet paper towel or silicone baking mat under the cutting board to keep it from sliding while you chop.
- Sharpen your knife, if it needs it.
- Set out a bench scraper to transfer chopped ingredients from one surface or vessel to another without mess.

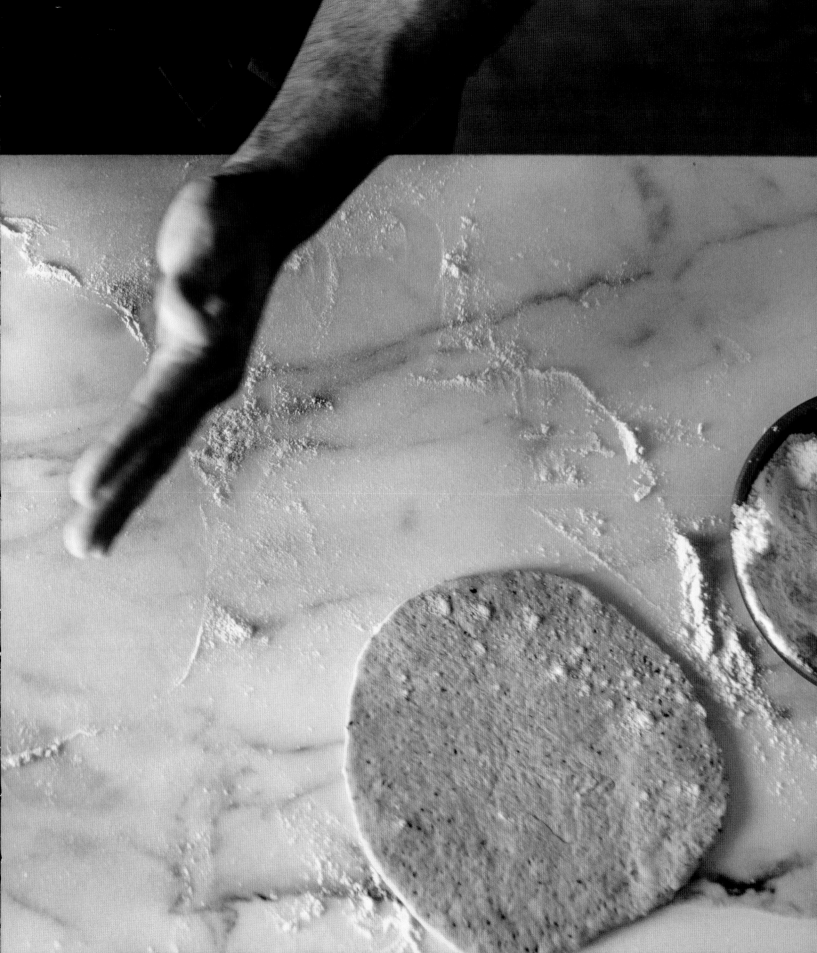

GETTING STARTED

All these recipes have been meticulously tested, so they'll turn out well if you follow them carefully. That said, here are six ways to make cooking with this book even more foolproof.

1.

Make the spice blend before you start cooking.

Choose which blend you want to use and prepare it. A kitchen scale (see page 33) is best for the job, but measuring spoons work too. I've provided both weight and volume measurements so you can use the type of tools you prefer. Have the blend ready before anything else. In fact, you can make a bunch of blends over the weekend or whenever you have time and keep them in labeled jars or airtight containers at room temperature so they're ready to use (see page 37 for information on how to store spices).

2.

Prep the ingredients.

If you followed the How to Be a Planner instructions on pages 24 to 25, you already have your ingredients on the countertop. Some people like to chop, mince, and measure all their ingredients in advance, but I'm a strong believer in prepping ingredients while cooking, and I have written those instructions into the recipes. For example, if onions need to sauté for 5 minutes, you can peel and slice your carrots during that time. Still, I like to prep any ingredients that are used in the first couple of steps of the recipe in order to start off smoothly—if the recipe is a quick one, or all the ingredients get added in the first step or two without much time between them, then, yes, of course, prep all your ingredients before you start cooking.

3.

Cook with your senses.

Even though I've given approximate cooking times and temperatures for these recipes, I know how widely people's stoves and ovens vary. Focus on my instructions for what an ingredient should look, smell, or feel like. Are the potatoes tender? The meat brown? The garlic aromatic? Most important: Are the spices burning? If you get even a whiff of spices beginning to burn, turn down the heat or remove the pan from the heat source entirely. In all cases, adjust the stove's or oven's heat to maintain whatever I call for—a gentle simmer, a steady sizzling. The timing I give may change, too, depending on how high your stovetop's BTUs go, or the thickness of your pan's bottom, so don't be tied to the times in a recipe procedure; rather, use them as guidelines. If a roast hits the desired internal temperature faster than what I say, take it out of the oven. If the greens haven't wilted when I say they should, keep cooking them.

4.

Season to taste.

Ingredients and salt change from place to place. One tomato may need more salt than another, and some salts are, well, saltier than others. When I ask you to season to taste, I'm emphasizing the taste part. You should actually take a spoonful, blow on it, and taste it. Keep adding more salt if needed, and taste after each addition. (And don't forget to stir what is in the pan or pot after adding salt and before tasting!)

5.

Know your variation.

If you're making one of the variations that follow the master recipe, remember which steps you're changing as you cook. In this case, prep any alternate ingredients before you start cooking and set them up in your cooking station in the order in which you're going to use them so you don't forget about them.

6.

Enjoy yourself.

Cooking is fun! Take pleasure in the process and in savoring every bite with those around your table.

STOCKING YOUR KITCHEN

A well-stocked kitchen has both the shelf-stable ingredients and the tools you need to cook a solid meal. Keep staples in your pantry, and all you really need to worry about on a weekly basis are the perishables: vegetables, fish, and meat (plus cheeses, milk, and eggs as needed). In addition to spices (see pages 253 to 261), having the following essentials on hand will make cooking from this book even more streamlined.

PANTRY

Salt. All salt is sea salt. It all comes from the sea, but it is processed and sold in different forms. I use kosher salt and fleur de sel both to season and as a finishing salt, because they're easier to pick up and sprinkle over or into dishes (plus, they are not as salty as table salt, so overseasoning is less likely). Kosher salt ranges in saltiness between brands and also between batches—I use Morton's brand at home, and it's what I tested these recipes with. Morton's is sometimes considered "saltier" than other brands of kosher salt, which is why you always need to add salt slowly and taste the dish continually as it comes together to add the amount of salt that tastes right to you. If you are using a spice blend that contains salt, you may choose to decrease the amount of salt you add to the dish to avoid making the food too salty (the same is true for salty ingredients like Parmigiano-Reggiano, anchovies, and soy sauce). I prefer the iodine flavor of fleur de sel, but it's more expensive than kosher salt and can be harder to find. For large roasts and preserving food, I use gray salt. I love its strong sea-salty taste and crystalline texture, which has more bite and is very intense. Because the crystals are larger, they don't dissolve on roasts and result in a crunchy crust. Whichever salt you

use, be sure to season as you cook. Don't wait until the end. Sometimes you need the salt to draw out moisture as well, as with onions when you want to caramelize them without browning. Everything should taste good on its own at each stage of cooking. You can't taste your food only at the end and expect miracles to happen. Seasoning and tasting as you cook will help you develop your palate too.

Extra-virgin olive oil. I keep extra-virgin on hand both for cooking and drizzling. Look for cold-pressed, single-origin oils. You can splurge on a really good one just for finishing dishes and use a less expensive one for cooking.

Grapeseed or other neutral oil. Sometimes you want a flavorless oil for cooking. I prefer grapeseed, sunflower, or safflower, but vegetable oil works too. For deep-frying, you can use canola oil.

Vinegars. For a potent acid note, use vinegar instead of citrus—its flavor lasts longer and comes through more strongly than lemon or lime juice. I stick with distilled white, white wine, red wine, rice wine, apple cider, and sherry vinegars.

Wine, beer, and liquor. A splash (or more) of alcohol can add a lot to a dish. I cook with red, white, and rosé wines; light beers such as pilsners; and spirits such as rum, port, and vermouth. You don't have

to cook with the highest-quality options, but you might as well buy what you like to drink.

Sweeteners. I always like a little sweetness in my dishes. I buy organic white and brown sugar (because organic makes me feel better about the environment and it still tastes good), honey, maple syrup, *silan* (date syrup), and pomegranate molasses.

Canned tomatoes. I like fresh tomatoes, but I often prefer the consistency, flavor, and convenience of canned tomatoes. That's been a switch from restaurant to home-cooking mentality. I'm not going to peel four cases of tomatoes at home, but I'll keep four cans of peeled tomatoes (whole, diced, or crushed) in my pantry.

Tomato paste. This concentrated paste both adds a vegetable sweetness to dishes and helps thicken sauces. You can buy it in tubes that you can recap or cans. If you have any left after opening a can, transfer it by the tablespoon to snack-size resealable plastic bags and freeze. You can pop them out any time you need some.

Olives and capers. The saltiness from olives and capers has an added briny note, which brings complexity to dishes. I keep black and green olives on hand, usually kalamata and Castelvetrano, respectively. I use brine-packed capers and rinse and drain them before using.

Dried fruit. I love cooking with dried fruit because it's a dense, concentrated type of natural sugar that adds a complex sweetness and soaks up cooking liquids, making the fruit moist, plump, and delicious to eat, while introducing a nice texture to a dish. Plus, spices work well with sweets. Keep raisins, cranberries, dates, and apricots on hand and try to avoid ones with sulfur, because it imparts a nasty taste.

Nuts. Crunchy and fatty, nuts add great texture and taste to savory and sweet dishes. I like to keep pistachios, almonds, pecans, walnuts, and pine nuts on hand. Because they go rancid with all that fat, keep nuts in the freezer for up to three months.

Grains. Rice (such as Bomba, Arborio, jasmine, basmati) and pasta (including couscous) are essential for instant meals. Whole grains such as farro and wheat berries go rancid within three months, so be sure to use them quickly or store them in the freezer for up to six months.

Legumes. I keep both dried and canned beans on hand because I don't always have time to cook the former. Even though dried beans keep for a long time, they can become stale (if you cook stale beans, their skins will come off, resulting in a messy dish, and they may end up unevenly tender). Use them relatively quickly after purchase. Canned beans, such as black beans and chickpeas, should be drained and rinsed before using.

Baking ingredients. Keep all-purpose flour, baking powder, baking soda, and pure vanilla extract on hand. Confectioners' sugar is nice for dusting and sometimes as a main ingredient in a dessert.

Bread crumbs. Coarse panko crumbs and fine plain crumbs work well for a range of dishes, from meatballs to fritters. You can—and should—make spiced bread crumbs too (see page 250). They add an instant hit of flavor and crunch.

Garlic. Look for young plump and juicy heads tightly wrapped in papery skins. If you're using older garlic, be sure to remove the green germ that runs from the root through the top. If you don't remove it, there will be an unpleasant aftertaste in whatever you cook.

FRIDGE

Salted butter. I like the flavor of salted butter much more than unsalted because it's almost like cheese. (Cultured butter is even better!) It's a matter of personal taste. For a time, some people thought salted butter wasn't as fresh as unsalted. Depending on your supermarket, that may be the case, but the salted variety isn't any older than unsalted; it just has a funkier flavor compared to the creamy sweetness of unsalted. I created and tested all the recipes in this book using salted butter, but you can use unsalted if you like. If you choose unsalted butter, you may want to increase the amount of salt in a recipe. Salted butter is especially tasty in baked goods, where salt is crucial to flavor. If the butter turns yellow on the outside, it's not a problem. It's like eating ripe cheese. If it smells rancid, though, toss it out and buy new butter.

Labne. You'll see me call for this strained yogurt throughout the book. Labne is from the Middle East and is almost as thick as cream cheese. It has a creamy, tangy taste and brings an incomparable richness to dishes. You can substitute plain Greek yogurt if you can't find labne; to mimic its texture, place plain full-fat Greek yogurt in a fine-mesh sieve lined with cheesecloth that you've set over a bowl and refrigerate it for a day. The excess liquid will strain out (discard whatever collects in the bowl) and leave you with something very similar to labne. Store the strained yogurt in an airtight container for up to one month. When cooking with labne or strained yogurt, keep the heat low. High heat or boiling will cause the labne or yogurt to break.

Cheese. It just makes everything better. Feta and goat cheese are my go-to options for crumbling into dishes, but I love Parmesan too.

Eggs. These are part of my weekly shopping list. Eggs should be part of yours, too, because they're just as good for dinner as they are for breakfast, and they are very important for baking.

Citrus. I put citrus in nearly everything because it offers sweetness, brightness, and bitterness. I always have lemons, limes, and oranges, and I buy organic because I like using and eating the peel. If the citrus is good, I scrape out the pulp to use with the juice.

Herbs. Cooking with spices means you don't need to buy fresh herbs. If you have them, great. When I buy them, I wash them right away, wrap them in damp paper towels, and put them in a resealable plastic bag to keep them fresh.

Vegetables. I prefer organic and local. It's very wasteful to dump trimmings, so I peel only inedible peels. I don't peel carrots, beets, sweet potatoes, or other thin-skinned vegetables. The skins on organic varieties have a lot of good nutrients and add nice texture too. I scrub the vegetables under warm water before chopping them.

Meat and seafood. I prefer organic and sustainably raised.

MUST-HAVE TOOLS

These are the tools and basic equipment that I consider necessary for a functioning kitchen.

Pots and pans. Buy good stainless-steel, copper, cast-iron, and nonstick pots and pans and you'll have them forever. Higher-quality cookware conducts heat better and more evenly. It's a bit of an investment, but it lasts so long. If it's a pretty piece, you can use it as servingware too. You definitely should have at least one large Dutch oven with a lid.

Lids. Using lids helps you (and your kitchen) stay neat while cooking, but it also speeds up low-heat cooking for tenderizing ingredients. Sometimes you should skip the lid if you want moisture to evaporate, as when searing a steak. More often, though, lids help capture flavor.

Roasting pans. One of my best purchases ever was a heavy Mauviel roasting pan, the kind usually reserved for a whole turkey. But it can roast anything, including vegetables, and be used to braise or as a bain-marie too. Pan sizes range, but don't go smaller than 10 × 15 inches, and make sure the sides are about 4 inches high.

Half sheet pans. These 11 × 17-inch pans with 1-inch-tall rims are as useful for roasting as they are for transporting goods. I use one under smaller baking dishes, too, to catch any drips.

Cutting board. Get a good solid wood or plastic one for all your vegetables, and keep separate ones for fish and meat to avoid cross-contamination. A nonstick baking mat (also called a silicone mat) is ideal for setting under the board to prevent it from sliding while you chop, but if you don't have one, you can center a wet paper towel under the board instead.

Knives. You need three: serrated, paring, and chef's. If you want more, great, but you don't need them. I'm a huge fan of serrated knives, because you don't have to sharpen them. They're good for soft fruit and vegetables and for bread. A paring knife is for peeling thick skins on produce and cutting small items, such as berries. Use chef's knives to butcher meat and fish and chop harder ingredients like carrots and other root vegetables. Keep paring and chef's knives sharp to make cutting faster and safer.

Graters. Both a standard box grater and a fine Microplane grater are essential.

Wooden spoons and silicone spatulas. I use these to stir whatever's simmering on the stove or roasting in the oven.

Food-service gloves. I prefer mixing by hand. If I'm cooking for my family, bare hands are fine. If I'm cooking for others, I use powder-free latex gloves for food-safety purposes. I also wear gloves when I'm chopping onions, garlic, or chiles to keep my hands from smelling. When I'm dealing with raw meat or seafood, I prefer having gloves on too.

Food-service plastic wrap. The small rolls from the supermarket are annoying. Invest in the thinner, more adhesive plastic wrap designed for restaurants and food service. It'll make wrapping anything easier and faster.

Parchment paper. This nonstick paper prevents any baked goods or savory food from sticking to the pan.

Kitchen twine. Twine ties roasts beautifully but has endless uses in the kitchen when you just need a piece of string.

Kitchen scale. This is essential for measuring spices (see page 38) and also helpful for weighing ingredients for baking or whenever you want exact results. I prefer scales used for measuring pour-over coffee, because they're precise and include half-gram increments.

Spice grinder. You can't really cook with this book without one (see page 37).

Stand mixer. Baking is infinitely easier with a stand mixer. You don't exactly need it, but you may want to invest in one if you want to bake more than once or twice a year.

Meat thermometer. This may seem esoteric, but it will ensure perfectly cooked meat and even homemade breads, everything from lamb roasts to challah. In my professional training, I learned how to test the doneness of meat just from the feel of it. After decades of doing that, I still know that an instant-read meat thermometer is the only way to be really sure of the internal temperature of meat.

Vegetable brush. This is another tool that's often neglected. Because I rarely peel vegetables, I use a brush and warm water to get rid of mud and grit.

UNDERSTANDING SPICES

If you care about food, spices should be part of the conversation, because spices often bring out the best in other ingredients.

Can you imagine chili without cumin? Or apple pie without cinnamon? I define spices as anything dried that I can use to season food and drink, sweet or savory. Dried herbs, vinegar powders, preserved fish, dehydrated barks and berries, all are worth exploring—I even consider salt a spice. To get into the world of spices, you need to smell and taste them before you ever cook with them. I recommend placing a little of the ground spice blend or a single spice on your tongue to taste it, or mixing it with a little neutral-flavored oil before trying it. Is it citrusy or smoky? Piney or earthy? Hot or musky? Not all spices taste great straight, but you'll get a sense of what they're like. Sumac tastes tangy, pimentón tastes smoky. If you don't want to eat spices plain, stir some into simmering vegetable or chicken broth and drink the broth to experience how higher temperatures accentuate the spice's depth. When you understand how spices taste, you'll be better able to predict how they will complement the recipe you plan to cook. Here are the essentials to buying, storing, and using spices.

BUYING SPICES

You probably already have spices, so you need to first determine which are worth keeping. You don't need an expert or even a best-by date to tell you when to replace your spices. That being said, I sometimes stage a spice intervention when someone asks me to evaluate the state of their spices. You can do it yourself at home too. Put all your spices out on a table. Smell them, taste them. If they still have a strong smell and taste like something, keep them. Otherwise, toss them. They're just powder. But keep the containers for storing homemade spice blends.

Since you're replenishing your spice stash, you should splurge on the good stuff. You don't have to buy spices from La Boîte, of course, but know that not all brands have high-quality spices in all their varieties. You can get spices from any shop as long as it's a place you trust with quick turnover in stock. A higher price may indicate higher quality. Some of that extra cost may be going to packaging, but most of it should be going to sourcing. If you pay more, you'll probably get a superior product with a more potent scent and intense, fresh flavor. If you pay less, your cheaper product may be fine, but then you'll need to add more to get the same effect as the pricier spice, so you don't actually save any money.

But don't go solely by the price tag. Determine which spices are fresh by looking for bright color. Dried herbs should be green, not brown. Even black peppercorns should be quite black. Generally, whole spices are fresher than pre-ground, but either is fine if you choose wisely. If a spice is sold whole but the jar has lots of dust at the bottom, don't buy it. If there's clumping in pre-ground spices, that's actually a good thing. It means there's moisture, which indicates freshness. That moisture evaporates more quickly in pre-ground spices, making them lose their scent and taste faster, but that's not an issue if you use them up in a short period of time. That's why you should buy smaller quantities more often. Don't buy huge containers—or even relatively larger jars—unless you're cooking huge volumes.

The freshest possible spices are ones you make yourself. It may sound intimidating, but it's actually quite easy. Instead of trashing fresh herbs that are about to go bad, put them on a cookie sheet to dry. You can do the same with chiles, citrus peel, and sliced ginger. If your oven has a dehydrating function, you can use that to make the process go faster. These are all simple solutions for not wasting food.

STORING SPICES

Well, *storing* is not quite the right word. Don't store them away—keep them where you can see them so you'll remember to use them. You're much more likely to cook with spices if you put them near where you prep ingredients. The back of the kitchen counter or a shelf above it are both nice spots. To maximize their freshness, keep them in airtight containers away from extreme sunlight and heat (so not above your stove or on a windowsill with intense daylight).

With your spices in plain sight, you'll likely use them at their peak freshness, which is within three months from harvest. Spices never spoil, and there's no rule about how long they keep, but one year from the date of purchase is as long as you want to store them, whether whole or pre-ground. When you bring new jars home, label them with the date of purchase, writing directly on the jars with a permanent marker or on tape that you stick to the jars.

USING SPICES

Once you become comfortable cooking with spices, you can spoon or sprinkle them right into your dishes by instinct and smell. Until you hit that point, however, measure them carefully using a scale. As we all know, the scale doesn't lie. Spices, whether whole or pre-ground, settle differently in measuring spoons, which can vary in size. Because spices are measured in such small quantities, a little change can make a big difference. The best scales are those designed for pour-over coffee. They are very accurate and often include half-gram units.

Once you've measured your spices, you can decide how to bring out their aroma and flavor. Toasting does bring spices back to life, but there's nothing wrong with not toasting spices. In fact, I don't toast dried herbs or oily spices, such as Aleppo pepper, because they'll burn and become bitter. Heating peppercorns kills their fruitiness, so they should be kept untoasted too.

I also don't toast spices when they're going to toast during the cooking process. When they're rubbed on a roast or tossed with vegetables that are going to be roasted for a long time, they'll toast while in the oven. In anything seared, the spices are making direct contact with a hot pan. If the spices are toasted beforehand, they will end up overtoasted or possibly burnt after searing, diminishing their nuanced tastes or developing an unpleasant bitterness. In Southeast Asia and India, spices are sizzled in oil, ghee, butter, or animal fat while stirring. A dish is then built upon those toasted spices.

For dressings, salads, or other applications in which whole spices won't be cooked, it's nice to toast them first. For small quantities, toast on the stovetop. It's easy and fast to shake spices in a small skillet while swirling the pan over medium heat until fragrant. It'll take three to four minutes. Don't walk away or they'll burn. Babysit that pan and pull it off the heat as soon as the spices smell good. It's better to take them off the heat early when the spices are fragrant because residual heat will keep toasting them. To ensure that doesn't happen, immediately pour the spices into the grinder or another bowl to stop any carryover heat.

For larger quantities (a cup or more), toast them in the oven. This provides a more even heat from every angle (versus the bottom-only heat of the stovetop). Spread the spices on a half sheet pan and bake at 350°F until fragrant, 8 to 10 minutes. Set a timer so you don't forget about them. If you're using the convection setting, cover the baking sheet with another so that the spices don't fly all over the inside of the oven. I'm giving general times here; you should rely on your eyes and nose to determine doneness. It's a very personal decision too. Maybe you like your spices barely toasted, or perhaps you push to the edge of brown. Just don't burn them.

Whether or not you've toasted whole spices, you need to decide if you want to grind them. There's no need to grind spices if you don't want to. You may want to keep spices whole or coarsely ground when you're looking for texture. Tiny bits and pieces can add complexity when you're working those spices between your teeth. Sometimes it's pointless to grind spices because they're so small already, like celery seeds. If you want to infuse a liquid, such as pickling liquid, simple syrup, or spirits, and you don't want to change the color of the liquid, you should keep spices whole as well. But when you do grind spices, you control the speed with which they dissolve in the dish and, therefore, in your mouth. How finely ground the spices are determines how quickly you'll taste them. Ground spices will affect the color of a dish too. Whole spices only add scent and taste.

If you decide to grind your spices, use an electric spice grinder. A mortar and pestle belong in the living room as decoration, not in the kitchen as a practical tool if you don't know what you're doing with them. They're beautiful and amazing tools, but they require skill to use properly. A spice grinder, often sold as a coffee grinder, is the best device for blending. It's great because you can control it without too much effort. I've tried every spice grinder out there and remain loyal to Krups. It works well and doesn't cost a lot. If you use it often, the lid or blade may break, and they can't be replaced. Just buy a new one.

Once you have your spice grinder and spices ready, you can follow my simple technique. If you're working with a single spice variety, just throw it into the grinder. If you're making a blend, here's my tried-and-true method for efficiently and neatly measuring spices and grinding them:

1. Gather all the spices you want to use.

2. Set out a scale, spice grinder, and two small bowls or ramekins.

3. Put one bowl on the scale and tare the scale to zero, with grams as the unit measurement.

4. Measure out one of the whole spices into the bowl on the scale. Be sure to measure only one type at a time so you can adjust the quantity or fix any measuring mistakes as needed.

5. Transfer the whole spices to a small skillet if toasting, the grinder if grinding, or the other bowl if keeping them whole. If you're measuring a pre-ground spice, put it in the other bowl after measuring it into the bowl on the scale.

6. Repeat with the remaining spices, transferring them to the correct vessel and taring the scale each time you put the empty bowl back on it.

7. If you're toasting spices (see page 37), toast them now.

8. If you've toasted spices, transfer them immediately to the grinder while they're hot, along with any other spices that should be ground. You should grind toasted spices right after they come off the heat. The residual heat helps them blend more evenly with other spices. If you haven't toasted any spices, grind whatever's in the grinder. If the whole spices are just spinning around the blade, start by gently shaking the grinder as you push the On button. If that doesn't work, add more or add ground spices to help everything move more evenly around the blade.

9. Immediately transfer the freshly ground spices to the bowl with the pre-ground spices, if there are any. Get the spices out of the spice grinder using a dry pastry brush. Brush out whatever's stuck to the lid too, and sweep the bristles around the edges of the grinder and blade.

10. Immediately mix all the spices in the bowl. The heat from grinding the spices helps them adhere to the pre-ground spices and keeps the blends in well-mixed suspension.

You can now use the spices right away or store them in an airtight container for up to two months. Use an empty spice jar or airtight container and label it with the contents and date. I'm all about efficiency when it comes to cooking, and I encourage you to make spice blends whenever you have time, and then keep them on hand. If a spice blend is ready to use, you'll use more of it.

If you're fanatical about cleaning, go ahead and clean your spice grinder. Otherwise, it's totally fine if there's a little flavor left from the blend. It's also fine to clean the grinder by simply wiping it out with a damp paper towel and air-drying.

Once you've made enough of the blends from this book, you'll be ready to spice dishes on your own. The best way to determine how much spice to add is to start by tasting the spice you're using and then tasting as you cook—something you should always do! If you don't try a spice before using it, you're gambling, and a lot could go wrong. Some spices have stronger scents than flavors, so you need to taste as you cook. If you don't, your dish could end up too bland from not adding enough or inedible from adding too much. In some cases, as with paprika, adding too much won't taste terrible, but it may make your sauce too thick. Anything with heat—namely ground chiles and peppercorns—should be added in small amounts. Some start subtle but develop more heat over time.

When tasting your dishes, be open to adventure and experimentation, remembering that specific spices aren't limited to particular uses. My goal—for both my company and this book—is to make single spices and spice blends a culinary tool for you to use however you want. Growing up in Israel, I wondered why the soup spice blend in every home's pantry was used only in soups. Why not on fish? Or vegetables? When I asked my mother, she replied, "Who do you think you are? You can't use this for something else. It was made only for soup by smart people." Okay, maybe. But no. I think spices—alone or in blends—are worth exploring in endless ways. That's how La Boîte started. I created blends with no specific uses. They weren't designed for a particular country's cuisine or for meat versus vegetables. I want cooks to feel inspired; I don't want to tell people how to use spices. If you don't say what the spice blend is meant for, people are more likely to experiment with it.

That philosophy worked well when I sold primarily to professional chefs. They're in the habit of tasting every ingredient and then intuiting how to proceed. When I started selling more to home cooks, I learned that they're afraid to experiment in the same way. But don't be. Go for it!

Not only should you be open to tossing different spices into dishes as you cook, you should boldly create your own blends too. When you're making a spice blend, don't worry about what I like or what anyone else likes—it's about what *you* like. Think of a spice blend as an idea. You're always looking for balance. First, decide which spices you'd like to put together. Next, decide which spices to toast, which to keep whole, and which to grind. If you're making a blend for a specific dish,

gather the other ingredients, then think of what could work and what won't. You can even substitute spices for fresh ingredients. This is especially true of onion, garlic, herbs, and chiles. There isn't an exact conversion for any of these ingredients, so start with a little and keep tasting until you end up where you want. Finally, taste again. When you taste a spice mix raw before using it, it's a good indication of how it will end up tasting in the dish. For example, if you barely get any heat from it, your resulting dish won't be spicy. If it's super hot, your dish will be too. At this point, you can still adjust the spices for balance to your taste.

The other thing you can adjust to your taste is salt. Many recipes out there say to season with salt and pepper. Not everything needs salt and pepper, but everything needs sodium and heat to taste good. I like to play around with how I add those. Ingredients such as soy sauce, feta cheese, capers, and celery seeds have a lot of sodium and mimic saltiness. Any form of peppercorns or chiles can deliver heat, as can the warming heat of mustard and ginger. You also need fat (such as oil), acid (like lemon or vinegar), sweetness (as in fruit and molasses), and bitterness (think coffee or turmeric).

After you've mastered using spices, you must remember one thing: don't burn them. You want a little bitterness to balance a dish's flavor profile, but it should never be from burnt spices. They can ruin a dish. When people tell me they don't like spices and describe what they taste, they're describing burnt spices. If you smell spices starting to burn on the stovetop, lower the heat or take the pan off the heat altogether. If they're scorching against a dry pan, add fat or water and scrape them up before they stick. If they're burning in the oven, stir or rotate the ingredients if they're burning on the bottom or tent them with foil if they're burning on top.

The other thing to remember is that you should try spices with everything you eat and drink, from coffee to dinner to dessert. Go ahead and try a little with different spices to get a better idea of how they can enhance a dish. If you don't like the taste of one spice with a particular dish, try another spice or sprinkle on a blend. I promise you that everything tastes better with spices.

The Philosophy and Flavors of My Recipes

The one thing all the recipes here have in common is spices. Other than that, they defy categorization. I was born and raised in Israel, trained as a chef in France and America, and now live in New York City. My ideas come from those experiences as well as from travel. I don't worry too much about sticking to traditions. Tradition is great, but you can create your own in the kitchen. Everyone adds something to the canon. I have a lot of respect for heritage and culture, but ingredients, technology, and everything else changes. It's okay—important, even—to uphold values, but express them in a different style. For example, I was raised with the Middle Eastern standard of hospitality. There was always enough food in the fridge for everyone in the community. Now in New York, I have enough in my freezer to feed fifty, but the food is totally different from what we had on the kibbutz.

Even in terms of classic dishes and seasonings, I believe that it's okay to change them or combine them with others. I don't think of it as fusion, though. It's more like infusion. For example, I love chipotle chile powder but don't restrict it to Mexican cuisine. It's still just chile, so I merge cultures and use it in shakshuka, a Middle Eastern dish.

Don't be afraid to experiment with spices from around the world in the kitchen. Don't worry about doing things the "right" way. You are you, and the sooner you understand that in the kitchen—and in life—the better. There are many countries I've never lived in or visited, so I'll never do true versions of their food. But that doesn't mean I can't be inspired by reading about their food, tasting it in restaurants, or getting to know chefs from those places. If you approach other cuisines, cultures, and, most important, people with respect and humility, you can use their seasonings any way you like with confidence.

Whichever spices you're using, you need to first consider balance. I want fat, acid, salt, bitter, and sweet. That's a complete flavor profile, but one or two can be more dominant than the others. I like as many layers of flavor as possible while still highlighting those one or two main ones. And I do so through technique as well as seasoning. It's a smarter way of cooking. For example, I roast or sauté vegetables to concentrate their flavor before putting them in soup (see page 78). You get complexity with acid and bitterness and think you're tasting more salt, which allows you to use less salt.

Once you have a handle on these basics, you can start playing with more complex combinations. You don't always need or want smoke, but if you use it, it needs to be balanced with sweet. Acid is something people tend to ignore, but its brightness and sharpness are as important as salt and heat. I always like a little heat, even if it's just in the form of ginger or mustard. That heat sensation complements salinity and sweetness. This flavor balance is the cornerstone for these recipes. Build on the foundation for an endless feast.

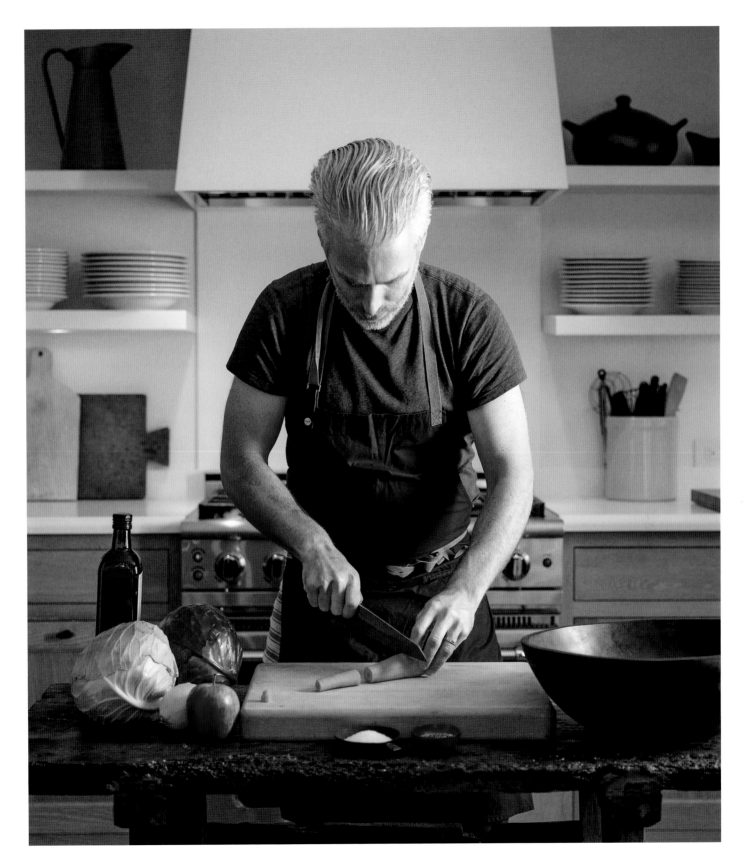

VEGETABLES

VEGETABLES

Even though I like eating meat, I primarily cook vegetables at home. Not only do I love their wide and delicious range of flavors and textures, I also value their flexibility—I can apply a variety of techniques to them. While it can sometimes be more challenging to coax satisfying flavors out of vegetables—they don't come with the built-in luscious fattiness of meat—it makes cooking them more exciting.

Spices can temper the sharpness of raw leaves in salads, brighten the mellow sweetness of roasted roots, add complexity to subdued potatoes, and turn water into flavorful vegetable broths. People who think they don't like carrots may discover they love them when they're blended with spices such as cumin and smoked paprika in soup (see page 74). Fans of roasted vegetables will be thrilled to find out how much tastier they can be when coated in spices like fennel seeds and cinnamon (see page 57).

Though vegetables themselves are fresh and need to be purchased regularly, the seasonings that go on them don't have to be. Rather than remembering to buy fresh herbs and then worrying about finishing them before they go bad, you can season vegetables with dried herbs and spices instead to bring a lot of bold flavor and character to the vegetables. The recipes that follow are the easy dishes that I make regularly at home. But I often stir spices into whatever vegetables I'm cooking, since their fresh flavors, whether naturally sweet or bitter, complement a range of spices so well.

MASTER SPICE BLENDS

for stirring into sautéed greens
5 tablespoons ajowan (15 grams)
2 tablespoons dried dill weed (5 grams)
½ teaspoon peperoncini (dried Calabrian chile; 1g)
3 tablespoons dried cilantro (3 grams)
2 teaspoons dried mint (2 grams)

Toast the ajowan (see page 37), then immediately mix with the dill and peperoncini. Crush the cilantro and mint with your fingers and stir them into the mix.

for vinaigrettes and creamy salad dressings
2 teaspoons dried onion slices (3 grams)
1 tablespoon plus 2 teaspoons dried mint (5 grams)
1½ teaspoons nigella seeds (5 grams)
2 tablespoons dried rose petals (1 gram)
½ cup dried za'atar leaves (15 grams)

Finely grind the onion slices, then immediately mix with the mint, nigella seeds, and rose petals. Crush the za'atar leaves with your fingers and stir into the mix.

for stirring into dips for crudités
1 scant cup dried tarragon (15 grams)
¼ teaspoon Muntok white peppercorns (1 gram)
3 tablespoons dried basil (3 grams)
2½ teaspoons dried dill weed (2 grams)
¾ teaspoon granulated dried lemon peel (2 grams)

Finely grind the tarragon and peppercorns together, then immediately mix with the basil, dill, and lemon peel.

SKILLET-BRAISED FENNEL

skillet-braised fennel with citrus, caraway, and celery seeds

In this master recipe, fennel seeds reinforce fresh fennel's bite. Celery and caraway seeds combine for a savory edge that complements the sweet orange and raisins.

SERVES 4 TO 6

MAIN SPICE BLEND

1 teaspoon fennel seeds (2 grams)
½ teaspoon caraway seeds (2 grams)
½ teaspoon celery seeds (1 gram)
½ teaspoon Urfa pepper (1 gram)

Mix together the whole fennel seeds, caraway seeds, celery seeds, and Urfa.

FENNEL

2 medium fennel bulbs, bottoms trimmed, cut
   into 8 (½-inch) wedges each
Extra-virgin olive oil
Kosher salt
1 orange, ends trimmed (leave the rest of the peel on),
   cut into 8 (½-inch) wedges
¼ cup golden raisins
Juice of ½ lemon
1½ tablespoons sherry vinegar

MAKE AHEAD

The pan-braised fennel can be refrigerated for up to 1 week.

Fennel is one of the most versatile vegetables, especially when pan-roasted and braised as it is here. Its fresh licorice-like bite mellows into a caramel sweetness, which tastes great hot, warm, or cold. It's good with rack of lamb (see pages 206 to 209), roast chicken (see pages 186 to 189), or roasted fish (see pages 154 to 157). For a vegetarian meal, pair it with any grain (see pages 94 to 101) or legume (see pages 114 to 125). Or turn it into a salad or sauce as in the recipes on page 53.

1. To prepare the fennel: Put the fennel wedges in a large bowl, drizzle with enough oil to evenly coat, and sprinkle with the main spice blend and a generous pinch of salt. Toss to coat.

2. Heat a 12-inch skillet over high heat for a minute. Add the fennel in a single layer, arranging the wedges in tight concentric circles, leaving no space between the pieces (reserve the bowl that held the spiced fennel). Reduce the heat to medium-high and cook until the fennel is deeply browned in spots but not burned, about 3 minutes.

3. Use tongs or a small offset spatula to flip all the fennel wedges and cook until the bottoms are browned, about 5 minutes. Flip the pieces again and reduce the heat to medium. Cook, flipping the pieces and rotating the skillet as needed to redistribute hot spots and prevent any burning, until the fennel wedges are evenly browned, about 2 minutes. Return the fennel to the reserved bowl.

4. Add enough oil to the skillet to coat the bottom (about 2 tablespoons) and place the orange wedges in a single layer, spacing them apart. Reduce the heat to medium and cook, turning once, until browned, about 2 minutes per side. Transfer to a plate.

5. Quickly return the fennel to the skillet, arranging it in the same tight concentric-circle pattern. Fit the orange between the fennel in concentric circles. Add ¼ cup water to the bowl that held the fennel and then pour it into the skillet along with any spices and accumulated juices.

6. Scatter the raisins on top, then add the lemon juice and sprinkle with the vinegar. Cover and adjust the heat to maintain a low simmer, turning the fennel and orange slices just once as they cook, until the fennel is tender with just a little bite and has an even caramel color, about 15 minutes. Uncover, remove the pan from the heat, and serve hot, warm, or at room temperature.

*caramelized fennel salad with pecorino, green olives, and almonds

SKILLET-BRAISED FENNEL

FIVE MORE RECIPES

caramelized fennel salad with pecorino, green olives, and almonds*

You can make this salad right after cooking and cooling the master recipe or up to a week later. The saltiness of the olives and cheese is really nice with the sweet vegetables and fruit.

Follow the braised fennel recipe on page 50. Cool completely, then transfer everything to a large bowl. Add ½ cup pitted and halved green olives and ⅓ cup toasted sliced almonds. Drizzle with olive oil to lightly coat and gently toss. Transfer to a serving platter and use a vegetable peeler to shave pecorino cheese on top.

white wine–braised fennel with dried cranberries

Using white wine instead of vinegar in this braise makes fennel even sweeter, but the tartness of dried cranberries balances it nicely. Dried basil and oregano bring a deep herbaceousness to the dish.

SPICE BLEND

¼ teaspoon freshly ground black pepper, preferably Tellicherry (1 gram)

½ teaspoon caraway seeds (2 grams)

1 tablespoon dried basil (1 gram)

2 teaspoons dried oregano (1 gram)

Mix together the pepper, whole caraway seeds, basil, and oregano. Use this spice blend instead of the main spice blend in the braised fennel recipe on page 50.

Follow the braised fennel recipe, substituting ¼ cup dried cranberries for the raisins and 2 tablespoons dry white wine for the sherry vinegar in step 6.

coconut milk–glazed fennel with turmeric and mint

Fennel goes golden with the addition of turmeric, which has a bitterness that is tempered by creamy coconut milk. Mint and lemongrass combine for a sunny freshness.

SPICE BLEND

1 teaspoon ground turmeric (1 gram)

1 teaspoon dried mint (1 gram)

½ teaspoon ground lemongrass (1 gram)

¼ teaspoon ground chipotle chile (½ gram)

Mix together the turmeric, mint, lemongrass, and chipotle. Use this spice blend instead of the main spice blend in the braised fennel recipe on page 50.

Follow the braised fennel recipe, adding ½ cup coconut milk along with the lemon juice and vinegar in step 6.

braised fennel with gremolata

Gremolata, an Italian garnish of bread crumbs, fresh parsley, and garlic, becomes more intense when made with dried spices. Here it's folded into the cooked fennel just before serving, rehydrating in the pan sauce while retaining its bite.

Follow the braised fennel recipe on page 50.

In step 6, after uncovering the pan, add ½ cup panko bread crumbs, 2 teaspoons dried parsley (2 grams), and 1 teaspoon finely ground dried garlic slices (2 grams). Fold the gremolata into the fennel mixture until evenly distributed and simmer for an additional minute before serving.

vegan fennel "aioli"

Soft braised fennel replaces egg in this vegan aioli, which is as creamy and smooth as mayonnaise, but with complex flavors from the spiced vegetables. This sauce is great with grilled meat or fish or crab cakes (see pages 170 to 173).

Follow the braised fennel recipe on page 50. Cool completely, then transfer 1 packed cup of the fennel wedges to a blender (save the citrus and raisins for another use), along with 1 garlic clove, 1 tablespoon apple cider vinegar, and 1 teaspoon Dijon mustard. Blend until smooth, scraping the bowl occasionally. With the machine running, add olive oil, 1 tablespoon at a time, until the mixture has the consistency of aioli (you'll need about 6 tablespoons, but the total amount will depend on the moisture in the fennel). Season to taste with salt.

Makes about 1⅓ cups

ROASTED MIXED VEGETABLES

sumac roasted vegetables with fennel seeds

The flavors in this master recipe are all about balance—whole fennel seeds soften in intensity and counter the heat of Aleppo pepper; sumac's tartness is rounded out by the warmth of cinnamon.

SERVES 8 TO 12

MAIN SPICE BLEND

1 tablespoon plus 1 teaspoon fennel seeds (10 grams)

2 teaspoons sumac (7 grams)

½ teaspoon pimentón (smoked paprika; 2 grams)

½ teaspoon Aleppo pepper (1 gram)

½ teaspoon ground cinnamon, preferably Vietnamese (1 gram)

Mix together the fennel seeds, sumac, pimentón, Aleppo pepper, and cinnamon.

VEGETABLES

3 tablespoons sherry vinegar

5 tablespoons extra-virgin olive oil, plus more to taste

Kosher salt

12 large Brussels sprouts, trimmed and halved lengthwise

6 large radishes, scrubbed and quartered

6 large garlic cloves, peeled

5 baby beets, scrubbed and quartered

5 baby turnips, scrubbed and cut into ½-inch wedges

3 medium carrots, scrubbed and cut into 1-inch chunks

3 large shallots, trimmed and cut into ½-inch wedges

1 medium sweet potato, scrubbed, quartered lengthwise, and cut crosswise into 1-inch-thick slices

1 large celery root, peeled and cut into 1-inch cubes

MAKE AHEAD

The roasted vegetables can be refrigerated for up to 1 week.

I used to be all about high-heat roasting, but the great chef Ana Sortun taught me to "slow it down, let it cook." That lesson applies here. By roasting the vegetables longer at a lower temperature, the spices infuse them without burning and the natural sugars caramelize beautifully. Because vegetables are so easy to prepare, inexpensive, healthy, and delicious, I purposefully roast them in big batches; they keep nicely in the refrigerator and are worth having on hand for dinner all week long. In fact, I pull them out of the fridge to eat straight from their containers for midday snacks and even breakfast. The produce mix here reflects my preferences, but you can use any combination of your favorite vegetables. The proportions are for about 5 pounds of raw vegetables total. While you want to cut all the vegetables into roughly the same size so they cook at the same rate, you can play with the shapes to make the dish look more interesting. Try slicing at an angle or cutting long sticks.

1. To roast the vegetables: Position racks in the upper and lower thirds of the oven and preheat the oven to 375°F. Line two half sheet pans with foil.

2. Combine the spice blend, vinegar, oil, and 1 teaspoon salt in a very large bowl and stir to mix well. Add the Brussels sprouts, radishes, garlic, beets, turnips, carrots, shallots, sweet potatoes, and celery root and toss well until evenly coated.

3. Divide the vegetables between the prepared pans and spread them evenly. Roast, stirring the vegetables and switching the positions of the pans halfway through, until tender, 45 to 60 minutes. Drizzle with more oil, season to taste with salt, and serve hot, warm, or at room temperature.

PAN-ROASTED POTATOES

crispy herbed skillet-fried potatoes

In this master recipe, the blend of garlic, bay leaves, sage, and thyme is reminiscent of classic American poultry seasoning (and would taste great on chicken or turkey).

SERVES 6 TO 8

MAIN SPICE BLEND

4 whole dried bay leaves

1 teaspoon dried sage (1 gram)

1½ teaspoons dried thyme (1 gram)

1 teaspoon Muntok white peppercorns (3 grams)

2½ teaspoons dried garlic slices (4 grams)

Finely grind together the bay leaves, sage, thyme, peppercorns, and garlic.

POTATOES

Extra-virgin olive oil

2 pounds Yukon Gold potatoes (about 3 medium), scrubbed and cut into ¾-inch chunks

Kosher salt

MAKE AHEAD

The potatoes can be refrigerated for up to 1 week. Reheat in a skillet or oven to crisp the outsides again.

This stovetop-roasting technique gets potatoes crisp on the outside and creamy on the inside in less than thirty minutes, start to finish, without the need to preheat the oven or dirty more than one pan. Spices create a flavorful crust and keep the potatoes tasty even after a week in the fridge. These easily turn into a creamy puree or a salad (see page 69).

1. To cook the potatoes: Coat the bottom of a large nonstick skillet with oil (3 to 4 tablespoons), then heat over high heat. When the oil shimmers, add the potatoes, season them very generously with salt, and spread them in a single layer (this will prevent the spices from hitting the hot oil directly and burning). Sprinkle the spice blend over the potatoes and stir well to evenly coat the potatoes.

2. Cover and cook, stirring and scraping up the browned bits from the bottom of the pan every 5 minutes or so, until the potatoes develop a deep brown crust and are almost tender, about 10 minutes. If the spices threaten to burn, reduce the heat. Every time you lift the lid, carefully tilt it to let the condensation on the lid drip back into the pan.

3. Carefully add ¼ cup water to the skillet, immediately cover, and reduce the heat to low. After the oil popping stops, uncover and stir the potatoes. Cover and cook until the potatoes are completely tender and a little glazed, about 5 minutes. Remove from the heat and serve hot or warm.

*crushed roasted potatoes with pistachios

PAN-ROASTED POTATOES
FIVE MORE RECIPES

spicy saffron and coriander crusted potatoes

Whole coriander and ajowan seeds toast along with the potatoes and offer great texture against the creamy saffron-infused potatoes.

SPICE BLEND

½ teaspoon peperoncini (dried Calabrian chile) or red pepper flakes (1 gram)

Pinch of saffron

2 teaspoons ajowan (2 grams)

1 teaspoon coriander seeds (2 grams)

Finely grind the peperoncini and saffron together and immediately mix with the whole ajowan and coriander seeds. Use this spice blend instead of the main spice blend in the pan-roasted potatoes recipe on page 58.

creamy herbed mashed potatoes

Classic French potato puree (aka American mashed potatoes), creamy with milk and butter, tastes so much richer and more complex with potatoes that have been roasted with spices first.

Follow the pan-roasted potatoes recipe on page 58 through step 2.

In step 3, add ⅔ cup whole milk after the potatoes are completely tender and a little glazed. Simmer, uncovered, stirring occasionally, until the potatoes are starting to fall apart, about an additional 5 minutes. Transfer to a food mill along with ½ cup cold salted butter cut into cubes. Pass through the food mill, then season to taste with salt. For a super-smooth puree, pass it through a fine-mesh sieve, if desired. Serve hot.

crispy duck fat potatoes

Duck fat makes potatoes taste better—period. It gives them a deep, meaty savoriness. Many markets sell rendered duck fat in the meat section.

Follow the pan-roasted potatoes recipe on page 58, substituting duck fat for the olive oil in step 1. You will need 3 to 4 tablespoons to coat the bottom of the skillet.

crushed roasted potatoes with pistachios*

Using a fork to gently crush crispy-tender potatoes creates cracks, so lemon juice and the spice-infused oil from the pan can seep into the fluffy center of each potato. For an even more indulgent dish, drizzle high-quality extra-virgin olive oil over the potatoes as well.

Follow the pan-roasted potatoes recipe on page 58 through step 2.

In step 3, after the potatoes are glazed, transfer them to a serving platter and gently crush with a fork. Drizzle with 1 tablespoon fresh lemon juice and then with the oil from the skillet. Top with ⅓ cup toasted chopped pistachios.

potato salad with bacon, nigella, and lime

Imagine regular potato salad with loads of crisp bacon and a creamy dressing with the pop of tasty seeds, and you'll have a sense of how good this is. The potatoes themselves carry a lot of savory flavor from the nigella and celery seeds, which are boosted with the tang of labne and lime juice and the saltiness of bacon.

Follow the pan-roasted potatoes recipe on page 58. Cool to room temperature, then transfer 3 cups of the potatoes to a large bowl. Eat the rest hot or save for another use. Add ⅓ cup labne or plain Greek yogurt, 1 tablespoon fresh lime juice, ¾ teaspoon nigella seeds (2 grams), ½ teaspoon celery seeds (1 gram), and 2 tablespoons crumbled cooked bacon. Fold until well mixed, then season to taste with salt. Top with more crumbled bacon, if you'd like.

POTATO GRATIN

rosemary and thyme potato gratin with bay leaves

In this master recipe, the mix of bay leaves, rosemary, thyme, garlic, and pepper tastes distinctly French. The resulting gratin ends up versatile enough for any menu.

MAKES ONE 8 × 11-INCH GRATIN
SERVES 8 TO 12

MAIN SPICE BLEND

5 whole dried bay leaves

2 tablespoons dried rosemary (2 grams)

1 tablespoon dried thyme (2 grams)

1 tablespoon dried garlic slices (5 grams)

½ teaspoon black peppercorns, preferably Tellicherry (2 grams)

Finely grind together the bay leaves, rosemary, thyme, garlic, and peppercorns.

GRATIN

1 tablespoon salted butter, plus more for the baking dish

2 medium yellow onions, finely diced

Kosher salt

¾ cup whole milk

¾ cup heavy cream

3½ pounds Yukon Gold potatoes (about 5 large), scrubbed

2½ ounces Gruyère cheese

MAKE AHEAD

The gratin can be refrigerated for up to 1 week.

This gratin is kind of French. It has the requisite butter, milk, and cream, but I use onions too—a debated addition—and, of course, spices. To infuse each layer of the potatoes with the spices and salt, I simmer both in the cream rather than sprinkle them on the potatoes. That trick works with whichever seasonings you choose from the options on page 65. Any leftovers taste even better when fried into crisp cubes, as on page 65.

1. To make the gratin: Preheat the oven to 350°F. Line a half sheet pan with parchment paper. Butter a 2-quart (8 × 11-inch) baking dish and set it on the lined half sheet pan.

2. Melt the butter in a large saucepan over medium heat. Add the onions and stir to coat with the butter, then add the spice blend and season with salt. Stir well, cover, and reduce the heat to medium-low. Cook, stirring occasionally, until the onions are soft, about 3 minutes.

3. Add the milk and cream, stir well, and reduce the heat to maintain a low simmer. Cook for about 5 minutes to infuse the liquids with the spices. Season very generously with salt. Taste it; it should taste very salty—the potatoes will remain unseasoned, so this mixture provides all the flavor.

4. While the cream simmers, cut the potatoes into 1/16-inch-thick slices using a mandoline, food processor fitted with a slicing blade, or very sharp knife. If you're still slicing after the cream has simmered for 5 minutes, simply turn the heat to low to keep it warm. Put the sliced potatoes in a very large bowl and pour the cream over them. Gently fold to ensure all the slices are coated. Let sit for at least 5 minutes to allow the potatoes to absorb the liquid and soften slightly.

5. To assemble the gratin, you can either go more freestyle, dumping all the potatoes and the cream into the prepared baking dish and pressing them down, or shingle the potato slices, along with any onions clinging to them, laying them in the pan in rows and overlapping them slightly. After each layer, press the potatoes flat. (I prefer the latter method because it ensures that the gratin will hold together.) Pour the spiced cream remaining in the bowl evenly over the potatoes. Set aside while you grate the Gruyère. Sprinkle the Gruyère evenly on top.

6. Bake until the top is dark golden brown, the liquid is bubbling, and the potatoes are tender, about 1½ hours. If you insert a metal cake tester or thin-bladed knife into the center, it should slide through easily.

*crunchy fried potato gratin cubes

POTATO GRATIN
FOUR MORE RECIPES

tomato sauce potato gratin with marjoram and mozzarella

You get an almost lasagna effect here with a marjoram-and-paprika-spiced tomato sauce binding together the thin layers and molten mozzarella across the top.

SPICE BLEND

1 tablespoon plus 1 teaspoon dried marjoram (2g)

½ teaspoon black peppercorns, preferably Tellicherry (2g)

1 teaspoon sweet paprika (2 grams)

½ teaspoon peperoncini (dried Calabrian chile) or red pepper flakes (1 gram)

Finely grind the marjoram and peppercorns together and immediately mix with the paprika and peperoncini. Use this spice blend instead of the main spice blend in the potato gratin recipe on page 62.

Follow the potato gratin recipe, adding 2 tablespoons tomato paste to the softened onions at the end of step 2 and stirring for 1 minute before adding the milk and cream.

At the end of step 5, substitute 4 ounces grated mozzarella for the Gruyère.

sweet potato and goat cheese gratin

The natural sugars in sweet potatoes make for a comforting gratin. Tangy goat cheese melts into each layer and creates a savory top.

Follow the potato gratin recipe on page 62, substituting 3½ pounds sweet potatoes (about 5 large) for the Yukon Gold potatoes in step 4.

In step 5, assemble the gratin layer by layer, sprinkling 2 ounces of finely crumbled goat cheese between each layer (you will need 8 ounces goat cheese total, including cheese for sprinkling on top).

In step 6, bake for about 20 minutes longer (1 hour 50 minutes total). Sweet potatoes take longer to soften. They're ready when a thin-bladed knife slides easily through the center.

dijon-gruyère potato gratin with basil and tarragon

Celery seeds and Dijon mustard add extra savory elements to this gratin, fragrant with garlic and the licorice scent of tarragon.

SPICE BLEND

1 tablespoon dried garlic slices (5 grams)

1 teaspoon celery seeds (2 grams)

1 teaspoon green peppercorns (2 grams)

1 tablespoon dried basil (1 gram)

1 tablespoon dried tarragon (1 gram)

Finely grind the garlic, celery seeds, and peppercorns together and immediately mix with the basil and tarragon. Use this spice blend instead of the main spice blend in the potato gratin recipe on page 62.

Follow the potato gratin recipe, whisking 2 tablespoons Dijon mustard in with the milk and cream in step 3.

crunchy fried potato gratin cubes*

The only thing better than a potato gratin is one fried crisp at the edges. When you let the cut sides of compressed cubes sizzle in fat, all the layers become crunchy shingles encasing a hot creamy center. This is also a great way to reheat any leftover gratin.

Follow the potato gratin recipe on page 62.

Cool completely. Set it on a clean half sheet pan and cover tightly with plastic wrap. Find a pan that fits snugly on top and put heavy cans or a small cast-iron skillet in it to weigh it down and compress the gratin. Refrigerate until very cold and set, preferably overnight or for up to 2 days. Unwrap and cut the gratin into 2-inch squares. Transfer the squares to a cutting board and trim any curved sides to form straight edges. (You can snack on the scraps!)

Heat a large cast-iron or nonstick skillet over medium heat until hot. Add 1 tablespoon olive oil and 1 tablespoon salted butter. As soon as the butter melts, add as many squares as will fit comfortably, cut-side down. Fry until golden brown on the bottom, about 2 minutes. Flip and brown another cut side. Repeat until all the cut sides are browned, 6 to 8 minutes total, adding more oil and butter as needed. Repeat with the remaining gratin. Drain on paper towels and serve hot.

SWEET POTATO PUREE

cumin and caraway sweet potato puree

Here I temper the vegetable's natural sweetness with a savory mix of cumin, garlic, and caraway and accentuate it with warming ginger and fresh orange juice. A bit of heat from cayenne ties it all together.

SERVES 4 TO 6

MAIN SPICE BLEND

1¼ teaspoons cumin seeds (4 grams)
2 teaspoons dried garlic slices (3 grams)
½ teaspoon caraway seeds (2 grams)
½ teaspoon ground ginger (1 gram)
¼ teaspoon cayenne pepper (½ gram)

Finely grind the cumin, garlic, and caraway together and immediately mix with the ginger and cayenne.

SWEET POTATO PUREE

Extra-virgin olive oil
1 medium yellow onion, halved and very thinly sliced
Kosher salt
1½ pounds sweet potatoes (about 2 large), peeled and cut into ½-inch chunks
½ cup fresh orange juice

MAKE AHEAD

The puree can be refrigerated for up to 1 week.

Sweet potatoes are like a blank canvas—you can top them with just about anything. I grew up with them in Israel, simply cooking them in the embers of campfires at my kibbutz, slashing them open, and then scooping out the hot, tender centers from the ashy skins. This live-fire style of cooking sweet potatoes is trendy in restaurants now, but I've been doing it since I was six years old. My favorite part, though, was the creamy center of the sweet potatoes. I re-create that texture and introduce bold new flavors with this spiced puree, which not only keeps well but can be used as the base for croquettes or a dip (see page 69).

1. To make the puree: Generously coat the bottom of a large saucepan with oil (1 to 2 tablespoons). Add the spice blend and set the heat to medium. Cook, stirring continuously, until tiny bubbles break the surface, 1 to 2 minutes.

2. Add the onion, season generously with salt, and stir well to evenly coat. Cover and cook, stirring occasionally, until the onion tenderizes a bit, 5 to 6 minutes.

3. Add the sweet potatoes, stir well to evenly coat, and cover. Reduce the heat to medium-low and cook, stirring often to prevent the spices from burning and the sweet potatoes from sticking, until the sweet potatoes start to break down into a semi-chunky mash, 13 to 15 minutes.

4. Stir in the orange juice, cover, and cook until the remaining sweet potato chunks are soft, 5 to 6 minutes. If all the liquid has evaporated before the sweet potatoes are soft, add water to the pan, 1 tablespoon at a time, to keep the mixture from drying out and burning. Remove from the heat.

5. Using an immersion or stand blender, food processor, or food mill, puree the sweet potatoes until smooth. Fold in 2 tablespoons oil, then season to taste with salt. If you prefer a thinner puree, you can fold in water, 1 tablespoon at a time, until they reach the desired consistency. Season to taste again, if needed. Serve hot or warm.

CABBAGE AND APPLE SLAW WITH CARROTS

spicy slaw with poppy and mustard seeds

A simple slick of lemon juice and olive oil brightens the savory-spicy duo of caraway and peperoncini. Whole poppy and mustard seeds add pop to every bite.

SERVES 6 TO 8

MAIN SPICE BLEND

¾ teaspoon caraway seeds (3 grams)

½ teaspoon peperoncini (dried Calabrian chile) or red pepper flakes (1 gram)

1¼ teaspoons poppy seeds (5 grams)

1 teaspoon yellow mustard seeds (5 grams)

Finely grind the caraway and peperoncini together and immediately mix with the whole poppy seeds and mustard seeds.

SLAW

2 cups very thinly sliced red cabbage

2 cups very thinly sliced green cabbage

2 large carrots, peeled and thinly sliced, julienned, or coarsely grated

1 large sweet tart apple, such as Lady Alice, Fuji, or Honeycrisp, cored and thinly sliced, julienned, or coarsely grated

Juice of 1 lemon, plus more as needed

1 tablespoon extra-virgin olive oil, plus more as needed

Kosher salt

MAKE AHEAD

The ingredients can be prepped and kept undressed up to 1 day ahead and the dressed slaw can be refrigerated for up to 5 days.

A hearty raw vegetable slaw holds well in the refrigerator, making this trio of cabbage, apples, and carrots ideal as a quick make-ahead salad or side dish. Given their sturdy texture, these three take to dressings like marinades, soaking up seasonings while staying crisp for hours. And anything goes with this trio, as you can see in the dishes on page 73. Depending on the season, you may even want to cook the vegetables as in the sautéed variation. This kind of simple and quick dish works so nicely with grilled or roasted meats or seared fatty fish in all seasons. It's a refreshing contrast to rich proteins.

1. To make the slaw: In a large bowl, toss the main spice blend with both cabbages, the carrots, and the apple.

2. Add the lemon juice, oil, and a generous pinch of salt. Stir and taste; add more lemon juice, oil, and salt to taste.

*creamy slaw with labne-tahini dressing

CABBAGE AND APPLE SLAW WITH CARROTS
FOUR MORE RECIPES

sesame-lime slaw with ginger

Sesame, in the form of both toasted seeds and oil, enriches this slaw and makes it a partner to any Asian-style dish, like Soy-Garlic Seared Salmon with Limon Omani (page 153).

SPICE BLEND

1½ teaspoons white sesame seeds, preferably unhulled (5 grams)

1 teaspoon nigella seeds (3 grams)

½ teaspoon ground ginger (1 gram)

½ teaspoon amchoor (dried mango powder; 1 gram)

Mix together the sesame seeds, nigella seeds, ginger, and amchoor. Use this spice blend instead of the main spice blend in the slaw recipe on page 70.

Follow the slaw recipe, substituting 2 tablespoons fresh lime juice for the lemon juice and adding 1 teaspoon sesame oil and 1 teaspoon fish sauce along with the olive oil in step 2.

slaw with anise seeds and tangy tamarind dressing

Both tamarind and sumac offer sour notes, the former with a funky fruitiness, the latter with floral notes. The combination makes this slaw ideal for pairing with sweet and savory main dishes.

SPICE BLEND

1½ teaspoons dill seeds (3 grams)

¾ teaspoon sumac (2 grams)

½ teaspoon Urfa pepper (1 gram)

¾ teaspoon anise (2 grams)

Finely grind the dill seeds, sumac, and Urfa together and immediately mix with the whole anise. Use this spice blend instead of the main spice blend in the slaw recipe on page 70.

Follow the slaw recipe, substituting 2 tablespoons tamarind paste for the lemon juice and 1 tablespoon grapeseed oil for the olive oil in step 2.

cabbage, carrot, and apple sauté with mustard seeds

Here the slaw vegetables are cooked until al dente. This hot side dish works well with any rich main dish—I think it is especially good with quick-seared pork chops (see page 194).

Follow the slaw recipe on page 70 through step 1. Coat a large, deep skillet or large, wide saucepan with olive oil (about 3 tablespoons) and heat over medium-high heat. When the oil is shimmering, add the slaw mixture, season generously with salt, and cook, stirring, until just wilted, about 5 minutes. Add the lemon juice, stir well, and season to taste with salt. Serve warm.

creamy slaw with labne-tahini dressing*

In my version of a creamy slaw, labne and tahini replace the traditional mayonnaise. The labne has a tangy edge and the tahini a nutty richness that make this salad very satisfying; use plain Greek yogurt if labne is not available.

Follow the slaw recipe on page 70 through step 1. In step 2, whisk 2½ tablespoons labne or plain Greek yogurt and 3 tablespoons tahini with the lemon juice, olive oil, and salt in a small bowl until well blended. Pour over the slaw and toss until evenly coated. Season to taste with salt.

CREAMY CARROT SOUP

smoky cumin and chipotle carrot soup

Both chipotle and pimentón deliver the smokiness of roasted chiles, which brings out the earthy sweetness of carrots that orange juice heightens as well. The floral zing of pink pepper ties the sweetness and smokiness together.

**MAKES ABOUT 7 CUPS
SERVES 4 TO 8**

MAIN SPICE BLEND

1¼ teaspoons cumin seeds (4 grams)

1 teaspoon pink pepper (2 grams)

⅛ teaspoon chipotle chile powder (¼ gram)

¾ teaspoon pimentón (smoked paprika; 2 grams)

Finely grind the cumin and pink pepper together and immediately mix with the chipotle and pimentón. (If you'd like more to sprinkle over the soup, make a double batch and reserve half for serving.)

SOUP

2 tablespoons extra-virgin olive oil, plus more to taste

5 large garlic cloves, smashed and chopped

2 large yellow onions, halved and thinly sliced

Kosher salt

9 medium carrots, scrubbed, halved lengthwise, and sliced

2 large celery stalks, halved lengthwise and sliced

½ cup freshly squeezed orange juice with pulp (from about 2 oranges)

MAKE AHEAD

Refrigerate the soup for up to 1 week or freeze for up to 3 months. The ingredients can be prepped the day before cooking.

The magic of this soup is that it's creamy without any cream. When the vegetables are blended together, they develop a luxurious silky texture and stay fresh and light with the addition of orange juice. Keep this soup—or any of its spin-off soups on page 77—in the fridge and freezer year-round to serve as a light lunch anytime or as part of a bigger meal. Or use leftovers to turn into another dish altogether, like Carrot Pasta with Poppy Seeds.

1. To make the soup: Heat the oil in a large saucepan over medium-low heat. When the oil is slightly warm but not hot, after about 30 seconds, add the spice blend and stir until the spices bloom and become very fragrant, about 30 seconds. Don't let the spices burn.

2. Add the garlic and cook, stirring, until sizzling and aromatic, 1 to 2 minutes. Add the onions, sprinkle generously with salt, and cook, stirring continuously, for 2 minutes. Cover and cook, stirring and scraping the bottom of the saucepan occasionally, to soften the onions a bit and let the spices infuse the onions, about 8 minutes.

3. Add the carrots and celery and stir well to coat with the spices. Cover and cook, stirring and scraping occasionally, to soften the carrots and infuse them with flavor, about 8 minutes.

4. Add the orange juice, stir well, and cover. Cook for 5 minutes. Add 3 cups cold water, stir well, and increase the heat to high. Bring to a steady simmer. Season to taste with salt, cover, and reduce the heat to maintain a low simmer. Cook, stirring occasionally, until the carrots are cooked through but still retain a fresh flavor, about 20 minutes.

5. Transfer the soup to a blender and blend until smooth, working in batches if needed and adding more water if you prefer a thinner soup. If you want an extra-smooth soup, pour it through a fine-mesh sieve. If you want a richer soup, blend in 1 to 2 tablespoons more olive oil. Season to taste with salt.

*carrot pasta with poppy seeds

CREAMY CARROT SOUP
FIVE MORE RECIPES

smoky carrot soup with cinnamon and crispy chorizo

Crispy fried chorizo is scattered on top of this soup before serving. The rendered fat from frying the chorizo is used to toast the spices and cook the vegetables, accentuating the smokiness of the pimentón.

SPICE BLEND

¾ teaspoon caraway seeds (3 grams)

1 teaspoon ground cinnamon, preferably
    Vietnamese (3 grams)

1 teaspoon pimentón (smoked paprika; 3 grams)

Finely grind the caraway and immediately mix with the cinnamon and pimenton. Use this spice blend instead of the main spice blend in the creamy carrot soup recipe on page 74.

Heat a thin sheen (about 1 tablespoon) of olive oil in the saucepan over medium heat. Add 8 ounces thinly sliced cured Spanish chorizo and cook, turning occasionally, until browned and crisp, about 5 minutes. Transfer the chorizo to paper towels to drain. Follow the creamy carrot soup recipe, starting with cooking the spice blend in the chorizo oil over low heat (remove from the heat if needed to prevent the spices from burning and turn the heat back on to proceed with the recipe). Top the finished soup with the crispy chorizo.

carrot pasta with poppy seeds*

This soup is thick enough to serve as a pasta sauce that kids—and adults—will love. Its natural sweetness is irresistible and complex with spices, and its creaminess lets it cling to noodles for a satisfying one-dish meal. It works well on both long noodles and short pasta shapes.

Follow the creamy carrot soup recipe on page 74. Transfer 3 cups of the soup to a large pot and set aside (save the rest for another use).

Boil 1 pound pasta until it is just shy of al dente (usually about 1 minute less than the package directions). Meanwhile, heat the creamy carrot soup over medium heat until bubbling. Drain the pasta and add it to the soup, tossing until the pasta is evenly coated and al dente. Divide among plates, drizzle with olive oil, and sprinkle with 1 tablespoon poppy seeds.

Serves 4

curried coconut carrot soup with green peppercorns

Warming cardamom and clove get a touch of acidity from amchoor and a welcome sharpness from fenugreek seeds. All together, the spices taste like curry, but green peppercorns add a unique tang. Creamy coconut milk binds all those flavors together with the carrots.

SPICE BLEND

1 teaspoon fenugreek seeds (5 grams)

¼ teaspoon whole cloves (½ gram)

1 teaspoon green cardamom pods (2 grams)

2½ teaspoons amchoor (dried mango powder;
5 grams)

½ teaspoon green peppercorns (1 gram)

Finely grind the fenugreek, cloves, and cardamom together and immediately mix with the amchoor. Use this spice blend instead of the main spice blend in the creamy carrot soup recipe on page 74.

Follow the creamy carrot soup recipe, substituting 1 cup coconut milk for the orange juice in step 4.

creamy tomato-carrot soup with basil, fennel, and oregano

The scent of this spice mix will make you feel as if you're at an old-school red-checkered-tablecloth Italian restaurant. Dried basil and oregano bring a welcome herbaceousness to sweet carrots, especially with an added hint of tomato paste.

SPICE BLEND

5 tablespoons dried basil (5 grams)

2½ teaspoons fennel seeds (5 grams)

2 teaspoons dried oregano (1 gram)

¼ teaspoon cayenne pepper (½ gram)

Finely grind the basil, fennel, and oregano together and immediately mix with the cayenne. Use this spice blend instead of the main spice blend in the creamy carrot soup recipe on page 74.

Follow the creamy carrot soup recipe, stirring 2 tablespoons tomato paste into the vegetables at the end of step 3.

chunky turmeric carrot soup with lime leaves

Carrot slices are set aside halfway through cooking and added later to give a fresh bite to this soup, which is made extra luxurious with cream and balanced by the heat of galangal, the acidity of ajowan (which has a distinct sour note), and the bitterness of turmeric.

SPICE BLEND

8 dried kaffir lime leaves

2½ teaspoons ground galangal or ginger
    (5 grams)

2 teaspoons ajowan (2 grams)

2 teaspoons ground turmeric (2 grams)

Finely grind the lime leaves and immediately mix with the galangal, ajowan, and turmeric. Use this spice blend instead of the main spice blend in the creamy carrot soup recipe on page 74.

Follow the creamy carrot soup recipe, substituting 1 cup heavy cream for the orange juice in step 4.

After the carrots have simmered for 10 minutes, use a slotted spoon to transfer half of them to a bowl. After blending the soup, stir the reserved carrots back into the soup and reheat before serving.

CHUNKY VEGETABLE SOUP

french country vegetable soup with sage and thyme

In this master recipe, limon omani (which is dried Persian lime) brings a welcome acidity without discoloring the vegetables the way fresh citrus juice would. It nicely complements the classic French flavors of pepper, sage, bay leaves, and thyme.

SERVES 6 TO 8

MAIN SPICE BLEND

1 whole limon omani (4 grams)

2 whole dried bay leaves

1 teaspoon dried sage (1 gram)

1½ teaspoons dried thyme (1 gram)

¾ teaspoon Muntok white peppercorns (2 grams)

Crack and crush the limon omani into smaller pieces by pressing it against a cutting board with your palm, then transfer to a spice grinder along with the bay leaves, sage, thyme, and white peppercorns. Finely grind them together.

SOUP

Extra-virgin olive oil

2 small leeks, tough green tops removed and discarded, cut into 1-inch-thick rounds

2 large celery stalks, halved lengthwise and cut crosswise into ½-inch-thick slices

2 medium yellow onions, cut into 1-inch chunks

2 large carrots, scrubbed and cut at an angle into 1-inch chunks

½ small savoy cabbage, cored and cut into 2-inch pieces

¼ large celery root, peeled and cut into ¾-inch chunks

1 tablespoon tomato paste

1 tablespoon soy sauce

½ small cauliflower, cored and cut into 2-inch florets

Kosher salt

MAKE AHEAD

Refrigerate the soup for up to 1 week or freeze for up to 2 months.

I like to sauté vegetables with spices before adding them to water to make soup. Concentrating the sweetness of the vegetables by sautéing them gives so much more flavor—between that step and the spices, you don't even need to use stock. Stovetop pan roasting is also a way to develop flavor without overcooking the vegetables. Another trick to creating a flavorful vegetarian stock is adding tomato paste and soy sauce. Both are rich in umami, which lends an almost meaty depth to the soup base. Vegetable soup is easy to turn into a hearty one-dish meal when served alongside legumes (see pages 114 to 125) or grains (see pages 94 to 101).

1. To make the soup: Heat a large Dutch oven or other heavy pot over medium-low heat. Add enough oil (about 3 tablespoons) to coat the bottom generously and add the leeks, celery, onions, carrots, cabbage, and celery root. Stir well and add the spice blend. Stir until all the vegetables are evenly coated with the spices, cover, and cook, stirring occasionally, until the onions are translucent around the edges, about 5 minutes.

2. Reduce the heat to low and add the tomato paste and soy sauce. Stir continuously for 2 minutes and then add 5 cups cold water. Cover the pot and raise the heat to high. When the liquid comes to a boil, reduce the heat to maintain a steady simmer.

3. Simmer, covered, until the vegetables are almost tender, about 8 minutes. Add the cauliflower and season to taste with salt. Stir, cover, and simmer until all the vegetables are tender, about 15 minutes. Remove from the heat, season to taste with salt, and serve hot.

*tumeric and coconut vegetable soup with ginger and cardamom

CHUNKY VEGETABLE SOUP
FIVE MORE RECIPES

turmeric and coconut vegetable soup with ginger and cardamom*

Turmeric, ginger, and cardamom—three common ingredients in curry—bring warmth and a welcome bitterness to this soup, while coconut milk adds richness. The heat of peperoncini brightens the entire mix.

SPICE BLEND

1 teaspoon green cardamom pods (2 grams)

2 teaspoons ground turmeric (2 grams)

1 teaspoon ground ginger (2 grams)

¼ teaspoon peperoncini (dried Calabrian chile) or red pepper flakes (½ gram)

Finely grind the cardamom and immediately mix with the turmeric, ginger, and peperoncini. Use this spice blend instead of the main spice blend in the vegetable soup recipe on page 78.

Follow the vegetable soup recipe, replacing 1 cup of the water with 1 cup coconut milk in step 2.

creamy vegetable soup

When all the vegetables are blended together, they become luxuriously creamy without any cream. You can garnish this with croutons (toasted nuts or seeds are delicious too) for a little crunch.

Follow the vegetable soup recipe on page 78. At the end of step 3, transfer the vegetables to a blender using a slotted spoon. Add just enough of the cooking liquid to barely cover the solids.

Blend the soup until very smooth and creamy, working in batches if needed and adding more of the cooking liquid if you prefer a thinner soup. (For an even more refined puree, strain the soup through a fine-mesh sieve.)

green lentil and jasmine rice soup with sautéed vegetables

The addition of lentils and rice make this a filling and very healthy one-bowl meal.

Follow the vegetable soup recipe on page 78. In step 2, add ½ cup rinsed and drained green lentils and an extra cup of water (for 6 cups water total). In step 3, add 1 cup rinsed and drained jasmine rice when you add the cauliflower. Simmer until the lentils and rice are tender, about 15 minutes.

When the soup is done, you can add additional water for more broth, if you'd like.

black bean and tomato tortilla soup

Caraway brings a surprising savory note to the mix of cumin and turmeric in this black bean soup that is sweetened with some tomatoes. Fried tortilla strips or chips are great for sprinkling on top or dipping in the hearty soup.

SPICE BLEND

1¼ teaspoons cumin seeds (4 grams)

½ teaspoon caraway seeds (2 grams)

¼ teaspoon black peppercorns, preferably Tellicherry (1 gram)

2 teaspoons ground turmeric (2 grams)

Finely grind the cumin, caraway, and peppercorns together and immediately mix with the turmeric. Use this spice blend instead of the main spice blend in the vegetable soup recipe on page 78.

Follow the vegetable soup recipe, adding 1 cup diced fresh or canned tomatoes along with the water in step 2. In step 3, stir in 1 (14.5-ounce) can rinsed and drained black beans. Simmer just until the beans are heated through, about 3 minutes. Stir in ⅔ cup chopped cilantro and serve with fried tortilla strips or tortilla chips.

comforting and quick chicken soup

Putting diced chicken thighs into the pot with the vegetables turns this into a satisfying chicken soup that is so quick to make, you can easily toss it together on a weeknight. The blend of saffron, cinnamon, and cardamom gives classic chicken soup a surprising yet comforting warmth reminiscent of a Moroccan-style stew. Chickpea flatbreads (see page 102) or store-bought flatbreads or pitas are an excellent accompaniment.

SPICE BLEND

2 teaspoons dried onion slices (3 grams)

1 teaspoon green cardamom pods (2 grams)

Pinch of saffron

¾ teaspoon ground cinnamon, preferably Vietnamese (2 grams)

Finely grind the onion, cardamom, and saffron together and immediately mix with the cinnamon. Use this spice blend instead of the main spice blend in the vegetable soup recipe on page 78.

Follow the vegetable soup recipe, adding 12 ounces diced boneless, skinless chicken thighs, seasoned with salt, to the hot oil with the vegetables in step 1.

PASTA, GRAINS, AND BREAD

PASTA, GRAINS, AND BREAD

The subtlety of pasta, grains, and bread takes well to all spices, and they become more delicious when cooked with a variety of aromas. In fact, spices soak into porous grains while they cook, giving them a depth of flavor you'll love. With the techniques that follow, you end up with snacks and dishes for any occasion, from weeknight meals to holiday feasts.

Most of these recipes start with pantry items, so if you've prepared spice blends ahead of time, you can cook quickly and efficiently. Keep the blends in small jars or containers, all labeled so you know what is in each one, and then whip up any of the dishes in this chapter on short notice. Better yet, do what I do and keep the fully cooked grains packed in an airtight container in the freezer. On crazy busy nights, I simply thaw and reheat them.

MASTER SPICE BLENDS

for seasoning pasta cooking water

1 tablespoon plus 1 teaspoon dried sage (5 grams)
¾ teaspoon juniper berries (2 grams)
½ teaspoon caraway seeds (2 grams)
1 tablespoon freshly grated nutmeg (3 grams)
½ teaspoon peperoncini (dried Calabrian chile) or
    red pepper flakes (1 gram)

Finely grind the sage, juniper, and caraway together and immediately mix with the nutmeg and whole peperoncini.

**for seasoning cooking water for hearty grains
(such as farro and barley)**

2 tablespoons plus 1½ teaspoons amchoor
    (dried mango powder; 15 grams)
1½ teaspoons pimentón (smoked paprika; 5 grams)
¾ teaspoon ground cinnamon, preferably
    Vietnamese (2 grams)
½ teaspoon Aleppo pepper (1 gram)

Mix together the amchoor, pimentón, cinnamon, and Aleppo.

for seasoning rice cooking water

1 whole limon omani (dried Persian lime; 4 grams)
5 tablespoons dried savory (15 grams)
1 teaspoon cumin seeds (3 grams)
1½ teaspoons coriander seeds (3 grams)
½ teaspoon cayenne pepper (1 gram)

Crack and crush the limon omani into smaller pieces by pressing it against a cutting board with your palm, then transfer to a spice grinder along with the savory, cumin, and coriander. Finely grind them together and immediately mix with the cayenne.

BAKED PENNE

garlic and tomato baked penne with rosemary and oregano

For the sauce, I start with dried garlic, rosemary, and oregano; it ends up tasting like the best jarred stuff imaginable.

SERVES 4 TO 6

MAIN SPICE BLEND

1 tablespoon plus ½ teaspoon dried garlic slices (6 grams)

1 tablespoon dried rosemary (1 gram)

2 teaspoons dried oregano (1 gram)

½ teaspoon black peppercorns, preferably Tellicherry (2 grams)

Finely grind together the garlic, rosemary, oregano, and peppercorns.

PASTA

Kosher salt

1 pound penne

1 (6-ounce) can tomato paste (⅔ cup)

1 tablespoon extra-virgin olive oil

8 ounces fresh mozzarella, preferably pearl-size balls or 1 large ball, cut into ½-inch pieces

3 ounces Parmesan cheese, preferably aged, finely grated

This old-school style of baked penne—coated with classically spiced red sauce, mozzarella, and Parmesan—is pure comfort food. My nostalgia for it comes straight from Italy, specifically to when my mom made it part of our weekly rotation while we lived in Rome (she learned the recipe from a friend there). It was such a family favorite that she continued to make it even after we moved back to Israel. I'll always think my mom's dish is better than anyone's, including my own, but my version is inspired by hers and floods me with wonderful and vivid childhood memories every time I eat it.

1. To make the pasta: Preheat the oven to 375°F.

2. Put one-quarter of the spice blend in a large pot of cold water and generously season it with salt; it should be as salty as seawater. Bring to a boil over high heat. Add the pasta and cook for a minute less than the package instructs for al dente. Reserve 1 cup of the pasta cooking water and then drain the pasta.

3. Scrape the tomato paste into a 3-quart baking dish. Add the oil, ⅔ cup of the reserved cooking water, and the remaining spice blend. Stir until very smooth, add the pasta, and fold until evenly coated. If the mixture seems dry, add more pasta water, a little at a time, until the noodles are evenly coated in sauce.

4. Add the mozzarella and half the Parmesan. Fold to distribute everything evenly, then smooth the top. Sprinkle the remaining Parmesan evenly on top.

5. Bake until the cheese melts and the top is golden brown, about 30 minutes. Let stand for 5 to 10 minutes and serve hot.

*eggplant and olive baked penne with feta

BAKED PENNE
FOUR MORE RECIPES

baked penne with sautéed italian sausage

For a meaty baked pasta, simply toss in cooked sausage. You can also make this with cooked slab bacon, crumbled meatballs (page 198), or shredded short ribs (page 202).

Remove the casings from 12 ounces of sweet or spicy Italian sausage. Cook the sausage in a skillet over medium-high heat until browned and cooked through, about 5 minutes, stirring often and breaking the meat into small bits, until browned.

Follow the baked penne recipe on page 86 through step 3. In step 4, add the cooked sausage along with the cheeses.

spicy and smoky baked penne with olive oil–packed tuna

In this recipe, I channel Southern Italy by mixing tuna with the pasta and the Middle East with za'atar. Tomato sauce spicy with peperoncini and smoky with pimenton gets a generous dose of onion too. Crumbled goat cheese melts into the mixture as it bakes, creating a decadent creaminess.

SPICE BLEND

3 tablespoons plus 2 teaspoons dried onion slices (15 grams)

¾ teaspoon pimentón (smoked paprika; 2 grams)

½ teaspoon peperoncini (dried Calabrian chile) or red pepper flakes (1 gram)

1½ teaspoons dried za'atar leaves (1 gram)

Finely grind the onion and immediately mix with the pimentón, peperoncini, and za'atar. Use this spice blend instead of the main spice blend in the baked penne recipe on page 86.

Follow the baked penne recipe, substituting 8 ounces crumbled goat cheese for the mozzarella and adding 1 (5-ounce) can flaked olive oil–packed tuna to the pasta along with the cheeses in step 4.

eggplant and olive baked penne with feta*

Olives and feta cheese add briny saltiness to this pasta, while the eggplant softens to tenderness while retaining a little bite.

Follow the baked penne recipe on page 86 through step 3, using the main spice blend.

In step 4, substitute 8 ounces crumbled feta cheese for the mozzarella and fold in 2 cups diced raw, skin-on eggplant and ½ cup pitted and sliced black olives.

creamy baked penne with halloumi

A splash of cream gives this sauce a little extra body, as does halloumi cheese. This cheese is as creamy as mozzarella in taste, but is firmer and has a higher melting point, so it stays intact even after baking. The combination of black mustard seeds and turmeric balances that richness nicely.

SPICE BLEND

1½ teaspoons dried onion slices (3 grams)

¾ teaspoon cumin seeds (2 grams)

½ teaspoon black mustard seeds (3 grams)

2 teaspoons ground turmeric (2 grams)

Finely grind the onion and cumin together and immediately mix with the whole mustard seeds and turmeric. Use this spice blend instead of the main spice blend in the baked penne recipe on page 86.

Follow the baked penne recipe, whisking ½ cup heavy cream into the tomato paste mixture in step 3. In step 4, substitute 6 ounces halloumi cheese (cut into ½-inch cubes) for the mozzarella.

STOVETOP PAELLA

summer harvest paella with saffron and coriander

The late summer abundance of peppers and zucchini turns this into a satisfying one-pan vegetarian meal. Dried garlic adds a punch of flavor, as do coriander seeds and oregano.

SERVES 4 TO 6

MAIN SPICE BLEND

¼ teaspoon saffron

¾ teaspoon pimentón (smoked paprika; 2 grams)

¼ teaspoon peperoncini (dried Calabrian chile) or red pepper flakes (½ gram)

1½ teaspoons coriander seeds (3 grams)

2 teaspoons dried oregano (1 gram)

2 teaspoons dried garlic slices (3 grams)

Finely grind together the saffron, pimentón, peperoncini, coriander, oregano, and garlic.

PAELLA

Extra-virgin olive oil

1 medium yellow onion, diced

Kosher salt

1 small red bell pepper, cut into 1-inch chunks

1 small green bell pepper, cut into 1-inch chunks

1 small zucchini, halved lengthwise and cut into ¾-inch-thick slices

1 small Italian eggplant, quartered lengthwise and cut into ¾-inch-thick slices

1 (14.5-ounce) can diced tomatoes

1½ cups Bomba rice

1 cup cooked chickpeas, homemade (page 114) or canned, drained and rinsed

My loose interpretation of Spanish paella infuses every element of the dish with flavor by adding a spice blend at each stage of the cooking process and then simmering the whole mix with the same blend. Bomba rice, a short-grain rice from Spain and the foundation for Spanish paella, absorbs liquid—and therefore seasonings—more readily than other varieties. You can find it online or in well-stocked markets. Also available online are paella pans. You don't need one, but it's the only way to get the signature *socarrat* crust on the bottom of the rice, a thin, crackly, browned layer that crisps on the pan's steel base. Even without the socarrat, this dish will be tasty. Every version of this paella is even better if served with a dollop of aioli (see page 246) for mixing in, as the Spanish do. If you have leftovers, try the Savory Pan-Fried Paella Cake on page 93.

1. To make the paella: Coat a large sauté pan with oil (2 to 3 tablespoons) and heat over medium heat. If you have a 16- to 18-inch paella pan, use it here; straddle the pan between two burners and rotate it occasionally to ensure even cooking. Add the onion, 2 pinches of the spice blend, and a pinch of salt. Stir well, spread in an even layer, and, if using a sauté pan, cover. Cook until the onion is just translucent, about 6 minutes.

2. Add the red and green bell peppers, 2 more pinches of the spice blend, and a pinch of salt and stir well. Cook, stirring occasionally, until the peppers are bright, about 4 minutes. Reduce the heat to low, cover (if using a sauté pan), and cook until the peppers are almost tender, about 3 minutes. If the vegetables seem like they're burning, add a little more oil. Transfer the vegetables to a plate.

3. Coat the pan generously with more oil (3 to 4 tablespoons) and raise the heat to medium-high. Add the zucchini and eggplant and season with salt. Stir well, spread in an even layer, and cover (if using a sauté pan). Cook, stirring occasionally, until crisp-tender, 5 to 6 minutes.

4. Raise the heat to high. Add the tomatoes, rice, chickpeas, the vegetables, 3 cups cold water, the remaining spice blend, and a large pinch of salt. Stir continuously until the mixture is bubbling and the rice absorbs some of the liquid, about 2 minutes. Reduce the heat to low and simmer, uncovered, until the rice is just cooked through, about 20 minutes. Raise the heat to high and cook until a crust forms on the bottom of the rice, about 5 minutes. Remove from the heat, tent loosely with foil, and let stand for 10 minutes before serving.

*chorizo and seafood paella with saffron and fennel

STOVETOP PAELLA
FIVE MORE RECIPES

savory pan-fried paella cake

Here paella is bound by eggs and cooked in the style of a Spanish *tortilla,* which stacks olive-oil-cooked soft potato slices bound by eggs into a thick round. This resulting cake—somewhere between a frittata and a tortilla—has a delicious crust all around and cuts into attractive wedges.

Follow the paella recipe on page 90. Transfer 3 cups to a large bowl and let cool (or use 3 cups chilled leftover paella). Add 2 beaten large eggs and stir until well mixed.

Coat an 8-inch nonstick skillet with olive oil (about 2 tablespoons) and heat over medium heat. Add the paella mixture and spread it in a single layer, pressing it into a compact cake with a silicone spatula. Cook until the bottom is evenly browned, 6 to 8 minutes. Place a large plate over the skillet (make sure its circumference is larger than the skillet's) and carefully flip the plate and skillet together. Wipe out the skillet and heat another coating of olive oil (about 2 tablespoons) in it. When the oil is hot, carefully slide the paella cake back into the skillet, browned-side up. Tuck in the edges with the spatula to form a neat cake. Cook until the bottom is browned and the center is hot, 5 to 7 minutes. Slide the cake onto a cutting board and let cool for 5 minutes before cutting into wedges and serving.

paella fried rice with scallions and eggs

Refrigerated leftover paella transforms into irresistible fried rice when stirred over high heat with scallions and eggs. Don't try this with fresh paella rice; it'll be too sticky to fry.

Follow the paella recipe on page 90. Transfer 5 cups to an airtight container and refrigerate until cold, preferably overnight.

Heat 2 tablespoons grapeseed oil in a large wok or Dutch oven over high heat. Add 1 bunch thinly sliced scallions (white and green parts) and a pinch of salt. Cook, stirring, until the greens are just wilted, about 1 minute. Add 3 beaten large eggs and a pinch of salt. Cook, stirring to scramble, until the eggs are just set, about 1 minute. Add the chilled paella and cook, stirring to separate the rice grains, until heated through, about 3 minutes. Serve hot.

Serves 4 as a side dish

chorizo and seafood paella with saffron and fennel*

Pimentón highlights the smokiness of chorizo sausage, while fennel and coriander seeds complement the seafood in this impressive dinner party dish.

SPICE BLEND
¼ teaspoon saffron
¾ teaspoon pimentón (2 grams)
¼ teaspoon peperoncini (dried Calabrian chile) or red pepper flakes (½ gram)
1½ teaspoons coriander seeds (3 grams)
2½ teaspoons fennel seeds (5 grams)
2 teaspoons dried garlic slices (3 grams)

Finely grind together the saffron, pimentón, peperoncini, coriander, fennel, and garlic. Use this spice blend instead of the main spice blend in the paella recipe on page 90.

Follow the paella recipe, but start step 1 by adding 4 ounces diced chorizo to the oil and cook over low heat, stirring often, until just browned, about 5 minutes. Transfer to a paper-towel-lined plate. Add the onion to the chorizo oil and cook as instructed.

In step 3, omit the zucchini and eggplant. In step 4, after the mixture has started bubbling, nestle 12 extra-large shell-on shrimp, 12 well-scrubbed clams, and 12 well-scrubbed mussels into the mixture. Scatter the chorizo all around. The seafood will be cooked through when the rice is done.

chicken paella with red and green peppers

The rendered fat from browned chicken thighs seared in the pan before cooking the vegetables seasons every part of this paella. If you're serving six, add two more thighs to the quantity here.

Follow the paella recipe on page 90. In step 1, heat 2 tablespoons olive oil over low heat. Sprinkle 2 large pinches of the spice blend over 4 bone-in, skin-on chicken thighs (1½ pounds) and season with salt. Place the thighs skin-side down in the oil and cook until the skin is browned, about 15 minutes, then flip and cook

for 5 minutes more. Transfer to a plate. Add the onion to the chicken fat, scraping any browned bits up from the bottom of the pan, and cook as instructed.

In step 3, omit the zucchini and eggplant. In step 4, after the mixture has started bubbling, nestle the chicken in the mixture, skin-side up, leaving the skin above the liquid line. Pour in any accumulated chicken juices from the plate. (The chicken will be cooked through when the rice is done.)

lemon and artichoke paella with pumpkin

To get all the pleasure of artichokes without the pain of preparing spiky fresh ones, I pop open a can. Of course, fresh artichokes taste, well, fresher, but for this dish, canned artichokes soak up the seasonings and meld into the rice beautifully. Pumpkin puree takes the place of tomatoes here, resulting in a creamier dish with an earthy warmth.

SPICE BLEND
2½ teaspoons coriander seeds (5 grams)
2½ teaspoons fennel seeds (5 grams)
Pinch of saffron
1 teaspoon ground turmeric (1 gram)
½ teaspoon Aleppo pepper (1 gram)

Finely grind the coriander, fennel, and saffron together and immediately mix with the turmeric and Aleppo. Use this spice blend instead of the main spice blend in the paella recipe on page 90.

Follow the paella recipe, substituting 1 (14-ounce) can drained quartered artichoke hearts and 1 lemon, diced with its rind and seeded, for the zucchini and eggplant in step 3, and swapping in ½ cup pumpkin puree for the tomatoes. Increase the water to 4½ cups total.

RISOTTO

rosemary and garlic risotto with mascarpone and parmesan

Celery seeds and garlic add a savory note to the natural sweetness of the rice and onion. Rosemary and fennel give this a classic Italian feel.

SERVES 4 TO 6

MAIN SPICE BLEND

½ teaspoon celery seeds (1 gram)

½ teaspoon fennel seeds (2 grams)

2 teaspoons dried garlic slices (3 grams)

1 tablespoon dried rosemary (1 gram)

½ teaspoon black peppercorns, preferably Tellicherry (2 grams)

Finely grind together the celery seeds, fennel, garlic, rosemary, and peppercorns.

RISOTTO

Kosher salt

Extra-virgin olive oil

1 large yellow onion, finely diced

1½ cups Arborio rice

1 cup dry white wine

2 tablespoons mascarpone cheese

3 tablespoons salted butter

1 cup grated Parmesan cheese (4 ounces)

MAKE AHEAD

See instructions in step 5.

My version of risotto adds the complex depth of spice at every stage of cooking. Because spices infuse the liquid, water is the base here, not stock. But the resulting dish still tastes rich with the addition of mascarpone and Parmesan. You can prepare most of the risotto ahead of time (see step 5). Whether you do that or go from start to finish, the timing may vary depending on the grains. Different brands and varieties of rice absorb liquid at different rates. Risotto is all about feel. You'll sense the push and pull of the rice as you stir, the liquid soaking into the grains and becoming a starchy sauce.

1. To make the risotto: Combine half the spice blend and a generous pinch of salt with 4½ cups cold water in a small saucepan. Bring to a boil over high heat, then reduce the heat to maintain a bare simmer.

2. Meanwhile, coat a large sauté pan with oil (2 to 3 tablespoons) and heat over medium-high heat. Add the onion, a pinch of the spice blend, and a pinch of salt and cook, stirring often, until sizzling, about 3 minutes. Reduce the heat to medium-low and cook, stirring often, until the onion is tender, about 5 minutes.

3. Add the rice, stir well, and spread it in a thin, even layer. Let sit for a minute, then stir it gently until the grains turn translucent at their ends and smell a little toasty, about 5 minutes. They shouldn't darken at all in color, and there shouldn't be any fat left in the pan.

4. Add the wine and stir well. The liquids should be thick at this point—that's the starch coming out of the rice. Add the remaining spice blend and stir until there's just a little wine still coating the pan.

5. Add ⅔ cup of the spice broth, stir well, and spread the rice in an even layer. Reduce the heat to maintain a low simmer. Let sit for a minute and stir again. Repeat until almost all the liquid is absorbed, about 5 minutes. Add ⅓ cup of the broth and repeat the spreading, sitting, and stirring, about 3 minutes. Repeat two more times. At this point, the grains should have doubled in size. Season to taste with salt. You're at the halfway point, and you can stop cooking now, transfer the risotto to an airtight container, and refrigerate it for up to 3 days before finishing (pick up the recipe at step 6).

6. If you're going to continue cooking, keep adding broth ⅓ cup at a time, stirring, spreading, sitting, and stirring again, until the rice is almost al dente. You should have about ⅔ cup broth left. You know the rice is ready at this point when you pull the spoon from the center to the edge of the pan and the mixture flows back like lava.

7. Fold in the mascarpone until incorporated and then add another ⅓ cup of the broth and stir well. Add the butter and stir until melted. Remove from the heat and stir in the remaining broth and then the Parmesan. The rice should be al dente and the whole mixture should be quite loose. Season to taste with salt and serve immediately.

FARRO WITH TOASTED NOODLES

savory minted farro

A hint of mint freshens up the savory depth of garlic and the smokiness of pimentón in this simple side dish. It would pair well with any grilled meat or fish.

SERVES 6 TO 8

MAIN SPICE BLEND

1 tablespoon dried garlic slices (5 grams)

1 teaspoon dried savory (1 gram)

¼ teaspoon cayenne pepper (½ gram)

¾ teaspoon pimentón (smoked paprika; 2 grams)

1 teaspoon dried mint (1 gram)

Finely grind the garlic and savory together and immediately mix with the cayenne, pimentón, and the whole dried mint.

FARRO

1½ pounds farro (3¾ cups)

Extra-virgin olive oil

1 tablespoon salted butter

¾ ounce vermicelli or angel hair pasta, broken into 1-inch pieces (½ cup)

1 large yellow onion, finely diced

Kosher salt

1 small red bell pepper, finely diced

3 tablespoons apple cider vinegar

MAKE AHEAD

The farro can be refrigerated for up to 1 week.

Throughout Lebanon, Syria, and Turkey, rice is often cooked with broken bits of toasted vermicelli noodles, which are sometimes called *fideos* in Spain and Latin America. The resulting dish is like a pilaf, but with more layers of texture and taste. I learned the technique from an Armenian chef when I cooked in France and have since adopted it as my own, swapping in farro for rice, because I find that it has more character. I like the earthy taste and substantial bite of this ancient grain, which has become so popular it's easy to find in just about any supermarket. Fresh red bell pepper lends sweetness and a little acidity to the mix and pairs well with a range of seasonings (see page 101).

1. To make the farro: Place the farro in a large bowl and add enough cold water to cover by 1 inch. Let the farro soak for at least 10 minutes and up to 1 hour to speed up the cooking; drain well. Prep and cook the pasta and vegetables while the grains soak.

2. Coat the bottom of a medium pot with oil (2 to 3 tablespoons) and set over medium-low heat. Add the butter and swirl until melted. Add the pasta and stir well. Adjust the heat so you find that happy place where the fat bubbles and the noodles sizzle. Cook, stirring continuously, until the pasta is golden brown and smells toasty, about 5 minutes.

3. Add the onion and stir well. Add all of the spice blend and a pinch of salt. Stir well, mix in the red bell pepper, raise the heat to high, and add the drained farro. Stir well and add the vinegar and 4 cups cold water. Cover and bring to a boil. Reduce the heat to maintain a simmer and cook, stirring and scraping the bottom of the pot occasionally to prevent the spices from scorching, until the farro is tender and the water is absorbed, about 20 minutes.

4. Let sit, covered, for 10 minutes, then gently fold the mixture to evenly incorporate all the ingredients and serve.

*savory pan-fried farro cakes with goat cheese and cilantro

FARRO WITH TOASTED NOODLES
FIVE MORE RECIPES

savory pan-fried farro cakes with goat cheese and cilantro*

Turn leftover farro—or use some of your freshly cooked grains—to make these patties. Rich with goat cheese and fresh with cilantro, they are a great vegetarian main course served with a green salad on the side.

Follow the farro recipe on page 98. Transfer 2 cups to a large bowl and cool completely (save the rest for another use).

To the cooked farro, add 2 beaten large eggs, ⅓ cup crumbled goat cheese, ¼ cup chopped fresh cilantro, ½ cup panko bread crumbs, and a large pinch of salt. Gently fold until well mixed. Using a ¼-cup measuring cup, scoop the mixture and shape it into a 3-inch-round patty. Repeat with the remaining mixture to form 8 patties.

Coat a large nonstick pan with olive oil (2 to 3 tablespoons) and set over medium heat. When the oil is hot and shimmering, add the patties in a single layer, spacing them an inch apart. Cook, turning once, until browned on both sides and heated through, about 5 minutes total. Garnish with fresh cilantro and serve with lemon wedges for squeezing fresh juice on top.

Makes 8 patties

tomato and basil farro with oregano

Simmering the farro in tomato juice, along with basil, oregano, and garlic, results in a farro that tastes a bit like pizza. I like the satisfying wheaty chew with a bit of heat from the Aleppo pepper.

SPICE BLEND

2½ teaspoons dried garlic slices (4 grams)

1 tablespoon dried basil (1 gram)

2 teaspoons dried oregano (1 gram)

½ teaspoon Aleppo pepper (1 gram)

Finely grind the garlic and immediately mix with the whole basil, oregano, and Aleppo. Use this spice blend instead of the main spice blend in the farro recipe on page 98.

Follow the farro recipe, substituting 2 cups tomato juice for 2 cups of the water in step 3.

bacon and onion farro with ajowan

Smoky bacon and caraway with onion is a classic combination, made more interesting here with the warmth of cinnamon and ajowan. This would be great with roast chicken (see page 186).

SPICE BLEND

2 teaspoons dried onion slices (3 grams)

¾ teaspoon caraway seeds (3 grams)

2 teaspoons ajowan (2 grams)

¼ teaspoon ground cinnamon, preferably Vietnamese (1 gram)

Finely grind the onion, caraway, and ajowan together and immediately mix with the cinnamon. Use this spice blend instead of the main spice blend in the farro recipe on page 98.

Follow the farro recipe through step 1.

At the beginning of step 2, before adding oil to the pan, cook 3 strips bacon in the medium pot over medium heat, turning them occasionally, until browned and crisp, 8 to 10 minutes. Drain the bacon on paper towels. Continue step 2 as instructed, adding the butter, enough olive oil to coat the bottom (about 1 teaspoon), and the pasta.

At the end of step 4, crumble the cooked bacon over the farro before serving.

wheat berry pilaf with raisins and almonds

Wheat berries tend to be a little sweeter than farro, making them ideal with raisins and almonds. You can swap in any of your favorite dried fruits and nuts for this pilaf.

Follow the farro recipe on page 98, substituting 1 pound wheat berries for the farro and omitting the soaking in step 1.

At the end of step 3, fold in ½ cup raisins and ½ cup sliced almonds.

Serves 4

farro salad with tomatoes, olives, and feta

Grain salads keep well, whether you're preparing them ahead of time or leaving them for hours on a table, making them perfect for barbecues and picnics. This mix, fresh with mint, would be delicious with grilled lamb or fish.

Follow the farro recipe on page 98, using the main spice blend. Transfer 2 cups of the farro to a large bowl and cool completely (save the rest for another use).

To the cooled farro, add ½ cup pitted and sliced green olives, ½ cup diced tomatoes, ¼ cup chopped fresh mint, and ½ cup crumbled feta cheese. Drizzle with olive oil and sprinkle with salt. Fold gently and season to taste with more oil and salt, if desired.

Serves 2 to 4

CHICKPEA FLATBREADS

sesame sumac flatbreads with nigella seeds

In this master recipe, the duo of nigella and sesame seeds brings crunch to every bite. Sumac adds a surprising tart note and tints the dough a beautiful shade of pink.

MAKES 8 FLATBREADS
SERVES 8 TO 12

MAIN SPICE BLEND

1 tablespoon plus 2 teaspoons dried savory (5 grams)

1 tablespoon plus ¼ teaspoon nigella seeds (10 grams)

1 tablespoon white sesame seeds, preferably unhulled (10 grams)

1 tablespoon plus ¼ teaspoon sumac (10 grams)

Finely grind the savory and immediately mix with the whole nigella seeds, sesame seeds, and sumac.

FLATBREADS

1¼ cups lukewarm water (280 grams)

1 packed tablespoon fresh yeast (15 grams), or 2¼ teaspoons active dry yeast (7 grams)

3 tablespoons plus 1½ teaspoons sugar (45 grams)

2¾ cups all-purpose flour (380 grams), plus more for the work surface

⅔ cup chickpea flour (75 grams)

1½ teaspoons kosher salt (10 grams), plus more for sprinkling

2 tablespoons extra-virgin olive oil (20 grams), plus more for greasing and brushing

MAKE AHEAD

The kneaded dough can be refrigerated for up to 1 day before the second rise, rolling, and baking.

This flatbread, which is my take on pita, is tender thanks to the addition of chickpea flour. It also has loads of flavor since it's flecked with spices inside and topped with them as well. These are fun to make with kids and friends, because they're like pizza, especially with toppings (see page 105). On their own, they're great with hummus (see page 117), labne dip (see page 246), or anything saucy.

1. To make the flatbreads: Whisk the water and yeast with 1½ teaspoons of the sugar (8 grams) in a bowl. Let stand until foamy, about 10 minutes.

2. Meanwhile, combine both flours, the salt, oil, half the spice blend, and the remaining 3 tablespoons sugar (37 grams) in the bowl of a stand mixer. Add the yeast mixture and knead with the dough hook on low speed, scraping the bowl occasionally, until an elastic and sticky ball forms, about 5 minutes.

3. Lightly grease a large bowl with oil. Scrape the dough into the bowl and turn it to coat with oil. Cover with a clean kitchen towel and let it rise in a warm, draft-free spot until doubled in bulk, about 1½ hours. Even better, cover with plastic wrap and refrigerate for up to 24 hours for a more complex and flavorful dough. (If chilled, remove the dough from the fridge and let it stand at room temperature for 1 hour before continuing to step 4.)

4. Arrange a rack in the center of the oven and place a pizza stone or baking sheet on it. Preheat the oven to 400°F.

5. Divide the dough into eight equal portions (about 100 grams each). Shape each piece into a smooth ball and place on a lightly floured work surface. Cover with the kitchen towel and let rest for 20 minutes.

6. Use a rolling pin to roll each ball into a 6-inch-round, ¼-inch-thick disk, flouring only as needed to prevent the dough from sticking to the surface or to the rolling pin. Use a fork to poke a few holes in the top of the dough.

7. Carefully take out the hot pizza stone or baking sheet from the oven and place two or three dough disks on it, spacing them at least an inch apart. Keep the remaining rounds covered with the kitchen towel.

8. Bake until the flatbreads are golden brown in spots on the top and bottom and baked through, 8 to 10 minutes. Transfer to a cooling rack and place more dough rounds on the hot pizza stone or baking sheet. Repeat until all the rounds are baked.

9. When the flatbreads come out of the oven, brush them while they're still warm with a thin sheen of olive oil and sprinkle some of the remaining spice blend and a little salt on top. Serve warm or at room temperature.

YOGURT CHALLAH

golden turmeric challah with nigella seeds

Turmeric tints the dough gold while nigella seeds add an aromatic crunch to every bite.

MAKES TWO 9-INCH LOAVES

MAIN SPICE BLEND

2½ teaspoons nigella seeds (7 grams)

1½ teaspoons ground turmeric (3 grams)

Mix together the nigella seeds and turmeric.

CHALLAH

1 cup lukewarm water (210 grams)

1 tablespoon active dry yeast (11 grams)

¼ cup sugar (50 grams)

2¾ cups all-purpose flour (500 grams)

3 tablespoons extra-virgin olive oil (35 grams), plus more for the bowl

1 tablespoon plus 1 teaspoon labne or plain whole milk Greek yogurt (25 grams)

1 teaspoon kosher salt (4 grams)

2 large eggs (120 grams), at room temperature

¼ cup white sesame seeds, preferably unhulled (40 grams), for sprinkling

MAKE AHEAD

The baked challah can be wrapped tightly in plastic wrap and kept at room temperature for up to 2 days or in the freezer for up to 1 month. Thaw before reheating it in the oven or cutting slices and toasting.

Growing up in Israel, I had challah every Friday for Shabbat and on most days in between. After trying countless recipes, I discovered my favorite in baker Uri Scheft's brilliant book *Breaking Breads*. He figured out the perfect proportions, so why reinvent it when he graciously let me share his formula here? I add labne to make the dough even richer, while olive oil lends a savory flavor. If you want a dairy-free dough, omit the labne. What you can't leave out are spices. They deliver both extra flavor and texture. Nowadays, I bake challah every week with my sons, switching up the seasonings and shapes (see page 109) throughout the year.

1. To make the challah: Whisk the warm water, yeast, and 1 teaspoon of the sugar (5 grams) in a medium bowl. Let stand until foamy, about 10 minutes.

2. Combine the flour, oil, labne, salt, 1 of the eggs, the spice blend, yeast mixture, and the remaining sugar (45 grams) in the bowl of a stand mixer fitted with the dough hook. Mix on low speed, scraping the bowl occasionally, until the dough comes together in a firm, stretchy mass, about 7 minutes.

3. Turn out onto a clean work surface and knead to form a tight ball, about 2 minutes. Lightly oil the mixer bowl, return the dough to it, and cover with a clean kitchen towel. Let rise in a warm spot until doubled in size, about 1 hour.

4. Line a half sheet pan with parchment paper. Turn the dough out onto a clean unfloured work surface and divide it into six equal pieces (about 108 grams each). Roll each into a 12-inch-long rope, pressing and rolling the ends to taper them.

5. Place two ropes parallel to each other, spacing them 3 inches apart. Cross the ropes once, leaving an inch free at the ends. Lay a third rope over the point at which the others cross. Braid the three ropes, tucking in the ends. Repeat with the remaining three ropes to form a second loaf. Transfer both braids to the prepared pan, spaced at least 5 inches apart. Cover with a clean kitchen towel and let rise in a warm place until puffed and the volume increases by about a third, about 45 minutes.

6. Position a rack in the center of the oven and preheat the oven to 400°F. Beat the remaining egg with a few drops of water and gently brush it over the loaves to lightly coat. Sprinkle with the sesame seeds.

7. Bake until browned and well risen, 19 to 20 minutes. Cool completely on a wire rack.

*hazelnut chocolate babka with nutmeg

YOGURT CHALLAH

FIVE MORE RECIPES

smoky cheddar challah with pepitas

Challah tends to be on the sweet side, but here I make it savory by seasoning the dough with ground cumin and smoked paprika. Whole mustard seeds and Cheddar cheese lace the loaves, delivering savory notes with their respective crunchiness and creaminess.

SPICE BLEND

¾ teaspoon cumin seeds (2 grams)

2 teaspoons yellow mustard seeds (10 grams)

1 teaspoon pimentón (smoked paprika; 3 grams)

Finely grind the cumin and immediately mix it with the whole mustard seeds and pimentón. Use this spice blend instead of the main spice blend in the challah recipe on page 106.

Follow the challah recipe, adding ½ cup grated Cheddar cheese (112 grams) at the end of step 2, kneading until everything is evenly distributed.

In step 7, substitute ½ cup pepitas (shelled pumpkin seeds; 68 grams) for the sesame seeds.

raisin walnut challah with cinnamon

Chewy, sweet raisins and crunchy walnuts stud these cinnamon-scented loaves. Toast slices and slather with butter for breakfast.

SPICE BLEND

1¼ teaspoons caraway seeds (5 grams)

1½ teaspoons fennel seeds (3 grams)

1 teaspoon ground cinnamon, preferably Vietnamese (3 grams)

Mix the caraway and fennel seeds with the cinnamon. Use this spice blend instead of the main spice blend in the challah recipe on page 106.

Follow the challah recipe, adding ½ cup raisins (42 grams) and ½ cup chopped walnuts (59 grams) to the kneaded dough at the end of step 2, mixing until evenly distributed.

hazelnut chocolate babka with nutmeg*

A touch of heat from ancho chile amplifies the chocolaty indulgence twisted into this cinnamon-and-ginger-scented dough. Challah dough isn't buttery like traditional babka dough, making this bread as suitable for weekday breakfasts as for brunch. Forming these loaves is a bit of a project, but one well worth trying.

SPICE BLEND

¾ teaspoon ground cinnamon, preferably Vietnamese (2 grams)

½ teaspoon ground ginger (1 gram)

½ teaspoon ground ancho chile (1 gram)

1 teaspoon freshly grated nutmeg (1 gram)

Mix together the cinnamon, ginger, ancho, and nutmeg. Use this spice blend instead of the main spice blend in the challah recipe on page 106.

Follow the challah recipe through step 3.

In step 4, substitute two greased 9 × 5-inch loaf pans for the parchment-lined half sheet pan. Divide the dough in half.

In step 5, flatten one ball into a rectangular shape. With a rolling pin, roll it into a 9 × 12-inch rectangle (1). Use an offset spatula or butter knife to spread ⅓ cup Nutella (95 grams) or other chocolate-hazelnut spread over the dough (2). Sprinkle ½ cup chocolate chips (90 grams) evenly over the spread. Starting from one long side, roll the dough tightly into a long log (3). Cut the log lengthwise in half (4). Twist the two halves together, keeping the exposed chocolate layers facing up, and push in the ends to form a 9-inch-long twist (5). Transfer the twist to one of the prepared pans. Repeat with the remaining dough. Cover both pans with a clean kitchen towel and let rise in a warm place until the dough has risen to the pans' rims, about 45 minutes.

In step 7, omit the sesame seeds.

In step 8, bake until golden brown, 30 to 35 minutes. A cake tester should slide through with no resistance and come out without any raw dough, though there may be melted chocolate clinging to it. If the top begins to brown too much, tent it lightly with foil. When the loaves are done, immediately brush the tops with 2 tablespoons honey mixed with 1 teaspoon water. Cool completely in the pans (6).

garlic knots

Dried garlic delivers a more potent aroma without fresh garlic's risk of burning or tasting steamy. Dried herbs do the same and are especially good under a shower of Parmesan.

SPICE BLEND

1 teaspoon dried garlic slices (2 grams)

2 tablespoons dried rosemary (2 grams)

1 tablespoon dried basil (1 gram)

2 teaspoons dried oregano (1 gram)

¼ teaspoon peperoncini (dried Calabrian chile) or red pepper flakes (½ gram)

Finely grind the garlic and rosemary together and immediately mix with the basil, oregano, and whole peperoncini. Use this spice blend instead of the main spice blend in the challah recipe on page 106.

Follow the challah recipe through step 3.

In step 4, divide the dough into twelve pieces (54 grams each). Roll each into a tight ball.

In step 5, place the balls on the prepared pan, spacing them 2 inches apart. Cover with a clean kitchen towel and let rise in a warm place until the volume has increased by a quarter, about 35 minutes.

In step 7, substitute olive oil for the egg wash and ½ cup finely grated Parmesan cheese (56 grams) for the sesame seeds.

In step 8, bake until golden brown, about 15 minutes. Serve warm or at room temperature.

challah sandwich loaves

Fine-grained and pleasantly chewy, challah is ideal for sandwiches. These loaves will give you the perfect shape to slice for sandwiches.

Follow the challah recipe on page 106 through step 3.

In step 4, substitute two greased 9 × 5-inch loaf pans for the half sheet pan. Divide the dough into six pieces (108 grams each). Roll each into a tight ball.

In step 5, place three balls of dough in each prepared pan. Cover with a clean kitchen towel and let rise in a warm place until the dough has risen to the pans' rims, about 45 minutes.

In step 8, bake until golden brown, about 30 minutes. Serve warm or at room temperature.

LEGUMES
AND EGGS

LEGUMES AND EGGS

Vegetables are the foundation of much of my cooking. Sometimes, I'll eat them with a bit of meat, but often I'll turn vegetables into a hearty, satisfying meal by adding legumes or eggs. In this chapter, you'll find options for bean- and egg-based vegetarian main dishes that only need other vegetables, a salad, great bread, or grains (pages 94 to 101) to make a complete, satisfying dinner. Spices bring such complexity and depth to both beans and eggs that going meatless is easy. They penetrate the thin walls of dried legumes as they cook, infusing them and their cooking liquid with flavor—and spices can be introduced to eggs at almost any stage, from whisking them into scrambled eggs to sprinkling over fried ones.

Before cooking legumes, it's a smart practice to rinse them to wash off sediment, debris, or dust—this is also a good time to remove any tiny pebbles. After soaking, good dried beans should plump in cold water and stay at the bottom of the container; be sure to discard any beans that float or are shriveled. After cooking, the beans can be stored in their cooking liquid in the refrigerator for up to a week or in the freezer for up to three months so they'll be on hand to add instant protein to a meal.

Eggs are so quick to prepare that they are often my go-to for easy weeknight meals and definitely what I turn to for simple yet delicious weekend brunches. On weekday mornings—or even nights—I'll make some basic eggs, toss in a spice blend, and have a really satisfying dish. Here are a few of my favorite mixes.

MASTER SPICE BLENDS

All of these blends can also be added to the cooking water for dried beans/legumes, stirred into them before serving, or pureed with beans/legumes to make a dip or spread.

for sprinkling on fried eggs
¾ teaspoon caraway seeds (3 grams)
1 tablespoon black sesame seeds (10 grams)
1 tablespoon plus 1½ teaspoons white sesame seeds, preferably unhulled (15 grams)
1½ teaspoon sumac (5 grams)
½ teaspoon Urfa pepper (1 gram)

Finely grind the caraway and immediately mix with the whole black and white sesame seeds, sumac, and Urfa.

for stirring into scrambled eggs
2½ teaspoons fennel seeds (5 grams)
2 tablespoons dried rosemary (2 grams)
2 tablespoons plus 1½ teaspoons peperoncino (dried Calabrian chile) or red pepper flakes (15 grams)
2 tablespoons dried marjoram (3 grams)

Finely grind the fennel and rosemary together and immediately mix with the whole peperoncino and marjoram.

for sprinkling on boiled or poached eggs
2 tablespoons plus 1½ teaspoons green peppercorns (15 grams)
1½ teaspoons anise (5 grams)
½ teaspoon yellow mustard seeds (3 grams)
1 teaspoon celery seeds (2 grams)

Finely grind together the peppercorns, anise, mustard seeds, and celery seeds.

for folding into an omelet
1 teaspoon coriander seeds (2 grams)
¼ teaspoon black peppercorns, preferably Tellicherry (1 gram)
2½ teaspoons celery seeds (5 grams)
½ cup dried parsley (15 grams)
2 tablespoons dried tarragon (2 grams)

Finely grind the coriander, peppercorns, and celery seeds together and immediately mix with the whole parsley and tarragon.

CHICKPEAS

smoky chickpeas with garlic and ginger

The rounded heat of ginger and Aleppo pepper is balanced by the warmth of cinnamon and pimentón in these chickpeas. Dried garlic gives the chickpeas a more pronounced yet less sharp allium taste.

MAKES ABOUT 6½ CUPS
SERVES 12

MAIN SPICE BLEND

2½ teaspoons dried garlic slices (4 grams)

½ teaspoon ground ginger (1 gram)

¾ teaspoon ground cinnamon, preferably Vietnamese (2 grams)

1 teaspoon pimentón (smoked paprika; 3 grams)

½ teaspoon Aleppo pepper (1 gram)

Finely grind the garlic and immediately mix with the ginger, cinnamon, pimentón, and Aleppo.

CHICKPEAS

1 pound dried chickpeas

2 tablespoons extra-virgin olive oil, plus more for serving

Kosher salt

MAKE AHEAD

The chickpeas can be cooled completely in the cooking liquid and then refrigerated in their cooking liquid for up to 1 week or frozen for up to 3 months.

While canned chickpeas are passable, they'll never be as tasty as these freshly cooked ones. I like to cook chickpeas just to have them around. They're so easy to prepare, and they're just as good cold as they are hot. It's best to soak them in the fridge overnight to make cooking go quickly, but if you forget, you can still soak them first thing in the morning and they'll be ready for dinner that evening. Once they're done, keep them on hand; they have endless uses (see page 117). Here the spices penetrate the chickpeas while they're cooking, so they taste nuanced even when eaten on their own.

1. To make the chickpeas: Put the chickpeas in a large airtight container and add enough cold water to cover by 2 inches. Cover and refrigerate for at least 6 hours or up to overnight.

2. Drain the chickpeas well and put in a large pot. Add enough cold water to cover by 2 inches and add 2 tablespoons oil. Cover and bring to a boil over high heat. Uncover, skim off any foam that's risen to the surface, and reduce the heat to maintain a simmer. Stir in half the spice blend. Reserve the remaining spice blend for serving.

3. Simmer until the chickpeas are tender all the way through, about 50 minutes. Sample one; it should be very soft now (chickpeas will harden as they cool).

4. Serve the chickpeas warm or at room temperature, seasoning to taste with the remaining spice blend, olive oil, and salt.

*cumin and garlic hummus (top) and chickpea salad with raisins, orange, and celery (bottom)

CHICKPEAS
FIVE MORE RECIPES

chickpea salad with raisins, orange, and celery*

Sweet with raisins and orange and savory with celery and shallots, this all-purpose salad keeps well for a week in the fridge. You can snack on it anytime or serve it as a light main course or as a side dish with grilled chicken or fish.

Follow the smoky chickpeas recipe on page 114. Drain well and transfer the chickpeas to a large bowl.

Add 1 cup golden raisins. 2 finely diced large shallots, 2 finely diced large celery stalks, the zest and diced fruit of 1 orange, 2 tablespoons olive oil, 2 tablespoons sherry vinegar, and the remaining spice blend. Gently fold together and season to taste with salt. Serve immediately or refrigerate for up to a day; the salad tastes best when it sits for at least an hour before serving.

cumin and garlic hummus*

Way smoother, creamier, and more flavorful than the store-bought stuff, this will likely be the best hummus you've ever tasted. Using dried garlic provides all the aroma without the sharpness of raw cloves.

SPICE BLEND

1¼ teaspoons cumin seeds (4 grams)

1 teaspoon dried garlic slices (2 grams)

Finely grind together the cumin and garlic. You will use this for seasoning the hummus.

Follow the smoky chickpeas recipe on page 114, using the main spice blend. Transfer 2 cups of the cooked chickpeas to a small saucepan with enough cooking liquid to cover by ½ inch. Bring to a boil over high heat and then reduce the heat to maintain a simmer. Cover and simmer until the chickpeas are mush, about 20 minutes. Refrigerate the chickpeas in an airtight container until cold.

Drain the chickpeas and transfer to a food processor along with 1 cup high-quality tahini and the spice blend for seasoning the hummus. Pulse until the chickpeas are very finely chopped, scraping the bowl occasionally. With the machine running, add 4 to 8 tablespoons ice-cold water 1 tablespoon at a time until the mixture becomes a thick puree. Process, scraping the bowl occasionally, until very smooth. Season to taste with salt.

crisp fried chickpeas with ajowan and amchoor

Already infused with spices, these chickpeas also get a spice crust that ends up crunchy after a sizzle in olive oil. They're tasty enough to snack on alone but can be served with meat or fish, or over yogurt.

SPICE BLEND

¾ teaspoon cumin seeds (2 grams)

1 teaspoon ajowan (1 gram)

1 teaspoon amchoor (dried mango powder; 2 grams)

⅛ teaspoon pimentón (smoked paprika; ½ gram)

Finely grind the cumin and ajowan together and immediately mix with the amchoor and pimentón. You will use this for frying the chickpeas.

Follow the smoky chickpeas recipe on page 114, using the main spice blend. Drain 2 cups of the cooked chickpeas well, transfer them to paper towels, and roll them around to dry completely. If you have time, refrigerate the chickpeas overnight on a paper-towel-lined plate to dry even more thoroughly.

Coat a large skillet with olive oil (3 to 4 tablespoons) and add the spice blend for frying the chickpeas. Cook over medium heat, stirring, until the spices are sizzling, about 30 seconds. Add the chickpeas and fry, stirring and turning to coat evenly with the spices, until golden brown and crisp, about 5 minutes. Transfer to paper towels to drain.

chickpea fritters with mint and cilantro

These are reminiscent of falafel, but they're heartier in texture. They're great on their own but also nice with a smear of labne or dollop of yogurt.

Follow the smoky chickpeas recipe on page 114. Drain 2 cups of the cooked chickpeas well.

Coat a small saucepan with olive oil (1 to 2 tablespoons) and heat over medium-high heat. Add 1 very finely chopped medium yellow onion and sprinkle with 1 teaspoon celery seeds (2 grams) and a pinch of salt. Cook, stirring occasionally, until tender, about 5 minutes. Transfer to a plate to cool to room temperature.

Pulse the chickpeas in a food processor until ground to the texture of coarse sand. Add the onion mixture, ½ cup chopped fresh cilantro, ¼ cup chopped fresh mint, 1 large egg, and a large pinch of salt. Pulse until blended and transfer to a large bowl. Stir until evenly mixed.

Fill a medium saucepan with grapeseed or another neutral-tasting oil to a depth of 2 inches. Heat over medium heat to 350°F. Using a small ice cream scoop or a tablespoon, pack the chickpea mixture into the scoop and carefully release or push it into the hot oil. Repeat to make three or four balls; do not crowd the pan. Fry, turning to cook evenly, until golden brown and heated through, 3 to 4 minutes. Drain on paper towels and immediately sprinkle with salt. Repeat with the remaining chickpea mixture.

lemon and turmeric chickpea soup

Because it's seasoned with spices, the chickpea-cooking liquid is tasty enough to drink as soup. Simply throw in some onion and garlic and finish the soup with lemon juice. You can also add more diced vegetables if you'd like.

SPICE BLEND

¾ teaspoon cumin seeds (2 grams)

1 tablespoon ground turmeric (3 grams)

1½ teaspoons sweet paprika (3 grams)

1 teaspoon ground ginger (2 grams)

¾ teaspoon ground cinnamon, preferably Vietnamese (2 grams)

Finely grind the cumin and immediately mix with the turmeric, paprika, ginger, and cinnamon. Use this spice blend instead of the main spice blend in the smoky chickpeas recipe on page 114.

Follow the smoky chickpeas recipe, adding 1 medium chopped yellow onion and 2 chopped garlic cloves at the beginning of step 3.

In step 4, stir in the juice of 1 lemon and the remaining spice blend, and season to taste with salt. Divide among bowls and serve hot as soup.

BRAISED WHITE BEANS WITH CHARRED SPINACH

tunisian braised white beans with charred spinach, fennel, and cumin

Bay leaves reinforce the taste of green spinach leaves, while cumin and fennel lend their aromas to the mix. You can eat these beans straight, over rice or couscous, or scooped onto flatbreads (see page 102).

SERVES 6 TO 8

MAIN SPICE BLEND

4 whole dried bay leaves
1½ teaspoons fennel seeds (3 grams)
1 teaspoon cumin seeds (3 grams)
¼ teaspoon cayenne pepper (½ grams)

Finely grind the bay leaves, fennel seeds, and cumin seeds together and immediately mix with the cayenne.

BEANS

1 pound dried cannellini beans
Extra-virgin olive oil
1 (5-ounce) package fresh baby spinach (make sure the spinach is not wet)
1 medium yellow onion, finely diced
Kosher salt
1 tablespoon balsamic vinegar

MAKE AHEAD

The beans can be cooled completely in their cooking liquid and then refrigerated in their cooking liquid in an airtight container for up to 1 week or frozen for up to 2 months.

These braised white beans are the most flavorful white beans you'll ever taste. Spices penetrate the beans while they cook in a liquid infused with charred spinach. Inspired by the traditional Tunisian dish *pkaila*, this braise starts with frying dry spinach leaves in oil until they're nearly blackened. Not only does cooking down spinach make it delicious by concentrating its essential green flavor, it also shortens the beans' cooking time. Honestly, I don't understand the chemistry behind why that happens; I just know it works. The combination takes to a range of seasonings, and the cooked beans can be used in countless ways, from casseroles to spreads (see page 121).

1. To make the beans: Place the beans in a large container, add enough cold water to cover by 2 inches, and cover tightly. Refrigerate for at least 12 hours and up to 16 hours. Drain well, rinse, and drain again.

2. Heat a very large Dutch oven or other heavy pot over medium-high heat. Add enough olive oil to cover the bottom (4 to 5 tablespoons) and heat until very hot, shimmering, and almost smoking, about 2 minutes. Add the spinach and quickly spread it in an even layer. You want a really nice char on the spinach. Sear, using a wooden spoon to stir and smush the spinach and scraping the pot as needed. Keep cooking and adding more olive oil (up to 4 tablespoons more) if the spinach threatens to burn. The spinach is done when it's a bunch of crisp green bits and the olive oil turns dark green, which should take about 10 minutes.

3. Add the onion, stir well, and season generously with salt and half the spice blend. Cook, stirring, for 2 minutes. Add the vinegar and stir well. Add the drained beans and the remaining spice blend. Stir well and add enough water to cover (3 to 4 cups).

4. Raise the heat to high, cover, and bring to a simmer. Reduce the heat to maintain a simmer and cook until the beans are tender, 40 to 60 minutes. Remove from the heat and season to taste with salt. Serve hot, warm, or at room temperature.

*baked white beans with feta and spiced panko bread crumbs

BRAISED WHITE BEANS WITH CHARRED SPINACH

FIVE MORE RECIPES

tomato-and-spinach-braised beans with aleppo and ginger

Crushed tomatoes thicken the braising liquid beautifully while making it a little tangy. The heat of ginger and Aleppo pepper balance that sweet tartness nicely.

SPICE BLEND

1 teaspoon ground ginger (2 grams)

2 tablespoons dried cilantro (2 grams)

½ teaspoon Aleppo pepper (1 gram)

Mix together the ginger, cilantro, and Aleppo. Use this spice blend instead of the main spice blend in the braised white beans recipe on page 118.

Follow the braised white beans recipe, adding ½ cup canned crushed tomatoes along with the drained beans in step 3.

baked white beans with feta and spiced panko bread crumbs*

Dried garlic and parsley make the crunchy panko topping on these beans savory and irresistible. Under that crisp layer, feta cheese melts into a bubbling casserole of tender beans. Serve this as a comforting vegetarian main dish or as the side dish to a nice roast.

SPICE BLEND

1 teaspoon dried garlic slices (2 grams)

1½ teaspoons dried parsley (1 gram)

Finely grind together the garlic and parsley. Transfer to a small bowl and add 1 cup panko bread crumbs, 2 tablespoons extra-virgin olive oil, and a pinch of salt. Stir until evenly combined.

Follow the braised white beans recipe on page 118, using the main spice blend. Transfer 4 cups of the cooked beans with their braising liquid to a large bowl (save the rest for another use) and fold in ½ cup crumbled feta cheese. Spread evenly in a shallow 1½-quart baking dish or casserole. Sprinkle the panko mixture in an even layer on top.

Bake in a preheated 400°F oven until the crumbs are golden brown and the bean liquid is bubbling, about 25 minutes. Serve hot or warm.

mushroom and rosemary braised white beans with charred spinach

When finely ground, dried shiitake mushroom gives these beans a concentrated earthy flavor. Here the shiitakes are paired with the classic duo of garlic and rosemary.

SPICE BLEND

1 dried shiitake mushroom (3 grams), broken

1 tablespoon dried garlic slices (5 grams)

2 tablespoons dried rosemary (2 grams)

¼ teaspoon black peppercorns, preferably
   Tellicherry (1 gram)

Finely grind together the shiitake, garlic, rosemary, and peppercorns. Use this spice blend instead of the main spice blend in the braised white beans recipe on page 118.

Follow the braised white beans recipe, using the mushroom spice blend in step 3.

bacon-and-cider-braised beans

With a hint of the sweetness and smokiness of campfire baked beans, these make a nice addition to a cookout or barbecue.

Follow the braised white beans recipe on page 118 through step 1.

At the beginning of step 2, place 2 slices diced bacon in a dry, very large Dutch oven or other heavy pot. Cook over medium heat, stirring, until the fat renders from the bacon, 3 to 4 minutes. Proceed with the recipe, leaving the bacon and fat in the Dutch oven.

In step 3, add ¼ cup apple cider right before adding the water.

white bean spread with walnuts and yogurt

Whole mustard seeds crunch with a hot little pop in this spread, rich with toasted walnuts and creamy yogurt. It's delicious with crudités, smeared on toast or crackers, or served as a condiment for grilled fish.

Follow the braised white beans recipe on page 118. Transfer 1½ cups of the cooked beans with their braising liquid to a food processor and cool to room temperature (save the rest for another use). Add ⅓ cup toasted chopped walnuts and pulse until smooth, scraping the bowl occasionally. Add ¼ cup labne or plain Greek yogurt and 1 tablespoon white balsamic vinegar. Pulse until smooth. Season to taste with salt and fold in 1 teaspoon yellow mustard seeds (5 grams).

LENTILS

garlicky le puy lentils with mustard seeds

In this master recipe, limon omani adds a citrus note to brighten the earthy taste of the lentils. Garlic, celery seeds, and mustard seeds make these lentils work with any meal, but they're special alongside French ones in particular.

SERVES 6 TO 8

MAIN SPICE BLEND

1 whole limon omani (dried Persian lime; 4 grams)

1 tablespoon dried garlic slices (5 grams)

½ teaspoon celery seeds (1 gram)

1¼ teaspoons yellow mustard seeds (6 grams)

1 teaspoon Urfa pepper (2 grams)

Crack and crush the limon omani into smaller pieces by pressing it against a cutting board with the palm of your hand and transfer to a spice grinder along with the garlic. Finely grind them together and immediately mix with the whole celery seeds, mustard seeds, and Urfa.

LENTILS

Extra-virgin olive oil

1 large yellow onion, finely diced

Kosher salt

1 large carrot, finely diced

1 tablespoon tomato paste

1¼ cups French Le Puy lentils (8 ounces)

MAKE AHEAD

The lentils can be refrigerated for up to 1 week or frozen for up to 3 months.

Le Puy lentils are small, nearly black, and, when uncooked, hard as little stones. Unlike green lentils or red lentils, these French ones don't burst when boiled, meaning they're nearly impossible to overcook and they just about always keep their firm, toothsome texture. Their earthy taste gets even better when they simmer with spices. If you try to season them—or any beans—only after they're cooked, it's hard to get flavor into them. Seasoned Le Puy lentils, however, are good enough to eat by the spoonful alone and even better when turned into soups or stews with the addition of vegetables (pages 50 to 73). I also like stirring them into grains (see pages 94 to 101) for a salad or grain bowl, or eating them alongside pork with mustard and vinegar, as I did when I was a young cook in France.

1. To make the lentils: Coat the bottom of a large saucepan with oil (2 to 3 tablespoons). Set over medium heat and add 1 tablespoon of the spice blend. Cook, stirring continuously, until sizzling, about 30 seconds. Add the onion, season with salt, and stir well. Cover and cook, stirring occasionally, until the onion is translucent, about 5 minutes.

2. Add the carrot and cook, stirring occasionally, until barely tender, about 3 minutes; you want the carrot to keep a nice bite. Add the tomato paste and stir for 1 minute, then add the lentils and stir for 1 minute.

3. Add 3 cups cold water, raise the heat to high, and stir in the remaining spice blend. Bring to a boil, then season to taste with salt. Cover and reduce the heat to maintain a simmer. Cook, stirring and seasoning with salt occasionally (so the lentils are seasoned and cook evenly), until the lentils are just tender, about 45 minutes. (There should be only a tiny bit of liquid left in the pan.) Season to taste with salt and serve.

*carrot and tomato lentil soup with lemon yogurt

LENTILS

FIVE MORE RECIPES

lentil veggie burgers with scallions and cilantro

You can layer these tender veggie patties with whatever you'd like. I like them on a bun with a smear of aioli (see page 246), soft lettuce leaves like butter lettuce, and juicy tomato slices. If you want a cheeseburger, put a slice of your favorite cheese (I prefer Cheddar) on the browned side of the patties after the first flip.

Follow the lentils recipe on page 122. Drain 2 cups of the cooked lentils well and reserve the rest for another use.

Pulse the lentils in a food processor until finely ground to the texture of coarse, wet sand. Add ½ cup panko bread crumbs, ⅓ cup chopped scallions (white and green parts), ⅓ cup chopped fresh cilantro, 1 large egg, and a large pinch of salt. Pulse just until blended and transfer to a large bowl. Stir until evenly mixed.

Using a ½-cup measuring cup and damp hands, scoop the mixture and form it into a 4-inch-round patty. Repeat with the remaining mixture to form 4 patties total.

Coat a large nonstick pan with olive oil (2 to 3 tablespoons) and heat over medium heat. When the oil is hot and shimmering, add the patties in a single layer, spaced about an inch apart. Cook, turning, until browned on both sides and heated through, about 5 minutes per side. Serve on burger buns, layered with the toppings of your choice.

lentil salad with cornichons and mustard vinaigrette

Sweet peppers and salty cornichons add a fresh crunch to lentils. With a simple Dijon vinaigrette, this turns into the ultimate French picnic salad, delicious with charcuterie or a buttered baguette.

Follow the lentils recipe on page 122. Transfer 2 cups of the drained lentils to a large bowl (save the rest for another use), cover, and refrigerate until cold. Stir in ¼ cup chopped cornichons, ¼ cup diced red bell pepper, 1 tablespoon Dijon mustard, and 2 teaspoons red wine vinegar. Season to taste with salt.

lentil and carrot coconut curry

Most lentil curries use red or yellow lentils that fall apart into a savory porridge. Here the lentils stay plump and whole in a coconut broth seasoned with a heady blend of fenugreek and cardamom.

SPICE BLEND

1 tablespoon dried fenugreek leaves (1 gram)
½ teaspoon green cardamom pods (1 gram)
½ teaspoon ground ginger (1 gram)
½ teaspoon ground turmeric (1 gram)

Finely grind the fenugreek and cardamom together and immediately mix with the ginger and turmeric. Use this spice blend instead of the main spice blend in the lentils recipe on page 122.

Follow the lentils recipe, adding ⅓ cup coconut milk with the water in step 3.

carrot and tomato lentil soup with lemon yogurt*

When blended, Le Puy lentils turn into a hearty soup. You can make it as smooth or chunky, thick or thin, as you like. A dollop of yogurt sauce on top makes each spoonful really satisfying.

Follow the lentils recipe on page 122. With the lentils over low heat, use an immersion blender to puree them to your desired consistency (or, alternatively, ladle some into a blender, puree, and then stir it back into the saucepan). While blending, add cold water, ¼ cup at a time, until the soup is as thin or thick as you like it. Season to taste with salt. The soup can be refrigerated for up to 1 week or frozen for up to 3 months.

Whisk ½ cup plain Greek yogurt with 1 tablespoon extra-virgin olive oil and 2 teaspoons fresh lemon juice. Season to taste with salt. Dollop over the soup when serving.

smoky lentils with garlic, bacon, and cinnamon

Rich rendered bacon fat infuses the lentils with a sweeter meatiness when the bacon is cooked just until the fat is translucent. For an even more indulgent dish, top the lentils with additional bacon that's been fried until crisp and then crumbled.

SPICE BLEND

2 teaspoons dried garlic slices (3 grams)
¾ teaspoon cumin seeds (2 grams)
¾ teaspoon pimenton (smoked paprika; 2 grams)
¼ teaspoon ground cinnamon, preferably Vietnamese (1 gram)

Finely grind the garlic and cumin together and immediately mix with the pimenton and cinnamon. Use this spice blend instead of the main spice blend in the lentils recipe on page 122.

Put 2 chopped bacon slices into the dry saucepan. Cook over medium heat, stirring, until the fat renders, about 2 minutes. Add enough olive oil to completely coat the bottom of the saucepan (1 to 2 tablespoons) and proceed with the lentils recipe.

BAKED FRITTATA

zucchini and arugula frittata with feta and oregano

I like to take advantage of zucchini's ability to soak up other flavors. The slices still stay a bit crisp around the eggs and highlight the mix of cumin and coriander.

**MAKES ONE 10-INCH FRITTATA
SERVES 4 TO 6**

MAIN SPICE BLEND
¾ teaspoon cumin seeds (2 grams)
2½ teaspoons coriander seeds (5 grams)
2 teaspoons dried garlic slices (3 grams)
½ teaspoon Aleppo pepper (1 gram)
2 teaspoons dried oregano (1 gram)

Finely grind the cumin, coriander, and garlic together and immediately mix with the Aleppo and oregano.

FRITTATA
Extra-virgin olive oil
1 yellow onion, cut into ½-inch dice
Kosher salt
8 large eggs
½ cup heavy cream
1 small zucchini, quartered lengthwise and cut into
   ½-inch-thick slices
4 cups baby arugula
4 ounces feta cheese, crumbled (1 cup)

Starting the frittata on the stove and finishing it in the oven gives spices a chance to bloom with sautéed onions and greens and thoroughly season the eggs. Plus, using that two-step technique means the eggs won't stick to the pan or overcook, because even, low heat surrounds them in the oven. Even though there's cream and cheese in this base, the result tastes light and works well with different add-ins (see page 129). This is one of the best dishes for using up leftovers—I've added everything from salmon to kale—so feel inspired to toss in whatever you need to use up in your fridge.

1. To make the frittata: Preheat the oven to 375°F.

2. Heat a 10-inch cast-iron or other oven-safe nonstick skillet over medium-high heat. Coat with oil (2 to 3 tablespoons) and add the onion, sprinkle with half the spice blend, and season with salt. Cook, stirring occasionally, until browned around the edges but not translucent, about 7 minutes.

3. Meanwhile, whisk the eggs in a large bowl until blended and then whisk in the cream, a couple spoonfuls of the remaining spice blend, and a very generous pinch of salt.

4. Add the zucchini to the skillet along with half the remaining spice blend and a pinch of salt. Cook, stirring often, until lightly browned but still firm, 5 to 6 minutes. Add the arugula and stir until wilted, about 2 minutes. Stir in the remaining spice blend. If the pan is dry, add a drizzle of oil.

5. Reduce the heat to low and spread the vegetables in an even layer. Scatter half the cheese evenly on top and then slowly pour the egg mixture over the vegetables. Give the skillet a little shake to even out all the vegetables. Raise the heat to medium and scatter the remaining cheese on top. When the egg mixture starts to bubble—it will take a minute or so—transfer the skillet to the oven.

6. Bake until the eggs are just set in the center, about 25 minutes. Transfer to a wire rack and immediately run an offset or silicone spatula around the edges of the skillet to release the sides of the frittata. Serve hot, warm, or at room temperature, cut into wedges.

*mini potato, olive, and bell pepper frittatas

BAKED FRITTATA
FIVE MORE RECIPES

vegetable and feta cheese quiche

Quiche is frittata's richer cousin, baked into a crust. If you'd like, you can start with homemade pie crust. If you do, parbake it before filling and baking again.

Follow the frittata recipe on page 126 through step 1.

In step 2, increase the heavy cream to 2½ cups.

In step 5, divide the vegetables between two parbaked homemade or thawed frozen 9-inch pie crusts and scatter the crumbled feta cheese over the vegetables, dividing it evenly between the crusts. Divide the egg mixture between the two crusts and top with another 4 ounces (1 cup) crumbled feta, dividing it evenly.

In step 6, bake on the bottom rack of the oven until the crusts are golden brown and the egg is set, about 45 minutes. Serve warm or at room temperature.

bacon, cremini mushroom, and spinach frittata

Whole mustard seeds plump in the egg mixture, bringing a mellow-hot pop to every bite of juicy mushrooms and wilted spinach.

SPICE BLEND

½ teaspoon caraway seeds (2 grams)

½ teaspoon black peppercorns, preferably Tellicherry (2 grams)

¾ teaspoon pimenton (smoked paprika; 2 grams)

1 teaspoon yellow mustard seeds (5 grams)

Finely grind the caraway and peppercorns together and immediately mix with the pimenton and whole mustard seeds. Use this spice blend instead of the main spice blend in the frittata recipe on page 126.

Follow the frittata recipe, adding ⅓ cup diced slab bacon along with the onion in step 2.

In step 4, substitute 2 cups trimmed and halved cremini mushrooms for the zucchini and 4 cups baby spinach for the arugula.

asparagus and artichoke frittata with fennel seeds

Fennel seeds taste like spring and, along with za'atar leaves, highlight the grassy freshness of artichokes and asparagus in this frittata. If using canned artichoke hearts, drain them well and add with the asparagus.

SPICE BLEND

1 teaspoon fennel seeds (2 grams)

1 teaspoon freshly grated nutmeg (1 gram)

½ teaspoon peperoncini (dried Calabrian chile) or red pepper flakes (1 gram)

1½ teaspoons dried za'atar leaves (1 gram)

Finely grind the fennel and immediately mix with the nutmeg, whole peperoncini, and za'atar. Use this spice blend instead of the main spice blend in the frittata recipe on page 126.

Follow the frittata recipe, adding 1 cup peeled and diced fresh artichoke stems and hearts along with the onion in step 2.

In step 4, substitute 6 asparagus spears, trimmed and cut into ½-inch slices, for the zucchini.

In step 5, substitute goat cheese for the feta.

tuna and arugula frittata with fresh lemon juice

Be sure to use high-quality tuna packed in olive oil here. It's delicious when set into eggs with wilted peppery arugula.

Follow the frittata recipe on page 126 through step 3.

In step 4, omit the zucchini and add 12 ounces olive oil–packed tuna, flaked into chunks, along with the arugula.

In step 5, omit the feta.

In step 6, squeeze the juice of 1 lemon over the frittata before serving.

mini potato, olive, and bell pepper frittatas*

These individual frittatas are great for brunch parties. Potatoes make them a satisfying main course that needs just a salad to become a complete meal.

Follow the frittata recipe on page 126 through step 3, using the main spice blend.

In step 4, substitute 1 cup diced Yukon Gold potato and 1 cup diced red bell pepper for the arugula. Substitute ½ cup pitted and halved black olives for the arugula.

In step 5, divide the vegetables among six buttered 4½-inch (6-ounce) ovenproof ramekins and set on a half sheet pan. Divide half the feta cheese evenly among the ramekins and pour in the egg mixture. Top with the remaining feta.

In step 6, bake until the eggs are set, about 25 minutes.

SHAKSHUKA

tomato and pepper shakshuka with coriander and paprika

Savory celery seeds combine with the heat of chipotle and sweetness of paprika in a classic tomato and pepper shakshuka sauce, and the toasty aroma of coriander seeds helps all those seasonings work together.

SERVES 6

MAIN SPICE BLEND

2 teaspoons coriander seeds (4 grams)

1 teaspoon celery seeds (2 grams)

¼ teaspoon ground chipotle chile (½ gram)

2 teaspoons sweet paprika (4 grams)

Finely grind the coriander and celery seeds together and immediately mix with the chipotle and paprika.

SHAKSHUKA

Extra-virgin olive oil

3 large garlic cloves, thinly sliced

2 large shallots, thinly sliced lengthwise

Kosher salt

2 red bell peppers, very thinly sliced

2 green bell peppers, very thinly sliced

1 tablespoon tomato paste

1 (14.5-ounce) can diced tomatoes

6 large eggs, at room temperature

Challah, pita, or other bread, for serving

MAKE AHEAD

Before the eggs are added, the tomato sauce can be refrigerated in an airtight container for up to 1 week. Bring it back to a simmer in a sauté pan before adding the eggs. If the mixture has thickened, add a little water. The sauce should be as loose as when you first finished cooking it.

At its core, shakshuka is eggs cooked in a simmering sauce. It's one of Israel's most popular dishes, and I grew up eating it at least once a week. I've taken this one-pan meal and come up with endless variations for the sauce and its uses (see page 133). And remember that you don't have to use up all the sauce at once. You can reheat only as much as you want to eat, whether it's enough sauce for one egg, two, or more. Shakshuka is delicious any time of the day and can be served with salad or beans (pages 114 to 124). No matter what, be sure to have some challah (see page 106), flatbreads (see page 102), or other bread on hand. You'll want it to swipe up the sauce.

1. To make the shakshuka: Coat a large sauté pan (a straight-sided skillet) with oil (2 to 3 tablespoons). Set over medium heat and add the spice blend and garlic. Cook, stirring, until sizzling and fragrant, 1 to 2 minutes.

2. Add the shallots, season with salt, and stir well. Cover and reduce the heat to low. Cook, stirring occasionally, until translucent, 5 to 6 minutes. Add the red and green bell peppers, stir well, and cover. Cook, stirring occasionally, until the bell peppers are tender, about 10 minutes.

3. Add the tomato paste, raise the heat to medium, and stir for 2 minutes. Stir in the tomatoes and 1 cup water. Bring to a simmer and then reduce the heat to medium-low and cover. Cook for 5 minutes. Uncover and season to taste with salt.

4. Adjust the heat so the sauce maintains a steady simmer. Crack the eggs on top, spacing them apart. Cover and cook to your desired preference. I like my whites set and yolks runny, which takes 6 to 7 minutes. If you're not serving this right away, remember that the eggs will continue to cook in the sauce's residual heat. Serve with bread.

*tomato and pepper pizzas with sunny-side-up eggs

SHAKSHUKA
FIVE MORE RECIPES

shakshuka with halloumi and pistachios

Halloumi cheese softens a bit in the sauce but still keeps its tender bite. Pistachios add a nice crunch on top.

Follow the shakshuka recipe on page 130 through step 3, using the main spice blend.

At the end of step 4, when the eggs are just set, scatter 4 ounces diced halloumi around the eggs. Sprinkle ⅓ cup chopped roasted salted pistachios on top before serving.

italian sausage shakshuka with pimentón and cinnamon

Browned sausage makes this shakshuka especially satiating, as does a generous dose of smoky pimentón. You can use your favorite fresh sausage here, whether that is Italian-style links, breakfast sausages, or merguez lamb sausages.

SPICE BLEND

1 teaspoon ground cinnamon, preferably Vietnamese (3 grams)

2¼ teaspoons pimentón (smoked paprika; 7 grams)

¼ teaspoon cayenne pepper (½ gram)

Mix together the cinnamon, pimentón, and cayenne. Use this spice blend instead of the main spice blend in the shakshuka recipe on page 130.

Follow the shakshuka recipe, but start step 1 by cooking 8 ounces sausage links in the oil (before adding the garlic) until browned on all sides, about 5 minutes. Transfer to a cutting board and, when cool enough to handle, cut into ½-inch-thick slices.

In step 4, after cracking the eggs into the sauce, scatter the sausage slices around the eggs.

tomato and pepper pizzas with sunny-side-up eggs*

Shakshuka sauce tastes a lot like a good pizza sauce, so this is a natural extension of the original. If you want to try this but don't want to deal with fresh pizza dough, you can use good pita and skip the step of baking the dough to set it. Each pizza serves 2 to 4; I like to make six to serve a dozen guests.

Double the main spice blend recipe on page 130 and reserve half for sprinkling. Use the remaining (original) amount of the spice blend and follow the shakshuka recipe on page 130 through step 3. Let the sauce cool to room temperature.

Double the number of eggs in the master recipe for 12 large eggs total.

Divide 30 ounces homemade or store-bought pizza dough into six (5-ounce) pieces. Shape each into a ball and set aside on a lightly floured work surface, covered with a clean kitchen towel, until they have relaxed, about 15 minutes.

Preheat the oven to 500°F.

Roll one dough ball on a lightly floured surface into an 8-inch round. Put it on a large baking sheet and spread with ½ cup of the shakshuka sauce, leaving a ½-inch rim free of sauce. Bake until the dough is just set and dry to the touch, about 5 minutes.

Crack 2 large eggs on top and grate Parmesan cheese all over. Return the pizza to the oven and bake until the egg whites are cooked through and the yolks are still runny, 5 to 6 minutes longer. Sprinkle kosher salt and a pinch of the remaining spice blend over the eggs. Repeat with the remaining dough, sauce, and eggs. You can make multiple pizzas at one time, if you'd like.

green shakshuka with cumin and caraway

A common alternative to the iconic tomato-based shakshuka is one made with wilted greens. Here the greens taste even more savory with the trio of cumin, caraway, and yellow mustard seeds. Spinach is my personal favorite, but any dark leafy greens, from kale to chard, work too. Just cook them down before adding the eggs.

SPICE BLEND

1 teaspoon cumin seeds (3 grams)

¾ teaspoon caraway seeds (3 grams)

1 teaspoon yellow mustard seeds (5 grams)

Finely grind the cumin and caraway seeds together and immediately mix with the whole mustard seeds. Use this spice blend instead of the main spice blend in the shakshuka recipe on page 130.

Follow the shakshuka recipe, omitting the red bell peppers in step 2.

In step 3, after stirring in the tomato paste, substitute 2 pounds chopped fresh spinach for the can of tomatoes and omit the water. Cook the spinach, stirring, until wilted, about 2 minutes.

squashuka

Forgive the pun, but it's good, right? Butternut squash—or any other sweet winter squash—becomes an earthy sunset-hued sauce for cradling the eggs.

Follow the shakshuka recipe on page 130 through step 2.

In step 3, substitute 1½ pounds diced butternut squash for the tomato paste and tomatoes and add an additional 1 cup water (for 2 cups water total). Bring to a boil over high heat. Cover, reduce the heat to maintain a simmer, and cook, stirring occasionally, until the squash is very tender, about 25 minutes. Smash the squash with a fork into a chunky sauce, adding more water if needed. Season to taste with salt and spread the sauce in an even layer in the pan before adding the eggs.

OLIVE OIL DEVILED EGGS

labne deviled eggs with paprika and ginger

Labne in place of mayonnaise gives the filling a little tang. You'll still get classic creaminess, as well as mustardy heat. Starting with whole mustard seeds offers a more complex taste than using pre-ground mustard powder.

MAKES 10
SERVES 6 TO 10

MAIN SPICE BLEND

¾ teaspoon yellow mustard seeds (4 grams)

½ teaspoon black peppercorns, preferably Tellicherry (2 grams)

1 teaspoon ajowan (1 gram)

½ teaspoon sweet paprika (1 gram)

¼ teaspoon ground ginger (½ gram)

Finely grind the mustard seeds and peppercorns together and immediately mix with the ajowan, paprika, and ginger.

DEVILED EGGS

5 large eggs

3 tablespoons labne or plain Greek yogurt

2 teaspoons extra-virgin olive oil

Kosher salt

MAKE AHEAD

The deviled eggs can be refrigerated in an airtight container for up to 2 days.

They're a special thing, deviled eggs, and while they seem like a treat that someone took the time to make, at the end of the day, they're really very simple. I tend to think of them as composed egg salad, something I grew up eating a lot of (and they do make a great salad; see page 137). I play around with the fillings—spicing them up, of course, but also using different creamy elements (see page 137). To give traditional deviled eggs even more flavor, I sprinkle the usually bland whites with spices, too. It's as striking visually as it is taste-wise.

1. To make the deviled eggs: Put the eggs in a small saucepan and cover with cold water by 1 inch. Bring to a boil over high heat and then remove from the heat, cover, and let stand for 10 minutes.

2. Tilting the saucepan, pour out the hot water, holding back the eggs with a slotted spoon. Run cold water into the saucepan until it is cold. Cover the eggs with more cold water and let sit until the eggs are completely cold. Carefully peel the eggs and cut each in half lengthwise. To get clean cuts, use a very sharp knife and wipe the blade after each cut.

3. Pop out the yolks and place them in a medium bowl, and set the whites on a cutting board. Smash the yolks with a fork until crumbly and add the labne, oil, 1¼ teaspoons of the spice blend, and a pinch of salt. Mash and stir until smooth. Season to taste with salt.

4. Rub some of the remaining spice blend all over the cut sides and cavities of the egg whites to coat and set them cut-side up on a serving plate. Evenly divide the yolk mixture among the cavities and sprinkle with any remaining spice blend.

*deviled egg salad

OLIVE OIL DEVILED EGGS
FIVE MORE RECIPES

tahini and olive deviled eggs with mint and sumac

Nutty tahini and briny olives give this filling a savory jolt. The tang of sumac keeps it feeling light and adds a beautiful red hue.

SPICE BLEND

1 teaspoon dried mint (1 gram)

1 teaspoon sumac (3 grams)

¼ teaspoon black peppercorns, preferably Tellicherry (1 gram)

Finely grind together the mint, sumac, and peppercorns. Use this spice blend instead of the main spice blend in the deviled eggs recipe on page 134.

Follow the deviled eggs recipe, substituting 1 tablespoon tahini for the labne and adding 1 tablespoon finely chopped pitted black olives to the yolk mixture in step 3. If the mixture is too stiff, stir in 1 teaspoon olive oil.

walnut-scallion deviled eggs with coriander and turmeric

Toasted walnuts add a little crunch to the creamy yolk filling, which is freshened here with scallions. Dhania coriander has a lighter, grassier scent than regular, but whichever seeds you have on hand will work well here.

SPICE BLEND

1 teaspoon coriander seeds, preferably Dhania (2 grams), toasted (see page 37)

1 teaspoon ground turmeric (2 grams)

¼ teaspoon ground chipotle chile (½ gram)

Finely grind the coriander and immediately mix with the turmeric and chipotle. Use this spice blend instead of the main spice blend in the deviled eggs recipe on page 134.

Follow the deviled eggs recipe, substituting 2 tablespoons mayonnaise for the labne and adding ¼ cup chopped toasted walnuts and ¼ cup finely chopped scallions (white and green parts) to the yolk mixture in step 3.

deviled egg salad*

When I don't feel like stuffing deviled eggs, I still get to enjoy the taste by making this salad. It's as good by the spoonful as it is sandwiched between bread.

Follow the deviled eggs recipe on page 134 through step 3.

Coat a small skillet with olive oil and heat over medium heat. Add ½ cup chopped yellow onion, the remaining spice blend that would've been rubbed on the egg whites and sprinkled on top, and a pinch of salt. Cook, stirring occasionally, until the onions are almost tender, about 5 minutes. Transfer to a large bowl and cool completely.

Add the yolk mixture, egg whites, and ½ cup labne to the cooled onion. Stir with a fork, cutting up the egg whites, until well mixed. Season to taste with salt.

goat cheese deviled eggs with sesame seeds

Goat cheese brings a more pronounced tanginess and richer thickness to the filling, while sesame seeds add a nutty flavor and delicate crunch.

Prepare the main spice blend and mix in 1 tablespoon white sesame seeds, preferably unhulled (10 grams). Use this blend and follow the deviled eggs recipe on page 134 through step 2.

In step 3, substitute 3 tablespoons softened goat cheese for the labne and increase the olive oil to 2 tablespoons.

tuna and caper deviled eggs

Like a cross between tuna salad and egg salad, these savory deviled eggs can be served as a main dish at lunch. All you need are a green salad and bread to complete the meal.

Follow the deviled eggs recipe on page 134 through step 2.

In step 3, add ¼ cup finely flaked olive oil–packed tuna and 1 tablespoon chopped capers to the yolk mixture.

SEAFOOD

SEAFOOD

Pairing seafood with spices is an exercise in extremes. Some seafood, such as flaky, mild white fish like cod, can border on bland if cooked without spices or some kind of seasoning. For these types of fish, you don't want seasonings that overpower in either taste or scent. Other varieties, like oily salmon or sea-salty mussels, have a lot of personality, and these need stronger spices like chiles or fennel that can stand up to their assertiveness. The cooking technique makes a difference too—if you're searing on the stovetop over high heat or using another direct-heat cooking method like grilling, you want the spices to hold up to the flames, so you should use hardier whole spices (like caraway seeds or fennel seeds) that won't burn early. For indirect or low-heat or liquid-based cooking such as poaching or braising, you can apply more delicate spices like dried herbs.

When I was a young cook training in France, I asked my teacher, "How do you know when fish is ready?" He answered, "If you think it's ready, it's already overcooked." Once you understand that idea, your approach to cooking seafood will change. You should always be aware of the fish as it's cooking, remembering that most fish can be cooked to medium and will taste better that way. Fully opaque fish is the clearest indication of well-doneness, so if you remove it from the heat before that point (when it is opaque at the exterior but still slightly transucent in the middle), you can be confident that carryover heat during the plating process will give you perfectly cooked fish.

Even though spices were once used to disguise less-than-fresh fish and meat, nowadays you're much better off just finding a great source for fresh fish—whether that is a fish market or a good seafood counter at the supermarket. Don't be shy about asking to smell whatever you want. Fresh fish should smell a little sweet; if it smells like dirty marina docks, choose something else (or go fishing!). Fish should look pristine, firm, and shiny with no gaps in the flesh. Shellfish should be shut tight, and shrimp should be perky and taut, not floppy.

These spice blends are quite flexible and fun to have on hand for a quick and healthy way to add flavor and spice to seafood. As you learn the principles behind my blends by cooking and tasting these recipes, you can try mixing and matching them with other types of seafood and, better yet, start creating your own.

MASTER SPICE BLENDS

for sprinkling on fish before broiling (any fish will do—buy whatever is freshest)

1 teaspoon yellow mustard seeds (5 grams)
½ teaspoon black peppercorns, preferably Tellicherry (2 grams)
6 tablespoons dried oregano (9 grams)
7 tablespoons dried thyme (14 grams)
2½ teaspoons sweet paprika (5 grams)

Finely grind the mustard seeds and peppercorns together and immediately mix with the oregano, thyme, and paprika.

for sprinkling on fish before baking (like cod or mackerel)

¾ teaspoon coriander seeds (1½ grams), toasted (see page 37)
¾ teaspoon dried garlic slices (1½ grams)
5 tablespoons dried basil (5 grams)
1 tablespoon dried mint (3 grams)

Coarsely grind the coriander, garlic, basil, and mint together.

for sprinkling on fish before grilling (like salmon or swordfish)

¾ teaspoon cumin seeds (2 grams)
5 tablespoons ground turmeric (15 grams)
2½ teaspoons ground ginger (5 grams)
1 teaspoon ground cinnamon, preferably Vietnamese (3 grams)
½ teaspoon cayenne pepper (1 gram)

Finely grind the cumin and immediately mix with the turmeric, ginger, cinnamon, and cayenne.

for sprinkling on shellfish (like shrimp or crabs)

2 teaspoons yellow mustard seeds (10 grams)
¾ teaspoon caraway seeds (3 grams)
1 tablespoon plus 2 teaspoons pimentón (smoked paprika; 15 grams)
3 tablespoons dried oregano (5 grams)

Finely grind the mustard seeds and caraway together and immediately mix with the pimentón and oregano.

SUGAR-AND-SALT-CURED SALMON

dilled cured salmon with mustard and caraway seeds

Using the whole seeds of gravlax's classic dill and mustard seasonings flavors the salmon all the way through. Caraway is reminiscent of rye bread, which would be the ideal toast on which to serve this version.

SERVES 6 TO 8

MAIN SPICE BLEND

1½ teaspoons dill seeds (3 grams)

¾ teaspoon yellow mustard seeds (4 grams)

½ teaspoon caraway seeds (2 grams)

1 teaspoon green peppercorns (2 grams)

Coarsely grind the dill, mustard seeds, caraway, and green peppercorns.

SALMON

3 tablespoons gray salt, or 2 tablespoons kosher salt

1 tablespoon sugar

6 sprigs fresh dill

1 (1-pound) boneless, skinless salmon fillet (1½ inches thick)

MAKE AHEAD

The cured salmon can be refrigerated for up to 1 week.

Spices and time are all it takes to end up with delicious home-cured salmon. Because salmon is so fatty, it takes well to curing in sugar and salt. Silkier than store-bought lox, this supple-textured cured salmon is based on gravlax. Usually, it's made with whole sides of salmon, but I prefer to make a small 1-pound batch since it's best eaten within a week (unless you are having a party, in which case, double or triple the recipe). While gravlax is commonly made with skin-on salmon, I find that the spices flavor the fish much more readily when both sides are skinless. Of course, the better the salmon, the better the result. If you can't get a piece of salmon that's 1½ inches thick all the way across (ask for the fillets cut from the belly section of the fish), cut off the thinner part of the salmon and cure it in a separate container for only 12 hours. Serve the salmon on toast, with rice, in a salad, or chopped and mixed into scrambled eggs (see page 145), or use it to make a delicious dip, like Salmon and Scallion Labne Spread (page 145).

1. To make the salmon: Mix the salt and sugar with the spice blend in a small bowl. Place 3 dill sprigs in the bottom of a dish or container that will hold the salmon snugly. Sprinkle half the salt mixture over the dill and then place the salmon on top. Pat the remaining salt mixture all over the top of the salmon and then lay the remaining dill on top. Cover tightly with a lid or plastic wrap.

2. Refrigerate until the salmon is firmer and a deeper shade of orange, about 18 hours (some liquid should be pooling in the container). Rinse the salmon under cold water, discarding the dill and any remaining salt mixture, and pat it dry with paper towels. When ready to serve, cut the salmon into thin slices across the grain.

*salmon and scallion labne spread

SUGAR-AND-SALT-CURED SALMON

FIVE MORE RECIPES

sumac-and-pernod-cured salmon with cilantro, cumin, and fennel

The citrusy tartness of sumac brightens this salmon cure and dyes the fish a beautiful shade of pink.

SPICE BLEND

¾ teaspoon cumin seeds (2 grams)

1½ teaspoons fennel seeds (3 grams)

¾ teaspoon Muntok white peppercorns (2 grams)

1¼ teaspoons sumac (4 grams)

Put the cumin and fennel seeds in a small skillet, set over medium heat, and toast, shaking the pan occasionally, until fragrant and golden, about 3 minutes. Immediately transfer the seeds to a spice grinder along with the white peppercorns and sumac and pulse until coarsely ground. Cool completely, then use this spice blend instead of the main spice blend in the cured salmon recipe on page 142.

Follow the cured salmon recipe, substituting 6 sprigs fresh cilantro for the dill. In step 1, rub the salmon with 1 tablespoon Pernod, pastis, or arak before sprinkling with the salt-sugar mixture.

salmon and scallion labne spread*

Lighter than a smoked salmon cream cheese, this spread is wonderful on bagels or any type of toast or cracker.

Follow the cured salmon recipe on page 142. Cut enough slices into ¼-inch dice to yield ½ cup diced cured salmon and transfer to a bowl. Add 1 cup labne or sour cream, the zest and juice of ½ lemon, and 1 tablespoon minced scallion (white and green parts). Fold until well mixed, then season to taste with salt and coarsely ground black pepper, preferably Tellicherry. Spread over toasts, flatbreads, or other bread or crackers. The spread can be refrigerated for up to 2 days.

juniper-and-orange-cured salmon

Combining piney juniper berries and rosemary with orange results in a blend that's reminiscent of mulled wine and other wintery treats, making this version an ideal appetizer for holiday parties and buffets.

SPICE BLEND

1½ teaspoons coriander seeds (3 grams)

2 tablespoons dried rosemary (2 grams)

1½ teaspoons juniper berries (5 grams)

¾ teaspoon granulated dried orange peel (2 grams)

½ teaspoon cayenne pepper (1 gram)

Toast the coriander seeds in a small skillet over medium heat, shaking the pan, until fragrant and golden, about 3 minutes. Transfer immediately to a spice grinder along with the rosemary and juniper and pulse until coarsely ground. Immediately mix with the orange peel and cayenne. Use this spice blend instead of the main spice blend in the cured salmon recipe on page 142.

Follow the cured salmon recipe, substituting 6 sprigs fresh rosemary for the dill.

seed-crusted cured salmon

A quartet of seeds pressed onto just-cured salmon adds a delicious crunch to every bite of the supple fish. To get the freshest pop from the seeds, enjoy this right away; however, the seeds on the salmon will retain a little crunch for a few days in the fridge.

SPICE BLEND

1 teaspoon yellow mustard seeds (5 grams)

2½ teaspoons poppy seeds (10 grams)

1 teaspoon celery seeds (2 grams)

1 teaspoon nigella seeds (3 grams)

Toast the mustard seeds in a small skillet over medium heat, shaking the pan occasionally, until fragrant and golden, about 2 minutes.

Immediately mix with the poppy seeds, celery seeds, and nigella seeds. Cool to room temperature. You will use this to coat the salmon.

Follow the cured salmon recipe on page 142, using the main spice blend. Immediately after rinsing the cured salmon, evenly press the seed spice blend onto the fish to coat. Slice and serve or refrigerate for up to 2 days.

scrambled eggs with cured salmon

Cured salmon pairs naturally with creamy scrambled eggs and is even better when cooked right into them. Here, a duo of flaxseeds and sesame seeds adds a tiny crunch to every bite.

SPICE BLEND

1 teaspoon flaxseeds (2 grams)

1½ teaspoons white sesame seeds, preferably unhulled (5 grams)

Toast the flaxseeds and sesame seeds in a small skillet over medium heat, shaking the pan occasionally, until fragrant and golden, about 5 minutes. Transfer to a medium bowl and cool completely. You will use this to coat the cured salmon.

Follow the cured salmon recipe on page 142, using the main spice blend. Cut enough slices into ¼-inch dice to yield ½ cup diced cured salmon. Add to the bowl with the toasted seeds and toss until evenly coated.

Beat 6 large eggs with a pinch of salt in a medium bowl. Heat 1 tablespoon extra-virgin olive oil and 1 tablespoon salted butter in a large cast-iron or nonstick skillet over medium heat. When the butter melts, add the beaten eggs and cook, stirring with a silicone spatula, until small curds form but the eggs are still quite wet, about 2 minutes. Fold in the salmon mixture and cook until the eggs are just barely set and still a little wet. Serve immediately.

POACHED SALMON

basil and garlic poached salmon

Basil and fennel bring brightness to earthy garlic in this salmon-poaching broth. Fresh shallots, caramelized until sweet, marries the heat of white pepper with the other spices.

SERVES 4

MAIN SPICE BLEND

2 teaspoons dried garlic slices (3 grams)
1 tablespoon dried basil (1 gram)
¾ teaspoon Muntok white peppercorns (2 grams)
½ teaspoon fennel seeds (1 gram)

Finely grind together the garlic, basil, peppercorns, and fennel.

POACHED SALMON

Extra-virgin olive oil
3 large shallots, thinly sliced crosswise (about 1 cup)
Kosher salt
4 (1-inch-thick) skin-on boneless salmon fillets
    (4 to 5 ounces each)
½ lemon, scrubbed, seeded, and finely diced (with its
    peel)
½ cup dry white wine

MAKE AHEAD

The salmon can be refrigerated in its poaching liquid for up to 3 days.

Poaching salmon keeps it extremely moist and makes it silky and flavorful—it's also incredibly easy and takes very little time to cook. Unlike most watery poaching broths, the one I use to poach salmon is *overly* seasoned so that the salmon ends up *perfectly* seasoned. The remaining poaching liquid becomes almost like a sauce—I actually like to eat the sliced shallots and diced lemon from the liquid, which soak up the seasonings, alongside the salmon. You can stir noodles, rice, or croutons into the rest of the liquid or just sip on it. Note that I call for skin-on salmon here because the skin holds the fish together in one piece. Skinless fillets work, too, but they may flake apart when you plate them.

1. To make the poached salmon: Heat a large saucepan, preferably 8 to 10 inches in diameter and at least 5 inches deep, over medium-low heat. Add enough oil to lightly coat the bottom (2 to 3 tablespoons). Add the shallots, 2 pinches of the spice blend, and a pinch of salt. Stir to evenly coat the shallots with the spices and cover. Cook the shallots, stirring occasionally, until translucent, about 10 minutes.

2. Meanwhile, sprinkle the remaining spice blend all over the salmon and set aside.

3. Add the lemon to the pan, stir well, and add the wine. Bring to a simmer over high heat. Season to taste with salt. Simmer until the wine has reduced by a third, about 3 minutes. Add 1½ cups water and season to taste with salt. Bring to a boil and then reduce the heat to maintain a steady and low simmer.

4. Season the salmon with salt, then nestle the fillets in the simmering liquid, skin-side up, in a single layer. The liquid should just cover the salmon skin. If it doesn't, add a little more water.

5. Poach until the salmon is opaque on the outside and barely cooked in the center, about 5 minutes. If you insert a cake tester or thin-bladed paring knife into the center, it should start by sliding through easily, then meet a little resistance. Transfer the salmon to individual serving dishes, peel off and discard the skin, and turn the salmon right-side up. Spoon the shallots and lemon all around.

6. Bring the poaching liquid to a boil and cook until it is reduced by a quarter, about 3 minutes. Reduce the heat to low and stir in a tablespoon of olive oil. Season to taste with salt. Spoon some liquid over the salmon and serve the remainder on the side.

*tomato-poached salmon with rosemary and aleppo pepper

POACHED SALMON
FIVE MORE RECIPES

tomato-poached salmon with rosemary and aleppo pepper*

A little tomato paste sweetens and thickens the poaching liquid, while rosemary adds an herbaceous note. This preparation would be great with pasta.

SPICE BLEND

2 tablespoons dried rosemary (2 grams)

1 tablespoon dried onion slices (4 grams)

1 teaspoon Aleppo pepper (2 grams)

Finely grind the rosemary and onion together and immediately mix with the Aleppo. Use this spice blend instead of the main spice blend in the poached salmon recipe on page 146.

Follow the poached salmon recipe, stirring in 1 tablespoon tomato paste with the lemon and before adding the wine in step 3.

flaked salmon salad with cornichons

You can use a leftover poached salmon fillet here or poach an extra one in the same liquid to have it on hand for this tasty salad. It's nice spread on toast or served over salad greens. This recipe makes enough to serve one or two; the recipe easily doubles, triples, or quadruples to serve many more.

Follow the poached salmon recipe on page 146. Refrigerate 1 salmon fillet until cold. Eat the rest hot or reserve for another use.

Mix 2 tablespoons mayonnaise, 1 tablespoon finely chopped cornichons, 1 teaspoon ground turmeric (1 gram), and the zest of ½ lemon in a medium bowl. Flake the chilled salmon into the bowl and gently fold in the mayonnaise mixture to evenly coat. Season to taste with salt.

butter-poached salmon with capers and green peppercorns

In French kitchens, butter rules. Here, poaching salmon in butter makes for an indulgent dish that—believe it or not—doesn't taste too heavy, especially when paired, as it is here, with spices like dill weed, tarragon, and mustard to lighten its taste.

SPICE BLEND

½ teaspoon yellow mustard seeds (2 grams)

1¼ teaspoons dried dill weed (1 gram)

1 tablespoon dried tarragon (1 gram)

½ teaspoon green peppercorns (1 gram)

Finely grind the mustard seeds, dill, tarragon, and peppercorns together. Use this spice blend instead of the main spice blend in the poached salmon recipe on page 146.

Follow the poached salmon recipe, substituting 2 tablespoons salted butter for the olive oil in step 1.

In step 3, add ¼ cup capers, rinsed and drained, with the lemon.

In step 6, substitute 2 tablespoons salted butter for the olive oil, stirring it in until it melts and emulsifies with the liquid.

cream-poached salmon with fennel seeds

While this sounds rich, it tastes surprisingly light. The cream gives the sauce a little body and is delicious with rice or bread.

Follow the poached salmon recipe on page 146 through step 2, using the main spice blend.

In step 3, substitute ½ cup heavy cream for ½ cup of the water.

In step 6, substitute 1 tablespoon salted butter for the olive oil, stirring it in until it melts and emulsifies with the liquid.

soy-poached salmon with coconut broth and shiitakes

Creamy coconut milk turns the poaching liquid into a rich broth that you'll want to spoon over steamed rice.

SPICE BLEND

1 whole dried shiitake mushroom (3 grams)

1½ teaspoons dried thyme (1 gram)

2 teaspoons dried garlic slices (3 grams)

¼ teaspoon anise (1 gram)

Finely grind the shiitake, thyme, garlic, and anise together. Use this spice blend instead of the main spice blend in the poached salmon recipe on page 146.

Follow the poached salmon recipe, omitting the lemon and substituting 1 tablespoon soy sauce and 2 tablespoons rice wine vinegar for the white wine and 1 (14.5-ounce) can coconut milk for the water.

SEARED SALMON

coriander-and-fennel-crusted seared salmon

In this master recipe, mild Muntok white pepper blends together aromatic coriander and fennel with slightly bitter caraway. A nice helping of dried onion provides a little allium sweetness.

SERVES 4

MAIN SPICE BLEND

2½ teaspoons coriander seeds (5 grams)

1½ teaspoons fennel seeds (3 grams)

¾ teaspoon Muntok white peppercorns (2 grams)

½ teaspoon caraway seeds (2 grams)

1 tablespoon plus ¾ teaspoon dried onion slices (5 grams)

Finely grind together the coriander, fennel, peppercorns, caraway, and onion.

SALMON

4 (1-inch thick) skin-on salmon fillets (7 ounces each)

Kosher salt

Extra-virgin olive oil

1 lemon, cut into 8 wedges

MAKE AHEAD

You can coat the salmon with the spice blend before salting it and refrigerate it for up to 4 hours before seasoning with salt and searing.

Salmon skin is delicious when pan-seared—it becomes as crisp as a potato chip—and it's even tastier when it's crusted with spices. Those same spices surround the salmon while searing, encasing the flesh to balance its richness. When the spices sear onto the salmon, they toast in the process and become more fragrant and flavorful. Cooking salmon to the perfect degree of doneness (I like mine medium-rare) is easy because the fish has its own built-in thermometer—just look at the side of the fillet to see when the flesh becomes opaque all the way from bottom to top. As soon as the sides lose their translucence, I pull the pan off the stove so the salmon doesn't overcook—that means the center's still nice and pink for medium-rare (for extra assurance, you can always insert a thin-bladed knife into the thickest part of the fish and peek at the center; it should still be slightly translucent). Crisp outside and silken inside, this salmon takes well to different spices, and leftovers can end up in other dishes, too, like an arugula salad or crispy Salmon Potato Patties (page 153).

1. To make the salmon: Place the salmon on a large half sheet pan. Sprinkle salt all over the salmon and then sprinkle the spice blend all over as well. Be sure to coat the sides as well as the top and bottom (the skin side). Turn the salmon over to coat and press the spice on to crust it.

2. Generously coat a large nonstick skillet with oil (3 to 4 tablespoons) and heat over medium-high heat until hot and shimmering. Add the salmon, skin-side down. Let it sit for a minute before gently lifting each fillet to make sure the oil runs under it. You want to develop a crisp skin without burning the spices, so lower the heat if the spices brown too quickly or smell as if they're about to burn. Cook until the skin is browned, about 5 minutes.

3. Use a thin spatula to carefully flip the fillets. Put the lemon wedges in the skillet between the fillets, cut-side down. You want the lemons to char and sizzle alongside the salmon. Sear the lemons until the bottoms are browned, about 3 minutes. Flip and sear the other sides, too, about 5 minutes.

4. Take out the salmon when the sides just lose their transparency and a metal cake tester or thin-bladed knife slides through the thickest part with a little resistance, about 5 minutes. They'll probably be done before the lemon.

5. Transfer the salmon to individual serving plates, skin-side up. When the lemons are done, transfer them to the plates too. Drizzle any accumulated pan juices around the fish. When the lemon wedges are cool enough to handle, squeeze them over the fish.

*arugula salad with salmon and sesame and nigella seeds

SEARED SALMON
FIVE MORE RECIPES

cornmeal-crusted seared salmon with fenugreek and sumac

Mayonnaise glues cornmeal onto salmon while adding an extra layer of richness beneath a crunchy crust. The tartness of sumac and the heat of Aleppo pepper balance salmon's fatty flesh.

SPICE BLEND

¾ teaspoon sumac (2 grams)

½ teaspoon Aleppo pepper (1 gram)

1 teaspoon fenugreek seeds (2 grams)

¾ teaspoon pimentón (smoked paprika; 2 grams)

Finely grind the sumac, Aleppo, and fenugreek together and immediately mix with the pimentón. Use this spice blend instead of the main spice blend in the seared salmon recipe on page 150.

Follow the seared salmon recipe through step 1.

Before step 2, brush the salmon fillets all over with 2 tablespoons mayonnaise to lightly and evenly coat. Dredge the fillets in ¼ cup fine stoneground yellow cornmeal to evenly coat all sides. Tap off the excess cornmeal, then proceed with step 2, adjusting the heat as needed to brown the crust without burning it.

chickpea flour–crusted seared salmon with savory and nutmeg

A little chickpea flour creates a tissue-thin crisp crust on salmon when mixed with herbal savory and anise.

SPICE BLEND

¾ teaspoon anise (2 grams)

1 teaspoon dried savory (1 gram)

1 teaspoon freshly grated nutmeg (1 gram)

¼ teaspoon Urfa pepper (½ gram)

1 tablespoon chickpea flour (5 grams)

Finely grind the anise and savory together and immediately mix with the nutmeg, Urfa, and chickpea flour. Use this spice blend instead of the main spice blend in the seared salmon recipe on page 150.

arugula salad with salmon and sesame and nigella seeds*

You can turn leftover salmon into a delicious salad simply by tossing it with peppery arugula and crunchy sesame and nigella seeds.

Follow the seared salmon recipe on page 150. When the salmon is cool enough to handle, flake 1 to 2 fillets to yield 1 cup salmon. Eat the rest hot or save for another use. Place the salmon in a large bowl and refrigerate until cold.

To the cold salmon, add 1 tablespoon white sesame seeds, preferably unhulled (10 grams), 1 tablespoon nigella seeds (9 grams), 1 teaspoon toasted sesame oil, and 5 ounces baby arugula. Gently toss until evenly coated. Season to taste with salt and serve.

Serves 2 to 4

salmon potato patties

Mashed potatoes bind leftover salmon and fresh scallions into exceptionally tasty patties. The outsides become crisp, the insides tender. These work well any time of day but are especially nice for brunch with a side of scrambled, poached, or fried eggs.

Follow the seared salmon recipe on page 150. When the salmon is cool enough to handle, flake 1 to 2 fillets to yield 1 cup salmon. Eat the rest hot or save for another use. Put it in a large bowl, cover, and refrigerate until cold.

To the cold salmon, add ¾ cup cold Creamy Herbed Mashed Potatoes (page 000) or other mashed potatoes and ⅓ cup finely chopped scallions (white and green parts). Fold gently until well mixed. Season to taste with salt.

Using a ¼-cup measuring cup and damp hands, scoop the mixture and form into a 3-inch-round, 1-inch-thick patty. Repeat with the remaining mixture to form 8 patties total.

Coat a large nonstick pan with olive oil (2 to 3 tablespoons) and heat over medium heat until hot and shimmering. Add the patties in a single layer, spaced an inch apart. Cook, turning once, until browned on both sides and heated through, about 5 minutes. Serve with lemon wedges.

Serves 4

soy-garlic seared salmon with limon omani

The best way to combine garlic and salmon is by rubbing dried garlic on the fish. Fresh garlic would burn, while the dried version blends well with citrusy limon omani, salty soy, and the subtle heat of mustard seeds.

SPICE BLEND

1 whole limon omani (dried Persian lime; 4 grams)

1 teaspoon dried garlic slices (2 grams)

¾ teaspoon cumin seeds (2 grams)

½ teaspoon yellow mustard seeds (3 grams)

Crack and crush the limon omani into smaller pieces by pressing it into a cutting board with the palm of your hand, then transfer the pieces to a spice grinder along with the garlic, cumin, and mustard seeds. Finely grind together. Use this spice blend instead of the main spice blend in the seared seared salmon recipe on page 150.

Follow the seared salmon recipe but rub 2 teaspoons soy sauce all over the salmon before salting the fillets lightly.

ROASTED WHOLE FISH

savory and aleppo pepper roasted fish with fennel and cherry tomatoes

Limon omani gives great acidity to the fish without adding extra liquid. Its tartness is complemented by garlic and bay leaves, along with the grassy freshness of savory and the rounded heat of Aleppo pepper.

**MAKES 2 WHOLE FISH
SERVES 4 TO 6**

MAIN SPICE BLEND

1 whole limon omani (dried Persian lime; 4 grams)

4 whole dried bay leaves

1 tablespoon plus 2 teaspoons dried garlic slices (8 grams)

1 teaspoon dried savory (1 gram)

1 teaspoon Aleppo pepper (2 grams)

Crack and crush the limon omani into smaller pieces by pressing it against a cutting board with your palm, then transfer the pieces to a spice grinder along with the bay leaves and garlic. Finely grind them together and immediately mix with the whole savory and Aleppo.

FISH

2 whole white fish (1 pound each), such as branzino, sea bass, dorade, or orata, gutted and scaled

Extra-virgin olive oil

Kosher salt

2 large shallots, halved and thinly sliced lengthwise

1 fennel bulb, halved, cored, and thinly sliced lengthwise

1 pint cherry or grape tomatoes

Lemon wedges, for serving

MAKE AHEAD

The spice-rubbed fish can be covered and refrigerated for up to 1 day before stuffing and roasting; proceed from step 3.

Whole fish are easy enough for a child to make—I know because that's when I first cooked one. After fishing with my dad, I'd stuff the trout we caught with lemon slices and throw it in the hot oven. This version isn't much more complex. Have the fish gutted and scaled at the store and, once home, coat the skin with oil and spices, which will roast into a very savory crust. A medley of vegetables in and under the fish turns into a natural side dish, making this a one-pan meal that you can walk away from while it's roasting. You really don't need anything else to make this a complete dinner, but good crusty bread or steamed rice never hurt.

1. To make the fish: Preheat the oven to 400°F.

2. Using a sharp knife, cut four or five 2-inch-long, ½-inch-deep slits on both sides of each fish. Drizzle and rub oil all over the fish to coat both sides. Sprinkle the spice blend all over the fish and inside their cavities.

3. Stuff some of the shallot and fennel slices inside the fish cavities. Put the tomatoes and remaining shallots and fennel in a small roasting pan, half sheet pan, or shallow baking dish. Generously drizzle with oil, season with salt, toss to coat, and spread in an even layer. Season the fish evenly with salt and place on top of the vegetables.

4. Roast until the flesh is opaque (you can tell if the flesh is opaque by peeking into the slits) and the blade of a paring knife inserted into the thickest part and removed feels warm when you touch it to your lips, about 25 minutes. Let the fish rest for a few minutes, then serve with the vegetables and lemon wedges for squeezing over the fish.

*sesame-roasted fish with olives and preserved lemons

ROASTED WHOLE FISH

FIVE MORE RECIPES

chimichurri roasted fish

Argentinian chimichurri sauce, which is a blend of herbs with chiles, olive oil, and vinegar, becomes more intense here with dried garlic and dried herbs. They rehydrate in the mix of oil and vinegar and give mild fish a welcome tangy freshness.

SPICE BLEND

2 teaspoons dried garlic slices (3 grams)

2 teaspoons dried parsley (2 grams)

2 tablespoons dried cilantro (2 grams)

1 teaspoon dried mint (1 gram)

½ teaspoon peperoncini (dried Calabrian chile)
    or red pepper flakes (1 gram)

Finely grind the garlic and immediately mix with the parsley, cilantro, mint, and peperoncini. Use this spice blend instead of the main spice blend in the roasted fish recipe on page 154.

Follow the roasted fish recipe, mixing the spice blend with ¼ cup extra-virgin olive and ¼ cup red wine vinegar and rubbing it all over the fish in step 2.

butter roasted fish with leeks, capers, and tarragon

The classic French combination of sweet leeks and salty capers comes together with plenty of butter in this treatment. Even in dried form, tarragon and dill deliver a fresh herbaceousness.

SPICE BLEND

2 tablespoons dried tarragon (2 grams)

2½ teaspoons dried dill weed (2 grams)

½ teaspoon green peppercorns (1 gram)

Finely grind the tarragon, dill, and peppercorns together. Use this spice blend instead of the main spice blend in the roasted fish recipe on page 154.

Follow the roasted fish recipe, adding 2 cups thinly sliced leeks along with the shallots and fennel in step 3 and omitting the tomatoes. Scatter ½ cup capers and ½ cup salted butter, diced, all over the fish and vegetables at the end of step 3.

tomato-roasted fish with sweet and hot peppers

Sweet and spicy peppers caramelize with tomato paste under the fish in this dish. Be sure to get a forkful of the saucy vegetables with each bite of saffron-scented fish.

SPICE BLEND

1 teaspoon black cumin seeds (3 grams)

Pinch of saffron

1 teaspoon ground ginger (2 grams)

Finely grind the cumin and saffron together, then immediately mix with the ginger. Use this spice blend instead of the main spice blend in the roasted fish recipe on page 154.

Follow the roasted fish recipe, using only half the spice blend to season the fish in step 2.

In step 3, omit the shallots and fennel. Instead, mix 1 sliced red bell pepper, 1 sliced green bell pepper, 1 sliced jalapeño, 1 tablespoon tomato paste, ¼ cup extra-virgin olive oil, and the remaining spice mixture. Stuff some of the mixture into the cavities of the fish and spread the remainder in the baking dish.

honey-vinegar-glazed roasted fish with star anise

Coating the fish with spiced honey and vinegar results in extra-flavorful fish reminiscent of Chinese-style steamed fish. Serve this over steamed rice for soaking up all the pan juices.

SPICE BLEND

2 teaspoons coriander seeds (4 grams)

¾ teaspoon cumin seeds (2 grams)

1 whole star anise (1 gram)

1 teaspoon cayenne pepper (2 grams)

Finely grind the coriander, cumin, and star anise together and immediately mix with the cayenne. Use this spice blend instead of the main spice blend in the roasted fish recipe on page 154.

Follow the roasted fish recipe, mixing the spice blend with ¼ cup honey, ¼ cup sherry vinegar, and 1 tablespoon extra-virgin olive and rubbing it all over the fish in step 2.

In step 3, omit the tomatoes.

sesame-roasted fish with olives and preserved lemon*

An already crackly spice crust gets more crunch from whole sesame seeds here. The funkiness of preserved lemons, together with black olives, gives this big, bold flavor.

SPICE BLEND

1½ teaspoons sumac (5 grams)

1 tablespoon dried za'atar leaves (2 grams)

¾ teaspoon Muntok white peppercorns
    (2 grams)

1 tablespoon plus 1½ teaspoons white sesame
    seeds, preferably unhulled (15 grams)

Finely grind the sumac, za'atar, and peppercorns together and immediately mix with the whole sesame seeds. Use this spice blend instead of the main spice blend in the roasted fish recipe on page 154.

Follow the roasted fish recipe, substituting 1 cup halved pitted black kalamata olives and ½ cup diced preserved lemon for the fennel in step 3 and omitting the tomatoes.

CHRAIME: SEAFOOD IN TOMATO SAUCE

cod simmered in turmeric-coriander tomato sauce

A quartet of coriander, cumin, turmeric, and Aleppo pepper evokes Moroccan cuisine in this version of chraime. To enhance the effect, serve over couscous.

SERVES 6

MAIN SPICE BLEND

1 teaspoon coriander seeds (2 grams)

1 teaspoon cumin seeds (2 grams)

2 teaspoons ground turmeric (2 grams)

½ teaspoon Aleppo pepper (1 gram)

Finely grind the coriander and cumin together and immediately mix with the turmeric and Aleppo. Or mix ¾ teaspoon pre-ground coriander and ¾ teaspoon pre-ground cumin with the turmeric and Aleppo.

CHRAIME

Extra-virgin olive oil

3 large garlic cloves, coarsely chopped

6 (4-ounce) boneless, skinless cod or halibut fillets (about 1½ inches thick)

1 lemon, ends trimmed, seeded, and cut into ¼-inch dice, plus 1 lemon cut into wedges for serving

¼ cup tomato paste

1 (28-ounce) can diced tomatoes, with their juices

Kosher salt

1 large bunch cilantro, stems thinly sliced and leaves coarsely chopped

MAKE AHEAD

The sauce can be refrigerated for up to 1 week or frozen for up to 2 months. The fish, rubbed with the spice blend, can be refrigerated for up to 6 hours before cooking.

Chraime is a traditional North African dish that's also popular in Israel and other Middle Eastern countries. It's essentially fish simmered in a thick tomato sauce. My mom prepared it only for the holidays and occasionally for Shabbat, but I make it all the time. The sauce—even the whole dish—can be done ahead, so it's easy for entertaining or weeknight dinners. To make my sauce more complex, I add spices, of course, but also diced lemon, rinds and all. The lemon pith lends a nice bite and intriguing bitterness to the tomatoes, which I cook only enough to retain a pop.

Pronounced *hraiy-may,* chraime is a great introduction to cooking mild white fish like cod and halibut. There's no risk of the fish sticking to the pan, and its mildness is infused with the tang of tomatoes. Just turn off the heat before the fish cooks all the way through, since the heat from the sauce continues to cook the fish as it sits.

Every part of this dish is even better when served with rice or challah (see page 106) to soak up all the sauce.

1. To make the chraime: Sprinkle half the spice blend all over the fish, cover with plastic wrap, and refrigerate until ready to use, up to 6 hours.

2. Coat the bottom of a large saucepan with oil (2 to 3 tablespoons). Add the garlic and turn the heat to medium-low. Cook, stirring occasionally, until the garlic is golden, about 3 minutes.

3. Add the remaining spice blend, stir well, and add the diced lemon. Cook, stirring often, for 3 minutes. Add the tomato paste and cook, stirring, for 4 minutes. Add the tomatoes with their juices, raise the heat to medium-high, and season to taste with salt. Cook, stirring occasionally, for 2 minutes. Reserve some cilantro for garnish and stir in the remainder of the cilantro. Cover, reduce the heat to medium-low, and simmer for 20 minutes.

4. Sprinkle the fish all over with salt. Uncover the sauce; it should be bubbling slightly. Push the fish into the sauce so that all but the very tops are submerged. Cover and cook until the fish is almost opaque throughout, about 5 minutes. Remove from the heat.

5. Divide the fish and sauce among individual serving dishes. Garnish with the reserved cilantro and serve with lemon wedges.

*stuffed squid in tomato sauce

CHRAIME: SEAFOOD IN TOMATO SAUCE
FIVE MORE RECIPES

stuffed squid in tomato sauce*

Inspired by the stuffed squid common in Spanish tapas, this dish immerses squid stuffed with cheesy crumbs in chraime sauce. The tang of tomatoes complements the pecorino cheese filling, smoky with pimentón.

Follow the chraime recipe on page 158, substituting 14 squid bodies and 14 squid tentacles for the cod in step 1. To stuff the squid, mix 2 cups panko bread crumbs, 1 cup grated Pecorino Romano cheese, 2 large eggs, 2 teaspoons pimentón (smoked paprika; 6 grams), and a pinch of salt until well blended. When you squeeze some of the mixture between your fingers, it should stick together like dough. Divide the mixture among the tubes of the squid bodies, using a small spoon to stuff the mixture into the cavities. Close the top of one body and hold it shut, then stick a toothpick through one side and back out through the other to secure the filling inside. Repeat with the remaining squid bodies and more toothpicks.

In step 4, coat a large skillet with extra-virgin olive oil (2 to 3 tablespoons) and heat over medium-high heat. Add the stuffed squid to the hot oil and sear, turning to evenly brown lightly, about 1 minute per side. Coat the skillet with more oil (1 to 2 tablespoons) and add the squid tentacles when it's hot. Sear until browned on one side, about 1 minute. Transfer all the squid to the bubbling chraime sauce, press into the sauce, cover, and cook until heated through, about 3 minutes.

chraime with clams, mussels, and shrimp

Shellfish are inherently saltier than fish, and the resulting dish is more fully flavored for it. Be sure to thoroughly clean the clams and mussels (see page 166) before cooking to avoid any grit.

Follow the chraime recipe on page 158, substituting 8 ounces clams, 8 ounces mussels, and 12 ounces shelled and deveined large shrimp for the fish. Thoroughly clean and scrub the clams and mussels (see step 1 on page 166) before adding and cook until they open and the shrimp are opaque, about 5 minutes. Discard any clams or mussels that don't open.

shrimp, olive, and tomato penne

Chraime sauce tastes much like pasta sauce, so here it's tossed with penne. Shrimp and olives turn it into a complete meal, but it's tasty without too.

SPICE BLEND

3 tablespoons dried rosemary (3 grams)

2½ teaspoons coriander seeds, preferably Dhania (5 grams)

1½ teaspoons fennel seeds (3 grams)

½ teaspoon black peppercorns, preferably Tellicherry (2 grams)

Finely grind the rosemary, coriander, fennel, and peppercorns. Use this spice blend instead of the main spice blend in the chraime recipe on page 158.

Follow the chraime recipe, substituting 1½ pounds large shrimp, peeled and deveined, for the cod in step 1.

While making the sauce in steps 2 and 3, boil 8 ounces penne pasta according to the package directions for al dente.

In step 4, coat a large, deep skillet with olive oil (2 to 3 tablespoons) and heat over medium-high heat. Add the shrimp in a single layer and cook for 1 minute. Add the tomato sauce, drained pasta, and ½ cup halved pitted kalamata olives. Cook, folding the ingredients, until evenly mixed and the shrimp is opaque and slightly curled, about 2 minutes. Squeeze the juice of ½ lemon over the pasta and serve.

Serves 2 to 4

grilled tomato toasts with anchovies and sardines

Leftover sauce works here just as well as a fresh batch, and the topping options are endless for toast. Anchovies and sardines are my favorites, but the chraime sauce alone would be good, as would an additional sprinkling of cheese or slices of charcuterie.

Follow the chraime recipe on page 158 through step 3.

Lightly rub a cut garlic clove all over 12 slices of 1-inch-thick good country bread, then drizzle with extra-virgin olive oil. Grill or broil both sides of the bread over medium-high heat until charred, about 2 minutes per side. Spoon the hot tomato sauce all over the bread, then top each toast with 1 jarred anchovy fillet and ½ tinned sardine fillet, or more to taste.

cod chraime with orange, apple, ginger, and thyme

Orange and apple bring sweetness to this savory stew, and the duo of ginger and cinnamon makes the combination of fruit and fish a natural one.

SPICE BLEND

2½ teaspoons dried garlic slices (4 grams)

1 tablespoon dried thyme (2 grams)

1 teaspoon ground ginger (2 grams)

¾ teaspoon ground cinnamon, preferably Vietnamese (2 grams)

Finely grind the garlic and thyme together and immediately mix with the ginger and cinnamon. Use this spice blend instead of the main spice blend in the chraime recipe on page 158.

Follow the chraime recipe, substituting 1 diced orange (with rind) for the lemon and adding 1 peeled and diced Fuji apple in step 3.

SEARED SEAFOOD WITH PAN SAUCE

thyme-seared scallops with capers and lemon

Thyme gives scallops an interesting mushroom-like note, and celery seeds add a welcome light bitterness. This spice blend makes light and buttery scallops taste almost meaty.

SERVES 2 TO 4

MAIN SPICE BLEND

¼ teaspoon black peppercorns, preferably Tellicherry (1 gram)

½ teaspoon coriander seeds (1 gram)

½ teaspoon celery seeds (1 gram)

¼ teaspoon dried thyme (½ gram)

Finely grind together the peppercorns, coriander, celery, and thyme.

SEAFOOD

8 extra-large (U10) dry-packed sea scallops

Kosher salt

Extra-virgin olive oil

1 tablespoon salted butter, cut into small pieces, at room temperature

1 tablespoon capers, drained

Juice of 1 lemon (about ¼ cup)

Searing seafood in a hot pan and then basting it with hot olive oil or butter may be the fastest way to a restaurant-worthy meal. The technique is actually easy and fast, and when the seafood is coated with spices, it develops a crackly shell. Basting the seafood with olive oil and butter while tilting the pan above the flame ensures the center of scallops, shrimp, or meaty fish like swordfish cooks through before the outside has a chance to burn. You make a sauce in the same pan, and it's all done in about five minutes. With salad, pasta, or rice on the side, you're all set for dinner.

1. To make the seafood: Sprinkle about half the spice blend on both sides of the scallops.

2. Heat a large skillet over medium-high heat. While the pan heats, sprinkle salt evenly all over the scallops. Add enough oil to coat the bottom of the skillet (2 to 3 tablespoons) and heat until it ripples on the surface. Add the scallops in a single layer so they do not touch and then tilt the skillet so that the oil runs under all of them evenly. Cook the scallops without moving them, using regular rotations of the pan to keep the heat distribution even, until they are golden brown on the bottom, about 2 minutes. Flip the scallops and add the pieces of butter to the pan. Tilt the skillet again to let the melted butter run under all the scallops and then hold the skillet at a 30-degree angle so the butter and oil pool toward one side. Push the scallops toward the other side of the pan and use a spoon to baste the scallops with the fat for 30 seconds. Set the skillet down and cook until the bottoms are golden and the scallops are still slightly undercooked, about 1 minute—if you squeeze the sides of a scallop gently, it should still give a little and not feel firm. Transfer the scallops to a serving plate.

3. Add the capers, lemon juice, and remaining spice blend to the skillet. Cook, stirring and scraping up the bits from the bottom of the pan, until the liquid has reduced into a glazy sauce, about 15 seconds. Spoon the sauce over the scallops and serve immediately.

STEAMED MUSSELS

steamed mussels with limon omani and bay leaves

Ground limon omani infuses the mussels and broth with a tangy citrus flavor without the hassle of squeezing fresh fruit. That sharpness is mellowed by savory dried garlic and sweet fresh shallots.

SERVES 4

MAIN SPICE BLEND

½ whole limon omani (dried Persian lime; 2 grams)

2 dried bay leaves

2 teaspoons dried garlic slices (3 grams)

1 teaspoon coriander seeds (2 grams)

¼ teaspoon peperoncini (dried Calabrian chile) or red pepper flakes (½ gram)

Crack and crush the limon omani into smaller pieces by pressing it against a cutting board with your palm. Transfer the pieces to a spice grinder along with the bay leaves, garlic, coriander, and peperoncini and finely grind them together.

MUSSELS

2 pounds mussels, scrubbed well

1 large shallot, minced

1 celery stalk, very finely diced

½ cup dry white wine

Extra-virgin olive oil, for serving

My wife, Lisa, and I like mussels a lot, especially when we're having friends over. It's a very social meal, best eaten with the pot in the center of the table so everyone can scoop their own servings. These shellfish are a great vehicle for any flavor—from coriander to sage—because they have a natural balance of salty and sweet. They easily become a complete meal with a salad and a loaf or two of crusty bread or, better yet, lots of fries—make sure to serve enough to soak up all the tasty juices from the pot. If you're having more than four people over, simply double the quantities, use a bigger pot, and increase the cooking time, turning off the heat once the mussels are open.

1. To cook the mussels: Place the mussels in a large bowl and cover with cold water. Let them sit for 1 minute to spit out any sand, then lift them out and set them into a colander (don't dump them with the water into the colander, otherwise the sand on the bottom of the bowl will go right back on the mussels). Discard any mussels with cracked shells. Pluck or cut off any beards, then rinse and scrub the shells well to thoroughly clean them. Repeat the process as needed until there is no more sand or grit left.

2. Heat a Dutch oven or wide pot over high heat for 5 minutes. Once the Dutch oven is really hot, add the mussels, shallot, celery, wine, and spice blend. Cover immediately and cook for 2 minutes. Uncover, stir well to mix everything evenly, cover again, and cook for another 4 minutes. Uncover, stir again, cover, and cook until the mussels open, 1 to 2 minutes more.

3. Remove the pot from the heat, stir well, and generously drizzle with some oil. Serve immediately with good bread to soak up the sauce (discard any mussels that don't open).

*spanish-style pickled mussels with coriander and pimentón

STEAMED MUSSELS
FIVE MORE RECIPES

vermouth-steamed mussels with lemon verbena, sage, and ginger

Vermouth is a fortified wine, meaning it's been mixed with a distilled spirit. It comes in red or white, and both varieties can be dry or sweet. Any kind works here, since the mussels release savory juices, and the blend of citrusy lemon verbena leaves and warm ginger complements vermouth well, so use whatever you have on hand.

SPICE BLEND

2 tablespoons dried lemon verbena leaves (2 grams)

2 teaspoons dried onion slices (3 grams)

1 teaspoon dried sage leaves (1 gram)

1 teaspoon ground ginger (2 grams)

Finely grind the lemon verbena, onion, and sage together and immediately mix with the ginger. Use this spice blend instead of the main spice blend in the steamed mussels recipe on page 166.

Follow the steamed mussels recipe, substituting ½ cup vermouth for the white wine in step 2.

steamed mussels with bacon and cabbage

Inspired by mussels' popularity in Belgium, where I first ate them when I lived there as a kid, this version becomes a complete meal with cabbage wilted into the cooking broth, which is also dotted with smoky bacon. Be sure to enjoy these with a good Belgian beer.

Follow the steamed mussels recipe on page 166 through step 1.

At the beginning of step 2, cook 2 slices diced bacon in the Dutch oven over medium heat, stirring occasionally, until browned, about 5 minutes. Add 3 cups thinly sliced green cabbage and a pinch of salt. Cook, stirring occasionally, until the cabbage is tender, about 5 minutes. Transfer to a bowl. Wipe out the Dutch oven, raise the heat to high, and cook the mussels as directed in step 2.

In step 3, return the cabbage-bacon mixture to the mussels and fold to evenly coat and heat through before serving.

spanish-style pickled mussels with coriander and pimentón*

In Spain, shelled cooked mussels are often served chilled in a sherry vinegar–olive oil bath. They take on richness from the olive oil and a complex brightness from the vinegar. The juicy mussels are then served as a cold starter, either with toothpicks for spearing and swirling in the sauce or piled onto toast with the sauce drizzled over. Both are delicious.

SPICE BLEND

1 teaspoon dried garlic slices (2 grams)

2½ teaspoons coriander seeds (5 grams)

¾ teaspoon pimentón (smoked paprika; 2 grams)

Finely grind the garlic and coriander together and immediately mix with the pimentón. Use this spice blend for pickling the mussels.

Follow the steamed mussels recipe on page 166 through step 2, using the main spice blend.

In step 3, after taking the pot off the heat, remove the mussels from their shells (reserve the cooking liquid) and place them in a small (1-pint) jar or other nonreactive container. Cover and refrigerate while preparing the pickling liquid. Strain the cooking liquid in the pot through a fine-mesh sieve and reserve.

Coat a small saucepan with olive oil (2 to 3 teaspoons) and add the spice blend for pickling the mussels along with a pinch of salt. Set the pan over medium heat and cook, stirring, until sizzling, about 1 minute. Add the reserved strained mussel cooking liquid, raise the heat to high, and bring to a boil. Boil until reduced by half, about 5 minutes. Remove from the heat and transfer to a small bowl. Set the small bowl over a larger bowl of ice and stir until cold. Stir in 1 tablespoon sherry vinegar, 1 tablespoon extra-virgin olive oil, and a pinch of salt. Pour over the chilled mussels in the jar, cover again, and refrigerate for at least 2 hours and up to 12 hours. Season to taste with salt before serving.

coconut milk–steamed mussels with thai chiles and lemongrass

Southeast Asian seasonings like lemongrass and galangal bring out the savory side of mussels, as do the South Asian spices turmeric and amchoor in this coconut milk broth.

Serve these over steamed sticky, basmati, or jasmine rice.

SPICE BLEND

2 whole dried Thai chiles (1 gram)

1½ teaspoons ground lemongrass (3 grams)

1 teaspoon ground galangal (2 grams)

2 teaspoons ground turmeric (2 grams)

1 teaspoon ground amchoor (2 grams)

Finely grind the chiles and immediately mix with the lemongrass, galangal, turmeric, and amchoor. Use this spice blend instead of the main spice blend in the steamed mussels recipe on page 166.

Follow the steamed mussels recipe, substituting 1 cup coconut milk for the white wine in step 2.

In step 3, omit the olive oil drizzle. Instead, stir in 1 tablespoon palm, coconut, or brown sugar; 1 tablespoon rice wine vinegar; and 2 teaspoons fish sauce until the sugar dissolves.

beer-steamed mussels with thyme and caraway

Mussels may sound fancy, but they're great as a casual meal, with beer in the broth and on the side. Use a pilsner here; other varieties pack too much complexity for the shellfish and may clash with the classic French combination of thyme, mustard seeds, and black pepper.

SPICE BLEND

1½ teaspoons dried thyme (1 gram)

½ teaspoon yellow mustard seeds (3 grams)

¼ teaspoon black peppercorns, preferably Tellicherry (1 gram)

½ teaspoon caraway seeds (2 grams)

Finely grind the thyme, mustard seeds, and peppercorns together and immediately mix with the whole caraway seeds. Use this spice blend instead of the main spice blend in the steamed mussels recipe on page 166.

Follow the steamed mussels recipe, substituting ½ cup pilsner or other light-flavored beer for the white wine in step 2.

In step 3, omit the olive oil drizzle. Instead, fold in 4 tablespoons salted butter until melted.

CRAB CAKES

crab cakes with sesame seeds and aleppo pepper

In this master recipe, sesame seeds add a nutty crunch to a spice blend that's savory with garlic and celery seeds. Aleppo pepper adds just a touch of heat; you can use more if you prefer spicy crab cakes. I like these with aioli on the side.

MAKES 15
SERVES 6 TO 8

MAIN SPICE BLEND

1 teaspoon dried garlic slices (2 grams)
1½ teaspoons coriander seeds (3 grams)
1 teaspoon fennel seeds (2 grams)
½ teaspoon celery seeds (1 gram)
½ teaspoon Aleppo pepper (1 gram)
1½ teaspoons white sesame seeds, preferably unhulled (5 grams)

Finely grind the garlic, coriander, and fennel together and immediately mix with the whole celery seeds, Aleppo, and sesame seeds.

CRAB CAKES

Extra-virgin olive oil
½ cup finely diced yellow onion
Kosher salt
¾ cup finely chopped fresh cilantro (leaves and stems)
Zest of 1 lemon (cut the zested lemon into wedges for serving)
1 pound fresh crabmeat, picked over for shells
1 large egg white
1 cup finely diced crustless challah or brioche
1 cup panko bread crumbs
Grapeseed oil
Lemon wedges

MAKE AHEAD

The shaped uncooked crab cakes can be refrigerated for up to 1 day before frying.

Crabmeat adapts to a range of spices, from sesame seeds to chipotle (see page 173), especially when shaped into savory cakes and then fried. A generous handful of cilantro—use the leaves and stems—keeps the patties tasting fresh, while a tiny dice of tender bread makes the texture delicate. The soft, rich bread in the center, along with the crab, gets a crunchy coating of panko bread crumbs. These were inspired by the fish *kefte* (like fish meatballs) of my childhood, the salt cod fritters from my years cooking in France, and the giant batches of crab cakes I'd churn out as the executive chef of Daniel Boulud's events company. You don't need to buy lump crabmeat, but you do want to get the freshest possible. These cakes taste great with lemon wedges but are even better with aioli (see page 246).

1. To make the crab cakes: Coat a small skillet with oil (about 1 tablespoon) and set over medium heat. Add the onion, a pinch of salt, and a few pinches of the spice blend. Cook, stirring occasionally, until translucent around the edges but still crunchy, about 3 minutes. Transfer to a large bowl and cool.

2. Add the cilantro, lemon zest, and remaining spice blend to the bowl. Gently fold in the crab and egg white; add the bread cubes and ½ teaspoon salt and gently toss to thoroughly mix but not smush the mixture.

3. Line a half sheet pan with parchment paper. Lightly wet your hands and gently press ½ ounce (about 3 tablespoons) of the mixture into a round by putting it on the fingers of one hand and using your other thumb and index finger to gently squeeze the edges of the round. While you carefully squeeze the sides, lightly pat the top flat with your other thumb to make a 2-inch patty (about ¾ inch thick). Don't pack the mixture tightly. Place the shaped patties on the parchment-lined pan.

4. Place the panko in a shallow dish. Put a patty in the panko and pat the crumbs all over to evenly coat. Return to the lined baking sheet and repeat with the remaining patties.

5. Fill a large nonstick skillet with grapeseed or other neutral-tasting oil to a depth of ⅛ inch and heat over medium-high heat. When the oil starts to shimmer, add enough patties to fit in the skillet, spacing 1½ inches apart. Fry until the bottoms are golden brown, about 2 minutes, then flip carefully. Cook until the other side is browned, 5 to 7 minutes longer. You're not trying to sear the patties so they have a charred crust—you just want them to get some nice color. Serve hot or warm with lemon wedges for squeezing.

*zucchini crab cakes with corn bread crust

CRAB CAKES
FOUR MORE RECIPES

chipotle corn and crab cakes

Both pimenton and chipotle are made with smoked peppers, giving these crab cakes a delicate hint of campfire that is balanced by the sweetness of fresh corn kernels.

SPICE BLEND

2 whole dried bay leaves

2 teaspoons dried onion slices (3 grams)

¾ teaspoon pimentón (smoked paprika; 2 grams)

½ teaspoon ground chipotle chile (1 gram)

Finely grind the bay leaves and onion together and immediately mix with the pimentón and chipotle. Use this spice blend instead of the main spice blend in the crab cakes recipe on page 170.

Follow the crab cakes recipe, adding ½ cup fresh corn kernels (from about 1 ear of corn) and ¼ cup mayonnaise along with the crab in step 2.

chorizo crab cakes with cumin and turmeric

Bits of chorizo bring a smoky, meaty richness to these crab cakes. Be sure to use Spanish-style fully cured chorizo and not fresh uncooked Mexican chorizo. Whether you go with mild or hot links is up to you.

SPICE BLEND

1 teaspoon dried garlic slices (2 grams)

¾ teaspoon cumin seeds (2 grams)

2 teaspoons ground turmeric (2 grams)

¼ teaspoon cayenne pepper (½ gram)

Finely grind the garlic and cumin together and immediately mix with the turmeric and cayenne. Use this spice blend instead of the main spice blend in the crab cakes recipe on page 170.

Follow the crab cakes recipe, adding ⅓ cup finely diced cured chorizo along with the crab in step 2.

fish cakes with fennel seeds

A mild white fish like cod, snapper, or haddock benefits from spices in these tasty savory cakes. Cutting the fish by hand gives you a loose, delicate patty, while chopping it in a food processor gives you firm ones that hold together tightly. I like them both ways.

Follow the crab cakes recipe on page 170 through step 1.

In step 2, substitute 1 pound skinless, boneless cod, snapper, or haddock, cut into ⅛-inch dice, for the crab and 1 whole egg for the egg white.

zucchini crab cakes with corn bread crust*

Packed with summer squash and corn bread, these taste like the end of summer, but you can enjoy them any time of year. Try to use small zucchini that aren't too seedy for the best flavor.

Follow the crab cakes recipe on page 170 through step 1.

In step 2, add ½ cup coarsely grated zucchini or other summer squash along with the crab and substitute 1 cup crumbled corn bread for the diced challah.

In step 4, substitute finely ground corn bread for half the panko, so you have ½ cup panko bread crumbs mixed with ½ cup finely crumbled corn bread in the dish for coating.

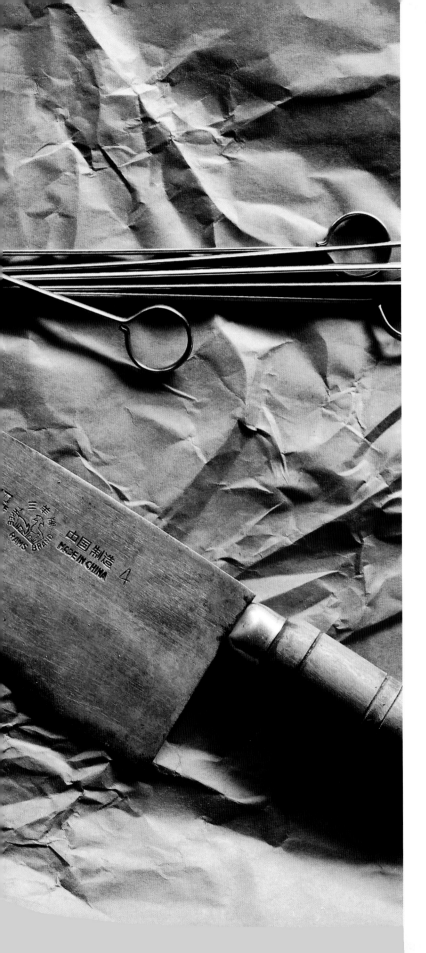

MEAT

MEAT

Meat is a natural vehicle for spices. Fat carries flavor, and meat is usually laced with plenty of fat. Meat also has enough moisture on its surface for spices to cling onto and then infuse it. Every recipe in this chapter essentially starts with rubbing spices onto meat, be it chicken, pork, beef, or lamb. How the meat is then cooked varies from roasting to pan-searing to poaching.

The techniques I've chosen to showcase here fall into two main categories: quick and slow. All are easy. Even the roasts that take a long time to cook require little time to prep. Quick dishes, like seared chicken breasts or pork chops, can end up on the table within half an hour from start to finish. They are ideal for days when you haven't had a chance to plan ahead. The slow dishes, like short ribs or roasted leg of lamb, are great for weekend cooking and entertaining and keep really well so you can reheat leftovers throughout the week or even eat them again cold.

To make prep even faster, you can blend the spices ahead of time whenever you have a moment. Just slip the pre-measured mix into a jar and label it with a permanent marker. When you're ready to cook, you'll have the bulk of your spice prep done. That quick, simple step of blending spices will instantly deliver layers of nuanced flavors that usually require hours to coax from fresh ingredients.

While I offer specific spice blends for different preparations, I encourage you to use them however you'd like. Know that they'll pair well with the same type of meat (any chicken spice will be good on any chicken preparation). Just make sure you stick to the techniques. They prevent you from burning the spices, which leads to bitterness in the finished dish.

MASTER SPICE BLENDS

for seasoning chicken wings

1½ teaspoons cumin seeds (5 grams), toasted (see page 37)
2 teaspoons dried garlic slices (3 grams)
2 teaspoons dried oregano (1 gram)
1 tablespoon plus 1½ teaspoons Aleppo pepper (15 grams)
¼ teaspoon sumac (1 gram)

Finely grind the cumin and garlic together and immediately mix with the oregano, Aleppo, and sumac.

for sprinkling on steak

3 tablespoons dried tarragon (3 grams)
1 tablespoon plus ¾ teaspoon black peppercorns, preferably Tellicherry (15 grams)
1 tablespoon dried mint (3 grams)
1 teaspoon yellow mustard seeds (5 grams)
½ teaspoon fleur de sel (1 gram)

Finely grind the tarragon and peppercorns together and immediately mix with the mint, mustard seeds, and fleur de sel.

for stirring into ground beef for burgers

2 teaspoon dried onion slices (3 grams)
1½ teaspoons sumac (5 grams)
2 tablespoons plus 1½ teaspoons Urfa pepper (15 grams)
1 teaspoon nigella seeds (3 grams)
1 tablespoon plus 1 teaspoon dried oregano (2 grams)

Finely grind the onion and sumac together and immediately mix with the Urfa, nigella, and oregano.

GLAZED SEARED CHICKEN BREASTS

coriander and black pepper chicken breasts with balsamic glaze

The well-loved pairing of coriander and cumin creates an irresistible crust on chicken breasts, which finish in a tangy, sticky balsamic vinegar glaze. The fruity heat of black pepper balances the sweetness of the pan sauce.

SERVES 4

MAIN SPICE BLEND

2½ teaspoons coriander seeds (5 grams)

¾ teaspoon black peppercorns, preferably Tellicherry (3 grams)

1 teaspoon cumin seeds (3 grams)

½ teaspoon ground ginger (1 gram)

Finely grind the coriander, peppercorns, and cumin together and immediately mix with the ginger. Or mix together 2 teaspoons pre-ground coriander, ½ teaspoon pre-ground black pepper, and ¾ teaspoon pre-ground cumin with the ginger.

CHICKEN

4 boneless, skinless chicken breasts (8 ounces each)

Kosher salt

Extra-virgin olive oil

2 tablespoons balsamic vinegar

MAKE AHEAD

You can refrigerate the cooked chicken for up to 5 days.

Chicken breasts become intensely flavorful and juicy with my easy technique: start spice-rubbed chicken in a *cold* pan. Not only does the slow rise in heat prevent the spices from burning, it also keeps the chicken from sticking to the pan. From a technical standpoint, it's great because you get a sous vide effect, with the meat cooking through evenly first while retaining its juices and developing a seared crust at the end. The chicken—along with its instant pan sauce—takes well to a range of flavors, from anise to green peppercorns.

1. To make the chicken: Sprinkle the spice blend all over the chicken to evenly coat. You can cook them right away or cover and refrigerate for up to 1 hour.

2. Season the spiced chicken with salt. Generously coat a large skillet or sauté pan with oil (2 to 3 tablespoons). Put the chicken in the pan in a single layer, smooth-side down, spacing the breasts apart, and set over medium heat. Cook nice and slow until the bottoms are golden, about 7 minutes. Using a spatula or tongs, carefully flip each piece.

3. Cook until an instant-read thermometer inserted into the thickest part of the breast registers 120°F, about 7 minutes. Flip again, reduce the heat to low, and cook until an instant-read thermometer inserted into the thickest part of the breast registers 160°F, about 6 minutes more.

4. Drizzle the vinegar all around the chicken. It should bubble and spatter immediately. Continuously turn the chicken to glaze it in the reducing vinegar until lightly coated, about 2 minutes. Remove from the heat. Let stand for a few minutes, drizzle the pan glaze over the chicken, and serve.

*balsamic chicken with sautéed cherry tomatoes

GLAZED SEARED CHICKEN BREASTS
FIVE MORE RECIPES

soy-and-orange-glazed chicken breasts

Salty soy sauce and sweet orange juice combine into a syrupy glaze for chicken crusted with an Asian-inspired mix of garlic, anise, ginger, and lemongrass. The heat of cayenne brings everything together. This would be delicious over steamed rice. Double or triple the glaze if you like your chicken breasts extra saucy.

SPICE BLEND

2 teaspoons dried garlic slices (3 grams)
¾ teaspoon anise (2 grams)
1½ teaspoons ground ginger (3 grams)
1 teaspoon lemongrass powder (2 grams)
¼ teaspoon cayenne pepper (½ gram)

Finely grind the garlic and anise together and immediately mix with the ginger, lemongrass, and cayenne. Use this spice blend instead of the main spice blend in the chicken breast recipe on page 178.

Follow the chicken breast recipe, substituting 1 tablespoon each soy sauce and fresh orange juice for the vinegar in step 4.

honey-dijon-glazed chicken breasts

The beloved combination of honey and mustard simmer along with cider vinegar for a sticky, sweet-tangy glaze on chicken.

Follow the chicken breast recipe on page 178.

In step 4, substitute 2 tablespoons apple cider vinegar for the balsamic vinegar. Add ¼ cup Dijon mustard and 1 tablespoon honey along with the vinegar.

chicken salad with black beans and cilantro

Traditional American-style chicken salad gets a twist with the addition of black beans and cilantro. Eat this on its own or wrap it in tortillas, sandwich it between bread, or spoon it into lettuce cups.

Follow the chicken breast recipe on page 178. When cool enough to handle, dice enough chicken (1 to 2 breasts) to yield 1 cup meat (save the rest for another use). Refrigerate until cold and then mix with 1 (14- to 15-ounce) can rinsed and drained black beans, ¼ cup mayonnaise, ¼ cup chopped fresh cilantro, and 1 tablespoon fresh lime juice. Season to taste with salt.

Serves 2 to 4

balsamic chicken with sautéed cherry tomatoes*

Here, cubes of chicken breast get a quick turn with balsamic-glazed cherry tomatoes. This is great served over a grain salad or with crusty bread to swipe the pan sauce.

Follow the chicken breast recipe on page 178 halfway through step 3. When the chicken registers 120°F on an instant-read thermometer, transfer it to a cutting board. Add 1 pint halved cherry tomatoes to the pan along with a pinch of salt. Raise the heat to medium-high and cook, stirring, for 3 minutes.

Cut the chicken into ½-inch chunks and return it to the pan along with any accumulated juices. Add the balsamic vinegar and cook, stirring continuously, until the chicken is just cooked through, about 3 minutes more.

chicken breasts with shiitake mushroom cream sauce

A finely ground shiitake mushroom becomes a spice that brings an earthy savoriness to chicken, along with onion, green peppercorns, and thyme. White wine and cream mellow out the mix.

SPICE BLEND

1 small dried shiitake mushroom (3 grams)
2 teaspoons dried onion slices (3 grams)
1½ teaspoons green peppercorns (3 grams)
1½ teaspoons dried thyme (1 gram)

Finely grind together the shiitake, onion, peppercorns, and thyme. Use this spice blend instead of the main spice blend in the chicken breast recipe on page 178.

Follow the chicken breast recipe, substituting 2 tablespoons dry white wine for the vinegar in step 4. After the wine has glazed the chicken, transfer the chicken to a serving dish. Add ¼ cup heavy cream to the pan and bring to a simmer. Simmer, stirring continuously, until thickened, about 2 minutes. Spoon over the chicken and serve.

BRAISED CHICKEN THIGHS

herb-braised chicken with dried apricots

A combination of garlic, rosemary, thyme, and oregano offers a taste of the Mediterranean here. Green peppercorns deliver an herbaceous heat that brings extra warmth and intensity to the dish.

SERVES 6

MAIN SPICE BLEND

2½ teaspoons dried garlic slices (4 grams)

2 tablespoons dried rosemary (2 grams)

1 teaspoon green peppercorns (2 grams)

1 tablespoon dried thyme (2 grams)

2 teaspoons dried oregano (1 gram)

Finely grind the garlic, rosemary, and peppercorns together and immediately mix with the whole thyme and oregano.

CHICKEN

6 skin-on, bone-in chicken thighs (2¾ pounds)

Kosher salt

Extra-virgin olive oil

1 medium yellow onion

2 large celery stalks

½ cup dried apricots

1 tablespoon honey

1 cup dry white wine

MAKE AHEAD

You can refrigerate the braise for up to 1 week or freeze for up to 2 months. Reheat before serving.

Chicken thighs are often seared fast and then braised slow, but I reverse the process by slow-searing and fast-braising for juicy meat under crisp spice-crusted skin. I start the chicken in a cold pan to build flavor and color and to render the fat slowly. If you put the meat in a hot pan, the skin will immediately stick and retract when it makes contact with the oil, and the spices risk burning. With slow-rendering, the skin becomes golden brown and crisp and stays that way since only the meat and not the skin is nestled in the liquid and the spices have a chance to toast rather than burn. This technique ultimately shortens the total cooking time, which is great for weeknights, but I often find myself cooking this way on weekends and then reheating leftovers on busy weeknights. The combination of savory celery and sweet dried apricots takes on a range of flavors from rosemary to rose petals. They're all deeply satisfying and delicious when served with crusty bread, rice, pasta, or just a simple side salad.

1. To make the chicken: Sprinkle the spice blend all over the chicken to evenly coat. You can cover and refrigerate the chicken for up to 1 day.

2. When ready to cook, season the chicken all over with salt. Coat a large sauté pan with oil (2 to 3 tablespoons) and add the chicken in a single layer, skin-side down. Set the pan over medium heat and cook, rotating the pan to ensure even browning, until the skin is deep golden brown, 10 to 15 minutes.

3. While the chicken skin renders and browns, prep the vegetables. Cut the onion in half lengthwise and thinly slice it crosswise. Trim the celery stalks, halve lengthwise, and thinly slice crosswise.

4. Flip the chicken carefully and cook the other side until browned, about 5 minutes. Transfer the chicken to a plate. Pour out all but 3 tablespoons of the fat from the pan (reserve the remaining fat for another use, if desired, or discard).

5. Add the onion, celery, and apricots to the pan. Stir well to coat with the fat, scrape up any browned bits from the pan, and cook until the onions start to soften, about 2 minutes. Add the honey and stir until it's bubbling hard, about 1 minute, and then add the wine and bring to a boil. Boil until the wine is reduced by half and the vegetables are soft, about 5 minutes.

6. Reduce the heat to low and add ½ cup water. Return the chicken and any accumulated juices to the pan, arranging the thighs on top of the vegetables, skin-side up, in a single layer. Raise the heat to bring the liquid to a boil and then reduce the heat to maintain a low simmer. Simmer until the chicken is cooked through, 15 to 20 minutes. Remove from the heat and let sit for a few minutes before serving.

*red wine and mushroom braised chicken with caraway and allspice

BRAISED CHICKEN THIGHS
FIVE MORE RECIPES

cumin and cardamom chicken tajine with preserved lemon

A blend of Moroccan spices, from warming cardamom and cinnamon to floral rose, pairs with funky sour preserved lemon in this braise. This tajine tastes best served over couscous.

SPICE BLEND

1½ teaspoons cumin seeds (5 grams)

¾ teaspoon allspice berries (3 grams)

¼ cup dried rose petals (2 grams)

1½ teaspoons green cardamom pods (3 grams)

1 teaspoon ground cinnamon, preferably
   Vietnamese (2 grams)

Finely grind the cumin, allspice, rose, and cardamom and immediately mix with the cinnamon. Use this spice blend instead of the main spice blend in the braised chicken recipe on page 182.

Follow the braised chicken recipe, adding ¼ cup finely diced preserved lemon with the water at the beginning of step 6.

red wine and mushroom braised chicken with caraway and allspice*

The classic French duo of red wine and mushrooms gets complexity from caraway and allspice here. Serve this with a baguette for sopping up the sauce.

SPICE BLEND

1 teaspoon caraway seeds (4 grams)

¾ teaspoon allspice berries (3 grams)

¾ teaspoon black peppercorns, preferably
   Tellicherry (3 grams)

4 whole dried bay leaves

Finely grind together the caraway, allspice, peppercorns, and bay leaves. Use this spice blend instead of the main spice blend in the braised chicken recipe on page 182.

Follow the braised chicken recipe, adding 8 ounces white button mushrooms, trimmed and halved, along with the onion and celery and omitting the apricots at the beginning of step 5.

At the end of step 5, substitute 1 cup dry red wine for the white wine.

braised tarragon chicken in creamy leek sauce

The heat of mustard seeds and white pepper balances the richness of this chicken's cream sauce, which is sweetened with leeks and made aromatic with dried tarragon.

SPICE BLEND

1 teaspoon yellow mustard seeds (5 grams)

1 teaspoon Muntok white peppercorns (3 grams)

2 tablespoons dried tarragon (2 grams)

1 teaspoon celery seeds (2 grams)

Finely grind together the mustard seeds, peppercorns, tarragon, and celery seeds. Use this spice blend instead of the main spice blend in the braised chicken recipe on page 182.

Follow the braised chicken recipe, adding 1 pound leeks, white and light green parts only, finely chopped, along with the onion and celery and omitting the apricots at the beginning of step 5.

At the end of step 5, add ½ cup heavy cream after adding the white wine.

chicken braised with carrots, grapes, and rosé wine

Grapes bring a welcome, warming sweetness to this braise, along with grated carrots and rosé wine. The carrots practically melt into the mix, making the sauce luxuriously thick.

Follow the braised chicken recipe on page 182. Add 1 cup halved red or green grapes and ½ cup grated carrots along with the onion, celery, and apricots at the beginning of step 5.

At the end of step 5, substitute 1 cup dry rosé wine for the white wine.

beer-braised chicken with bacon and cabbage

Ideal for fall but great any time of year, this braise balances the aromas of coriander, fennel, and juniper with the richness of bacon and the nuttiness of poppy seeds. Pretzel rolls or rye bread would be ideal accompaniments to this hearty dish.

SPICE BLEND

2½ teaspoons coriander seeds (5 grams)

2 teaspoons fennel seeds (4 grams)

¾ teaspoon juniper berries (2 grams)

2½ teaspoons poppy seeds (10 grams)

Coarsely grind the coriander, fennel, and juniper together and immediately mix with the whole poppy seeds. Use this spice blend instead of the main spice blend in the braised chicken recipe on page 182.

Follow the braised chicken recipe, but start by cooking ⅓ cup diced bacon in the sauté pan over medium heat, stirring often, until the fat has rendered, about 5 minutes. Transfer the bacon to paper towels to drain and reserve. Cook the chicken in the bacon fat, following the chicken browning technique in step 2.

At the beginning of step 5, add 1 cup thinly sliced green cabbage along with the onion, celery, and apricots.

At the end of step 5, substitute 1 cup pilsner-style beer for the white wine.

In step 6, scatter the bacon all over the chicken before serving.

ROASTED BUTTERFLIED CHICKEN

bay leaf and garlic roasted chicken with savory and paprika

In this master recipe, you taste the vegetal sweetness of peppers because it's highlighted by the paprika and peperoncini. Celery seeds add a salty edge, complemented by garlic and bay leaves.

SERVES 6

MAIN SPICE BLEND

5 whole dried bay leaves

2 tablespoons dried garlic slices (10 grams)

1½ teaspoons celery seeds (3 grams)

1 tablespoon dried basil (1 gram)

1 tablespoon dried savory (3 grams)

2½ teaspoons sweet paprika (5 grams)

½ teaspoon peperoncini (dried Calabrian chile) or red pepper flakes (1 gram)

Finely grind the bay leaves and garlic and immediately mix with the whole celery seeds, basil, savory, paprika, and peperoncini.

CHICKEN

Extra-virgin olive oil

Kosher salt

2 medium yellow onions, thinly sliced

1 whole chicken (5 pounds)

1 tablespoon silan (date syrup) or honey

¼ cup sherry vinegar

MAKE AHEAD

The chicken can be butterflied and coated with the oil, silan, and spices and refrigerated for up to 1 day. Do not salt the chicken until you're ready to cook it or it'll weep.

Crisp, flavorful brown skin over juicy meat is the mark of a good roast chicken. My technique of butterflying the chicken before roasting ensures both. Using dry spices instead of fresh herbs creates a crunchy crust, as does *silan* (date syrup) or honey. Not only do those natural sugars add a hint of sweetness, they also deliver a deep caramel color to the chicken skin, and with my butterflying technique, all the skin is exposed to the oven's heat to make it crackly and flavorful. Plus, butterflying eliminates the need for trussing the chicken and helps it cook more quickly. The onions cooked under the chicken make for an instant, delicious sauce, which would be even better spooned over noodles, potatoes, or cooked or raw greens. Any leftovers make for other great meals like salad or soup (see page 189).

1. To make the chicken: Preheat the oven to 400°F.

2. Coat a medium roasting pan with oil (3 to 4 tablespoons). Add the onions, one-third of the spice blend, and a pinch of salt. Toss until the onions are well coated and spread them in an even layer. Pour the vinegar over the onions.

3. Line a half sheet pan or other large rimmed pan with parchment paper and set the chicken on the pan. Using a very sharp knife or poultry shears, cut the chicken along one side of the backbone to split it in half. Open the chicken. Arrange the chicken breast-side up and press down on both sides of the breastbone to flatten it. Drizzle the chicken with oil to coat (1 to 2 tablespoons) and then with the silan. Rub the oil and silan all over the chicken and sprinkle with the remaining spice blend to evenly coat. Sprinkle salt all over the chicken and place it on top of the onions, skin-side up. Scrape any spices and juices from the prep pan over the chicken.

4. Roast, basting the chicken every 20 minutes, until the skin is evenly browned and a meat thermometer inserted into the thickest part of the breast registers 150°F, about 1 hour. When you stick the cooked chicken with the thermometer, its juices should run clear.

5. Remove the chicken from the oven and let it rest for 15 minutes before carving. Serve with the onions and pan sauce.

*chicken tacos with hummus and sesame-mint salsa

ROASTED BUTTERFLIED CHICKEN

FIVE MORE RECIPES

chicken tacos with hummus and sesame-mint salsa*

Leftover chicken turns into tacos with a Middle Eastern twist when the traditional condiments are swapped for hummus and a refreshing red onion, sesame, and mint topping.

Follow the roasted chicken recipe on page 186. When cool enough to handle, shred 3 cups meat.

To make the salsa, toss 1 thinly sliced small red onion with ¼ cup chopped fresh mint, 2 tablespoons fresh lemon juice, 1 tablespoon extra-virgin olive oil, and 1 tablespoon toasted white sesame seeds, preferably unhulled. Season the salsa to taste with salt.

Divide 6 tablespoons hummus among 6 warmed small flour tortillas (5 to 6 inches in diameter), spreading it down the center. Top each with the chicken, drizzle with 2 tablespoons tahini, and spoon on the topping.

za'atar roasted chicken with lemons and olives

Za'atar refers to both the dried leaves of the za'atar plant as well as a blend made with those leaves, sumac, and sesame seeds. Here I start with the pure oregano-like leaves and mix them into a from-scratch blend that's delicious roasted onto chicken. Lemon and olives roasted with the onions echo the tang of the sumac.

SPICE BLEND

2 tablespoons plus 1½ teaspoons dried za'atar leaves (5 grams)

1 tablespoon plus 2 teaspoons sumac (15 grams)

1 tablespoon plus 1½ teaspoons dried thyme (3 grams)

½ teaspoon black peppercorns, preferably Tellicherry (2 grams)

3 tablespoons plus 1½ teaspoons white sesame seeds, preferably unhulled (35 grams)

Finely grind the za'atar, sumac, thyme, and peppercorns together and immediately mix with the whole sesame seeds. Use this spice blend instead of the main spice blend in the roasted chicken recipe on page 186.

Follow the roasted chicken recipe, adding 2 lemons, cut into wedges, and ½ cup pitted black kalamata olives along with the onions in step 2.

chicken and white bean soup with turmeric and amchoor

Simply simmering a spice blend into store-bought chicken broth instantly turns it into a deeply flavorful soup. A mix of canned white beans and shredded leftover roast chicken makes this a hearty one-pot meal that comes together in minutes. If you have unseasoned homemade chicken stock on hand, definitely use it here.

SPICE BLEND

¾ teaspoon cumin seeds (2 grams)

¼ teaspoon black peppercorns, preferably Tellicherry (1 gram)

2 teaspoons ground turmeric (2 grams)

1 teaspoon amchoor (2 grams)

Finely grind the cumin and peppercorns together and immediately mix with the turmeric and amchoor. Or mix ¾ teaspoon pre-ground cumin and ¼ teaspoon pre-ground black pepper with the turmeric and amchoor. You will use this for seasoning the soup. Put this spice blend in a large saucepan.

Follow the roasted chicken recipe on page 186, using the main spice blend. When cool enough to handle, shred 3 cups meat.

Add 6 cups unsalted chicken broth to the saucepan with the soup spices and bring to a simmer.

Add the shredded chicken and 1 (14.5-ounce) can rinsed and drained cannellini beans. Simmer until heated through, season to taste with salt, and serve.

pomegranate-glazed roasted chicken with figs

The distinctive tang of pomegranate powder and limon omani is balanced by the sweetness of dried figs and pomegranate molasses in this take on roasted chicken.

SPICE BLEND

2 whole limon omani (dried Persian lime; 8 grams)

2 teaspoons green cardamom pods (4 grams)

1½ teaspoons pomegranate powder (5 grams)

1½ teaspoons dill seeds (3 grams)

Crack and crush the limon omani into smaller pieces by pressing them against a cutting board with your palm. Transfer the pieces to a spice grinder along with the cardamom. Finely grind and immediately mix with the pomegranate powder and whole dill seeds. Use this spice blend instead of the main spice blend in the roasted chicken recipe on page 186.

Follow the roasted chicken recipe, adding 1 cup whole dried figs along with the onions in step 2.

In step 3, substitute 1 tablespoon pomegranate molasses for the silan.

sautéed spinach and arugula with chicken and feta

Mixing leftover roasted chicken with sautéed greens and lemon juice makes for a light yet warming one-dish meal. Feta scattered on top adds a welcome salty richness.

Follow the roasted chicken recipe on page 186. When cool enough to handle, shred 3 cups meat.

Coat a large, deep skillet with olive oil (2 to 3 tablespoons) and heat over medium-high heat until hot and shimmering. Add 1 pound each baby spinach and baby arugula by the handful, stirring after each addition. Season with salt and cook, stirring, until just wilted, 2 to 3 minutes.

Add the shredded chicken and fold until heated through, about 2 minutes. Squeeze the juice from 1 lemon all over and transfer to a serving dish. Top with 1 cup crumbled feta cheese and drizzle with olive oil.

OVEN-ROASTED CHICKEN SOUP

limon omani roasted chicken soup with celery seeds

The citrus sourness of limon omani delivers brightness to this soup, celery seeds bring a classic taste, and ginger makes it warming.

MAKES 3 TO 4 QUARTS
SERVES 8 TO 12

MAIN SPICE BLEND

2 whole limon omani (dried Persian lime; 8 grams)

1½ teaspoons celery seeds (3 grams)

½ teaspoon ground ginger (1 gram)

½ teaspoon peperoncini (dried Calabrian chile) or red pepper flakes (1 gram)

Crack and crush the limon omani into smaller pieces by pressing them against a cutting board with your palm. Transfer the pieces to a spice grinder and finely grind. Immediately mix with the whole celery seeds, ginger, and peperoncini.

SOUP

1 whole (3-pound) chicken, quartered (or 2 bone-in, skin-on breasts, 2 bone-in, skin-on thighs, and 2 drumsticks)

Kosher salt

Extra-virgin olive oil

3 medium carrots

1 large parsley root or small celery root

2 small yellow onions

2 large celery stalks

2 Granny Smith apples

4 garlic cloves

MAKE AHEAD

You can refrigerate the chicken and broth for up to 1 week or freeze for up to 2 months. Reheat before serving.

Roasting chicken first and then braising it in the oven with sautéed vegetables makes for the best chicken soup. The oven gives the chicken a rotisserie-like tenderness, and the addition of fruit, a trick I learned in the South of France, transforms the broth with sweetness and acidity. This technique lends itself to the different additions like ancho chile powder, dried wakame seaweed, and fresh cilantro. It also leaves you with a broth rich enough to serve as the base of any noodle soup, from ramen to orzo.

1. Preheat the oven to 400°F. Line a half sheet pan with parchment paper. Cut the chicken into quarters: Use poultry shears or a sharp knife to cut along one side of the backbone and one side of the breastbone to halve the chicken. Cut each half into two pieces between the breasts and thighs. (If your store sells whole chickens already quartered, you can buy that and skip this step.)

2. Sprinkle half the spice mix all over the chicken, sprinkle with salt, and drizzle with oil to coat (1 to 2 tablespoons). Place on the prepared pan, skin-side down. Roast until golden brown, about 15 minutes. Flip the chicken pieces over and roast until the other side is browned, about 15 minutes more.

3. Meanwhile, scrub the carrots and peel the parsley root. Cut the carrots, parsley root, onions, and celery into 1½-inch chunks. Quarter and core the apples. Cut the garlic cloves in half.

4. Heat a large Dutch oven or other large oven-safe pot over medium-high heat. Coat the bottom with oil (2 to 3 tablespoons) and heat until shimmering. Add the vegetables, apples, and remaining spice mix. Stir well, season with salt, and cook, stirring often, until the onions are translucent, 10 to 13 minutes.

5. Reduce the heat to low and add 2 cups water. Stir and scrape up all the browned bits from the bottom of the pot. Nestle the chicken into the vegetables. (Keep the oven on.) Pour 1 cup water into the sheet pan to loosen any browned bits and pour into the Dutch oven. Add another 5 cups water. The liquids should just cover the solids. Bring to a boil over high heat, cover, and transfer to the oven.

6. Bake until the chicken and vegetables are tender, about 40 minutes. Transfer the Dutch oven to the stovetop. Uncover the pot and use a slotted spoon to transfer the chicken to another sheet pan. When cool, peel off the skin, pull out the bones, and return the skin and bones to the soup; shred the cooled meat and set aside.

7. Simmer the soup on the stovetop over low heat for about 25 minutes and then use a slotted spoon to remove (and discard) the skin and bones. Return the shredded meat to the soup, season to taste with salt, and serve hot.

*two-bean soup with chicken and cilantro

OVEN-ROASTED CHICKEN SOUP
FIVE MORE RECIPES

tomato-basil chicken soup with ancho and cumin

With a thicker and slightly sweeter broth than the master recipe because of the added tomato paste, this basil-and-oregano-seasoned soup works well with any Italian-inspired menu. Ancho chile offers a surprising and welcome smoky heat. This soup's delicious on its own or with garlic bread for dipping.

SPICE BLEND

2 tablespoons dried basil (2 grams)

1 tablespoon plus 1 teaspoon dried oregano (2 grams)

1½ teaspoons cumin seeds (5 grams)

1 teaspoon ground ancho chile (2 grams)

Finely grind the basil, oregano, and cumin together and immediately mix with the ancho chile. Use this spice blend instead of the main spice blend in chicken soup recipe on page 190.

Follow the chicken soup recipe, substituting 1 orange, cut into segments, for the apple in step 3.

At the end of step 4, add ⅓ cup tomato paste to the cooked vegetables and stir well for 2 minutes before proceeding to step 5.

two-bean soup with chicken and cilantro*

When I have about a half pot of soup left over, I like to turn it into a different meal—like this two-bean soup. Chickpeas and white beans make this chicken soup extra filling, while cilantro adds freshness. You can double the quantities here if you'd like to make a larger pot of soup based on the complete chicken soup recipe on page 190, which serves 8 to 12.

Follow the chicken soup recipe. When the roast chicken is cool enough to handle, shred 1 cup of the meat (save the rest for another use). Strain 6 cups of the broth and bring it to a simmer in a large saucepan (save the vegetables for another use). Stir in the shredded chicken, 1 cup cooked chickpeas (see page 114) or rinsed and drained canned chickpeas, 1 cup cooked cannellini beans (see page 118) or rinsed and drained canned cannellini beans, ¼ cup chopped fresh cilantro, and the juice of 1 lemon. Season to taste with salt. Serve hot.

Serves 4

sesame-shiitake chicken soup with galangal

With dried shiitakes, seaweed, and bonito flakes, this soup tastes a bit like the broth in miso soup, but it's even richer than that with chicken and the addition of sesame seeds. This is delicious on its own or with ramen, soba, or other noodles stirred in.

SPICE BLEND

2 dried shiitake mushrooms (5 grams)

2 tablespoons dried wakame seaweed (5 grams)

2 tablespoons plus 1½ teaspoons white sesame seeds, preferably unhulled (25 grams)

1 teaspoon granulated dried orange peel (3 grams)

2½ teaspoons ground galangal (5 grams)

Finely grind the shiitakes and wakame together and immediately mix with the whole sesame seeds, orange peel, and galangal. Use this spice blend instead of the main spice blend in the chicken soup recipe on page 190.

Follow the chicken soup recipe, adding ¼ cup bonito flakes and 1 tablespoon soy sauce along with the water at the end of step 5.

coconut-cilantro chicken soup with lemongrass

Creamy coconut milk gives this soup a luxurious richness, and fish sauce adds a savory depth. A Southeast Asian–inspired blend of cilantro, lemongrass, galangal, and chile comes together with the sweetness of palm sugar. If you don't have that on hand, coconut sugar or brown sugar lends a similar full-bodied sweetness. This soup is delicious on its own or with cooked rice noodles stirred in.

SPICE BLEND

1 tablespoon plus 2 teaspoons ground lemongrass (10 grams)

2 tablespoons dried cilantro (2 grams)

2½ teaspoons ground galangal (5 grams)

¼ teaspoon jalapeño powder (1 gram)

1 teaspoon palm sugar (5 grams)

Mix together the lemongrass, cilantro, galangal, jalapeño powder, and palm sugar. Use this spice blend instead of the main spice blend in the chicken soup recipe on page 190.

Follow the chicken soup recipe, substituting 1 (14.5-ounce) can coconut milk for 2 cups of the water at the beginning of step 5 and adding 2 tablespoons fish sauce at the same time.

creamy labne chicken soup with dill seeds

Labne yogurt and chickpea flour give this soup a creamy richness balanced by the bite of mustard and dill seeds. Fennel seeds deliver a hint of licorice. You only need 4 cups of broth to make this soup, which serves 2. You can double or triple the quantities to use the full chicken soup recipe on page 190 to serve up to 12 people.

SPICE BLEND

1 teaspoon dill seeds (2 grams)

1 teaspoon fennel seeds (2 grams)

½ teaspoon brown mustard seeds (3 grams)

Finely grind the dill and fennel seeds together and immediately mix with the whole mustard seeds. You will use this for seasoning the soup.

Follow the chicken soup recipe, using the main spice blend. When cool enough to handle, shred ½ cup chicken meat (save the rest for another use). Bring 4 cups strained broth to a simmer in a large saucepan (save the vegetables from the soup for another use). Stir in the shredded chicken and the dill-fennel spice blend. Whisk ½ cup labne or plain Greek yogurt and 2 tablespoons chickpea flour in a small bowl; while whisking, add 1 cup of the simmering broth in a steady stream. Add the mixture to the chicken soup and stir until heated through; do not let the soup boil. Serve hot.

Serves 2

QUICK-SEARED PORK CHOPS

brown sugar–seared pork chops with orange glaze

In this master recipe, the warming heat of mustard seeds and ginger becomes even more aromatic with a generous dose of dried onion and cumin.

SERVES 4

MAIN SPICE BLEND

1¼ teaspoons cumin seeds (4 grams)

1 tablespoon plus 1½ teaspoons dried onion slices (10 grams)

¾ teaspoon yellow mustard seeds (4 grams)

½ teaspoon ground ginger (1 gram)

1 teaspoon packed brown sugar (5 grams)

Coarsely grind the cumin, onion, and mustard together and immediately mix with the ginger and brown sugar. Or mix together ¾ teaspoon pre-ground cumin, 2½ teaspoons granulated onion, and ½ teaspoon pre-ground yellow mustard powder with the ginger and brown sugar.

PORK CHOPS

4 (1-inch-thick) boneless center-cut pork chops (1¾ pounds)

Kosher salt

Extra-virgin olive oil

1 cup fresh orange juice

MAKE AHEAD

The spice-rubbed pork without salt can be cooked immediately or covered and refrigerated for up to 1 day before cooking. Season with salt before cooking.

Searing pork chops over medium heat instead of high heat ensures that the meat cooks through evenly and stays juicy. A bit of sugar in the spice mix gives the pork a nice color and caramelized crust. The whole dish—chops plus a glazy sauce—comes together in under half an hour. The seasoning options are endless (think caraway seeds, turmeric, Aleppo pepper) and leftovers also taste great cold (see page 197).

1. Coat the pork chops with the spice mix on all sides and then season the chops with salt.

2. Heat a large skillet or sauté pan over medium-high heat. Add enough oil to coat the pan (1 to 2 tablespoons) and add the chops right away (you don't want the oil to get hot first). Reduce the heat to medium so the chops sizzle steadily. Cook, turning once, until nicely browned and an instant-read thermometer inserted into the thickest part of the chop registers 150°F, 5 to 6 minutes per side. Transfer the chops to a plate and let rest for 5 minutes.

3. Meanwhile, add the orange juice to the pan and cook, stirring and scraping up any browned bits from the bottom of the pan, until the juice reduces to a syrupy consistency, 3 to 5 minutes. Remove from the heat.

4. Slice the pork at an angle from top to bottom and drizzle the sauce on top.

*pork and pineapple salad with honey-lime dressing

QUICK-SEARED PORK CHOPS

FIVE MORE RECIPES

dijon mustard–crusted pork chops with rosemary

A thin smear of Dijon mustard seals the French-inspired blend of green peppercorns, rosemary, and caraway to the chops before cooking and gives them a savory edge.

SPICE BLEND

1 teaspoon green peppercorns (2 grams)
1 tablespoon dried rosemary (1 gram)
¾ teaspoon caraway seeds (3 grams)

Finely grind together the peppercorns, rosemary, and caraway. Use this spice blend instead of the main spice blend in the pork chops recipe on page 194.

Follow the pork chops recipe, spreading 1 teaspoon Dijon mustard over both sides of each of the chops before pressing in the spice blend to coat all sides. Cook the chops as instructed.

crumb-crusted smoky pork chops with apple glaze

Similar to schnitzel, these pork chops have a lighter crunchy crust, smoky with pimentón, hot with Aleppo pepper, and aromatic with coriander.

SPICE BLEND

1½ teaspoons coriander seeds (3 grams)
¾ teaspoon pimentón (smoked paprika; 2 grams)
½ teaspoon Aleppo pepper (1 gram)

Finely grind the coriander and immediately mix with the pimentón and Aleppo. Use this spice blend instead of the main spice blend in the pork chops recipe on page 194.

Follow the pork chops recipe, coating the chops with olive oil after salting them in step 2. Immediately press 2 tablespoons fine plain bread crumbs all over the chops to evenly coat before cooking.

In step 3, substitute 1 cup apple juice for the orange juice.

pork chops with peanut satay sauce

Pork satay takes a different form here when whole chops are seared and then sliced, but the peanut-coconut dipping sauce evokes this beloved Southeast Asian dish. To get a more pronounced satay effect, you can grill the chops over a medium-hot fire instead.

SPICE BLEND

2 teaspoons dried onion slices (3 grams)
2 teaspoons dried garlic slices (3 grams)
¾ teaspoon Muntok white peppercorns (2 grams)
¼ teaspoon cumin seeds (1 gram)
2 teaspoons ground turmeric (2 grams)

Finely grind the onion, garlic, peppercorns, and cumin together and immediately mix with the turmeric. Use this spice blend instead of the main spice blend in the pork chops recipe on page 194.

Follow the pork chops recipe, substituting ¼ cup rice wine vinegar for the orange juice in step 3. After the vinegar has reduced, add ⅓ cup coconut milk and 2 tablespoons peanut butter to the pan and cook, stirring, until thickened, about 2 minutes. Stir in ⅓ cup chopped toasted peanuts. Spoon the sauce over the pork.

pork and pineapple salad with honey-lime dressing*

Leftover pork chops taste great cold. While you can eat chilled chops straight, they're even better when tossed with juicy ripe pineapple, crunchy bell pepper, and a sweet-and-sour mix of honey and lime in a bright and fresh salad.

Follow the pork chops recipe on page 194. Dice enough pork to yield 1 cup of meat (1 to 2 chops; save the rest for another use) and refrigerate until cold. Toss the chilled diced meat with ½ cup diced fresh pineapple, ⅓ cup diced red bell pepper, 1 tablespoon honey, and 2 tablespoons fresh lime juice. Season to taste with salt and serve over 4 cups mixed salad greens.

cider vinegar–glazed pork chops with apples and raisins

The classic combination of pork and apples develops layers of flavors here—from tangy apples to sweet raisins to tart apple cider vinegar. The warming ginger in the spice rub complements the apples, as do the hot yellow mustard seeds.

Follow the pork chops recipe on page 194. In step 2, after cooking the pork chops on one side and flipping them, add 1 peeled Honeycrisp or Fuji apple, cut into wedges and cored. Cook the apples alongside the pork chops, turning once, until they are golden brown on both sides, 5 to 6 minutes. Transfer the pork chops to a plate to rest and add ⅓ cup raisins to the pan.

In step 3, substitute ¼ cup apple cider vinegar for the orange juice. Serve the apple-raisin glaze over the pork.

OVEN-ROASTED MEATBALLS

spicy garlic and oregano meatballs with blistered grape tomatoes

Cinnamon adds a bit of intrigue to the traditional Italian sausage seasonings—fennel, garlic, oregano, and chile—in these meatballs. Labne takes the place of creamy Italian cheese to keep these meatballs moist and tender.

MAKES 12
SERVES 4

MAIN SPICE BLEND

1½ teaspoons fennel seeds (3 grams)

2½ teaspoons dried garlic slices (4 grams)

2 teaspoons dried oregano (1 gram)

¼ teaspoon ground cinnamon, preferably Vietnamese (1 gram)

½ teaspoon peperoncini (dried Calabrian chile) or red pepper flakes (1 gram)

Finely grind the fennel and garlic together and immediately mix with the oregano, cinnamon, and peperoncini.

MEATBALLS

Extra-virgin olive oil

1 cup finely diced yellow onion

Kosher salt

1 pound ground beef chuck or sirloin (85% to 90% lean)

¼ cup labne or plain Greek yogurt

⅓ cup panko bread crumbs

1 large egg

1 pint grape tomatoes

MAKE AHEAD

The uncooked meatballs can be formed and refrigerated for up to 1 day before roasting.

My oven-roasting technique simultaneously cooks the meatballs and the grape tomatoes, which collapse into a fresh, light sauce. Inspired by the meatball kebabs I grew up with in Israel, these are hearty and well spiced, with a satisfying char from a few final minutes under the broiler. In addition to mixing up the seasonings and meat in combinations like lamb with feta and olives, you can turn these into a nice meaty sauce for pasta or crispy Parmesan-coated meatballs that are great as two-bite appetizers (see page 201).

1. To make the meatballs: Position one oven rack 6 inches from the broiler heat source and one in the center of the oven. Preheat the oven to 400°F.

2. Coat a large oven-safe skillet with 2 tablespoons oil and set over medium-high heat. Add the onion, 1 teaspoon of the spice blend, and ½ teaspoon salt. Cook, stirring occasionally, until the onion is just translucent but still has a little bite, about 5 minutes. Transfer to a large bowl to cool completely; reserve the skillet.

3. Add the ground beef, labne, panko, egg, remaining spice blend, 1 tablespoon olive oil, and 2 teaspoons salt to the bowl with onions. Mix with your hands until evenly blended.

4. Coat the skillet with oil (1 to 2 tablespoons). Form the meat mixture into 12 (2-inch) balls (about 2 ounces each). Put them in the skillet in a single layer and scatter the tomatoes all around, letting them fall between the meatballs.

5. Roast for 20 minutes on the center rack. Turn the broiler to High and move the skillet to the upper rack. Broil the meatballs until browned and an instant-read thermometer inserted into the center registers 160°F, 2 to 8 minutes more. The strength of broiler heat sources varies widely, so keep an eye on the meatballs and take them out when they're nicely browned. Serve hot, with the tomatoes.

*feta-stuffed meatballs with green olives

OVEN-ROASTED MEATBALLS

FIVE MORE RECIPES

tahini-parsley meatballs with paprika

Tahini enriches these meatballs with a faint nutty flavor, which pairs nicely with the tang of sumac and the grassy freshness of parsley.

SPICE BLEND

1 teaspoon sweet paprika (2 grams)

¾ teaspoon sumac (2 grams)

1½ teaspoons dried parsley (1 gram)

¼ teaspoon jalapeño powder or cayenne pepper (½ gram)

Mix together the paprika, sumac, parsley, and jalapeño powder. Use this spice blend instead of the main spice blend in the meatballs recipe on page 198.

Follow the meatballs recipe, substituting ¼ cup tahini for the labne in step 3.

feta-stuffed meatballs with green olives*

Feta delivers a salty, creamy surprise in the centers of these meatballs.

Follow the meatballs recipe on page 198. In step 4, after forming the balls, use your thumb to make a cavity in a ball and stuff it with a ¾-inch cube of feta cheese. Press the meat around the cheese and roll into a ball again, sealing in the cheese. Repeat with the remaining meatballs and eleven more cubes of cheese. Substitute 1 cup pitted green olives (such as Castelvetrano) for the tomatoes.

rose and ginger lamb meatballs with black olives

Ground lamb gives these meatballs a welcome juiciness (I prefer to buy ground shoulder meat because it's richer). The heat of ginger and ancho chile cuts through the fattiness, as do the briny olives. Rose petals add a subtle and complex floral scent that complements the cumin.

SPICE BLEND

¾ teaspoon cumin seeds (2 grams)

2 tablespoons dried rose petals (1 gram)

1 teaspoon ground ginger (2 grams)

½ teaspoon ground ancho chile (1 gram)

Finely grind the cumin and rose petals together and immediately mix with the ginger and ancho chile. Use this spice blend instead of the main spice blend in the meatballs recipe on page 198.

Follow the meatballs recipe, substituting 1 pound ground lamb shoulder for the beef in step 3.

In step 4, substitute ½ cup pitted black kalamata olives for the tomatoes.

crunchy parmesan meatballs

Crusted with crunchy bread crumbs and cheese, these meatballs work well as an appetizer for a party. You can even roll them smaller to make them bite-size.

Follow the meatballs recipe on page 198. Mix ¼ cup panko bread crumbs, ¼ cup grated Parmesan cheese, and 1 tablespoon extra-virgin olive oil in a small dish. After forming the balls in step 4, roll the balls, one by one, in the panko-Parmesan mixture to evenly coat. Omit the tomatoes and bake as instructed.

quick tomato meat sauce

You only need four leftover meatballs for this 10-minute tomato sauce. It's great over pasta or rice and can be doubled or tripled if you have more than four leftover meatballs or want to make a bigger batch.

Follow the meatballs recipe on page 198, using the main spice blend. Crumble 4 cooked meatballs (save the rest for another use). Coat a small saucepan with extra-virgin olive oil (1 to 2 tablespoons) and set over medium heat. Add the crumbled meatballs and stir until browned, about 1 minute. Add 1 cup canned crushed tomatoes, 1 tablespoon tomato paste, and ¾ teaspoon pimenton (smoked paprika; 2 grams). Stir well, bring to a simmer, and cook for 5 minutes, stirring occasionally. Season to taste with salt and serve over pasta.

Serves 2 to 4

BRAISED SHORT RIBS

citrus-braised short ribs with star anise and cocoa

The hint of chocolate in Urfa pepper is echoed by cocoa powder in this spice rub. Both bring out short ribs' richness, which is countered by tangy sumac and pomegranate juice.

SERVES 8 TO 12

MAIN SPICE BLEND

1¼ teaspoons caraway seeds (5 grams)

3 whole star anise (3 grams)

1 tablespoon plus ¼ teaspoon sumac (10 grams)

2 teaspoons Urfa pepper (4 grams)

1 tablespoon plus 1 teaspoon unsweetened cocoa powder (8 grams)

Finely grind the caraway and star anise together and immediately mix with the sumac, Urfa, and cocoa powder.

SHORT RIBS

4½ pounds bone-in short ribs, preferably 2 × 4-inch pieces with more meat than bone on each one

Kosher salt and freshly ground black pepper

Canola oil

2 oranges

2 medium yellow onions

3 medium carrots

6 medium or 4 large garlic cloves

2 cups unsweetened pomegranate juice

MAKE AHEAD

You can refrigerate the braise for up to 1 week or freeze it for up to 2 months. Reheat before serving.

NOTE

For a more elegant presentation, transfer the short ribs to a half sheet pan lined with parchment paper, discard the bones, and remove and discard any cartilage. Strain the braising liquid into an airtight container and refrigerate; discard the solids or save to eat another time. Chill the short ribs until cold and firm, about 3 hours or up to 1 week, and then trim and cut the cold short ribs into neat pieces. Pour the braising liquid into a large, deep skillet and bring to a simmer. Add the short ribs pieces to the liquid and reheat, spooning the sauce over to glaze the meat. Serve hot.

When I was a chef at Daniel Boulud's restaurant Daniel, I cooked four hundred pounds of short ribs a week. For a long time after I left, I couldn't even look at a short rib. Recently, I have come back to them and remembered why they are so great—achieving rich and complex flavor in the meat and braising liquid takes barely any effort at all. Here, orange wedges cut the meat's richness with the pulp's tang and the rind's pleasantly bitter edge, and they are delicious eaten along with the carrots in the sauce. Simple tweaks, like changing the braising base, make short ribs ideal for any dinner party menu.

1. To make the short ribs: Preheat the oven to 300°F. Line two half sheet pans with parchment paper.

2. Put the ribs on one of the prepared pans and season them very generously with salt and pepper on all sides. Heat a large Dutch oven or other heavy oven-safe pot over medium-high heat. Add enough oil to coat the bottom (2 to 3 tablespoons). Add enough short ribs to fit in a single layer. Sear to evenly brown, 4 to 5 minutes per side. Transfer to the other sheet pan. Repeat with the remaining short ribs.

3. While the short ribs are browning, cut the oranges into 1½-inch wedges (with their peel). Cut the onions into 1-inch chunks. Scrub and trim the carrots and cut one at an angle into a 1-inch piece. Rotate the carrot and cut another 1½-inch wide triangular piece at an angle. Repeat with the remaining carrots. Peel the garlic and cut any large cloves in half lengthwise.

4. Once the meat is done browning, add the oranges, onions, carrots, and garlic to the Dutch oven. Stir well and sprinkle with salt. Cook, stirring occasionally, until the onions have a little color, 5 to 8 minutes.

5. Sprinkle two-thirds of the spice blend over the orange mixture. Reduce the heat to low and stir to evenly coat. Don't let the spices burn. While stirring, add the pomegranate juice in a steady stream, scraping up any browned bits from the bottom of the pan (you want the cocoa to gradually thicken the liquid without clumping). Raise the heat to high and bring to a simmer.

6. While the liquid heats, sprinkle the remaining one-third of the spice mixture all over the short ribs. Nestle the ribs in the Dutch oven bone-side up. Pour ½ cup water into the sheet pan that held the meat, scrape up any spices and browned bits, and pour it all into the pot. Bring to a simmer, cover, and transfer to the oven.

7. Bake until the bones lift right out of the tender meat, 3 to 3½ hours. Discard the bones and cartilage and serve hot.

*short rib and potato hash cakes

BRAISED SHORT RIBS
FIVE MORE RECIPES

red wine–braised short ribs with black pepper and yellow mustard

Steak au poivre meets boeuf bourguignon in this braise. A generous dose of black pepper, along with the licorice notes of fennel and the warming heat of mustard and ginger, cuts through the meat's richness and delivers a rich complexity.

SPICE BLEND

2½ teaspoons black peppercorns, preferably Tellicherry (10 grams)

2 teaspoons yellow mustard seeds (10 grams)

1 tablespoon plus 2 teaspoons ground ginger (10 grams)

2½ teaspoons fennel seeds (5 grams)

1 tablespoon plus 1 teaspoon all-purpose flour (7 grams)

Coarsely grind the peppercorns and mustard seeds together and immediately mix with the ginger, whole fennel seeds, and flour. Or mix 1 tablespoon pre-ground black pepper and 2 teaspoons dry mustard with the ginger, fennel, and flour. Use this spice blend instead of the main spice blend in the short rib recipe on page 202.

Follow the short rib recipe, substituting 2 cups dry red wine for the pomegranate juice in step 5.

chili-and-tomato-braised short ribs with cinnamon

A hint of Southwestern-style chili powder comes through with the cumin-oregano rub on the meat and the tomatoes simmered into the mix, while white wine keeps the braising liquid light. Chickpea flour thickens the sauce nicely, but you can use all-purpose flour instead.

SPICE BLEND

1 tablespoon plus ¼ teaspoon cumin seeds (10 grams)

1½ teaspoons ground cinnamon, preferably Vietnamese (5 grams)

1 teaspoon peperoncini (dried Calabrian chile) or red pepper flakes (2 grams)

2 tablespoons dried oregano (3 grams)

1 tablespoon plus 1 teaspoon chickpea flour (7 grams)

Finely grind the cumin and immediately mix with the cinnamon, peperoncini, oregano, and chickpea flour. Or mix 1 tablespoon pre-ground cumin with the cinnamon, peperoncini, oregano, and chickpea flour. Use this spice blend instead of the main spice blend in the short rib recipe on page 202.

Follow the short rib recipe, adding 2 tablespoons tomato paste at the end of step 4, after stirring the vegetables until they are a little tender, about 1 minute.

In step 5, substitute 2 cups dry white wine for the pomegranate juice. After all the wine is stirred in, add 1 (14.5-ounce) can diced tomatoes with their juices.

vermouth-braised short ribs with warm spices and dried fruit

Both red vermouth and bits of dried fruit bring a jammy sweetness to this braise. Savory spices like bay leaves and white pepper balance the sugar, which is accentuated with warming allspice, anise, and bitter cocoa.

SPICE BLEND

5 whole dried bay leaves

1 tablespoon plus ¼ teaspoon Muntok white peppercorns (10 grams)

1¼ teaspoons allspice berries (5 grams)

1 tablespoon plus ¼ teaspoon anise (10 grams)

1 tablespoon plus 1 teaspoon unsweetened cocoa powder (8 grams)

Finely grind the bay leaves, peppercorns, and allspice together and immediately mix with the whole anise and cocoa powder. Use this spice blend instead of the main spice blend in the short rib recipe on page 202.

Follow the short rib recipe, substituting 3 cups red vermouth for the pomegranate juice in step 5. After all the vermouth is stirred in, add ¼ cup raisins, ¼ cup diced dried apricots, ¼ cup pitted and diced dates, and ½ cup dried cranberries.

carrot juice–braised short ribs with sweet potatoes

Carrot juice infuses short ribs with an earthy sweetness, echoed by chunks of sweet potatoes. The bitter edge of turmeric and cocoa brings complexity to the mix, along with the heat of ginger and cayenne and the tang of amchoor.

SPICE BLEND

3 tablespoons plus 1 teaspoon ground turmeric (10 grams)

2½ teaspoons ground ginger (5 grams)

2½ teaspoons amchoor (5 grams)

½ teaspoon cayenne pepper (1 gram)

1 tablespoon plus 1 teaspoon unsweetened cocoa powder (8 grams)

Mix together the turmeric, ginger, amchoor, cayenne, and cocoa. Use this spice blend instead of the main spice blend in the short rib recipe on page 202.

Follow the short rib recipe, adding 1 cup diced scrubbed sweet potatoes along with the vegetables in step 4.

In step 5, substitute 3 cups carrot juice for the pomegranate juice.

short rib and potato hash cakes*

These little patties are a great use of leftover short rib meat—all you need is ½ pound of shredded meat to make 15 two-bite hash cakes. And any of the short rib options (here and page 202) taste delicious. The crisp cakes are as good at brunch with poached eggs as they are at dinner with a salad.

SPICE BLEND

1 teaspoon yellow mustard seeds (5 grams)

1 teaspoon celery seeds (2 grams)

Finely grind together the mustard seeds and celery seeds. Transfer to a large bowl and mix in ½ pound (about 1½ cups) finely chopped cooked short ribs (page 202 or 205), ½ pound coarsely grated Yukon Gold potatoes, ½ finely chopped medium yellow onion, 1 beaten large egg, 1 tablespoon all-purpose flour, and ¾ teaspoon kosher salt. With damp hands, form the mixture into 15 (2-inch) round patties (1½ ounces each).

Coat a large cast-iron or nonstick skillet with canola oil (1 to 2 tablespoons). Heat over medium heat until hot and shimmering and then add as many patties as can fit comfortably in the pan. Cook, turning once, until nicely browned and heated through, 3 to 5 minutes per side. Repeat with the remaining patties.

ROASTED RACK OF LAMB

fennel-and-coriander-crusted rack of lamb with caramelized onions

In this master recipe, the Middle Eastern duo of cumin and fennel balances the gamy richness of the lamb. The spice-infused mustard smeared over the lamb delivers a nice heat.

MAKES ONE RACK (8 OR 9 CHOPS)
SERVES 2 TO 4

MAIN SPICE BLEND

2 teaspoons cumin seeds (6 grams)

1 tablespoon plus 1 teaspoon coriander seeds (8 grams)

1 teaspoon black peppercorns, preferably Tellicherry (4 grams)

1 tablespoon plus 1 teaspoon fennel seeds (8 grams)

Coarsely grind together the cumin, coriander, peppercorns, and fennel. Or mix 1¾ teaspoons pre-ground cumin, 2½ teaspoons pre-ground coriander, ¾ teaspoon pre-ground black pepper, and 1 tablespoon pre-ground fennel.

LAMB

1 frenched rack of lamb (1¾ pounds)

Kosher salt

6 tablespoons smooth Dijon mustard

Extra-virgin olive oil

2 medium yellow onions, halved and thinly sliced

Kosher salt

MAKE AHEAD

The lamb can be coated with the spice mixture and refrigerated for up to 12 hours before roasting.

This dish looks beautiful enough for a dinner party but is simple enough for a weeknight meal too. It'll make you look good either way. I skip the messy step of searing the lamb on the stovetop and just roast it in the oven. The spices crust onto the outside and the center ends up evenly medium-rare. In each variation, I use a liquid component to both glue the spices to the meat and add an extra-complex layer of flavor. The bed of vegetables under the meat both infuses it with flavor and ends up as a delicious side dish. One rack of lamb will provide two small chops per person if serving four—which is okay if you're presenting this alongside lots of sides, but if you're serving a crowd, you can cook up to three racks of lamb in a large roasting pan at one time. Ask your butcher to french the rack if you like the look of trimmed and pristine bones.

1. For the lamb: Let the lamb sit at room temperature for 15 minutes before starting your prep work so that it can be at room temperature for 30 minutes total before roasting.

2. Preheat the oven to 400°F. Place the spice blend in a small bowl and stir in 1½ teaspoons salt and the mustard. Spread the spice paste evenly all over the rack of lamb.

3. Lightly coat the bottom of a small roasting pan with oil (2 to 3 tablespoons). Spread the onions evenly over the pan and sprinkle with salt. Set the lamb over the onions, fat-side up.

4. Roast until a crust forms on the lamb and a meat thermometer inserted into the center registers 115° to 120°F for medium-rare, 35 to 40 minutes. Remove from the oven and let the lamb rest in the pan for 10 minutes before transferring it to a cutting board and slicing it into individual chops. Serve immediately, with the onions.

*tomato-glazed rack of lamb with eggplant

ROASTED RACK OF LAMB
FIVE MORE RECIPES

tomato-glazed rack of lamb with eggplant*

Eggplant goes tender in the oven and soaks up rich, meaty juices when roasted under a rack of lamb. This is an ideal centerpiece for any Italian-inspired meal.

SPICE BLEND

3 tablespoons dried oregano (5 grams)

2 tablespoons plus 1½ teaspoons dried thyme (5 grams)

5 tablespoons dried rosemary (5 grams)

Finely grind the oregano, thyme, and rosemary together. Use this spice blend instead of the main spice blend in the rack of lamb recipe on page 206.

Follow the rack of lamb recipe, substituting 6 tablespoons tomato paste for the mustard in step 3.

In step 4, substitute 1 small eggplant, trimmed and cut into 1-inch dice, for the onions.

paprika and ginger rack of lamb with caramelized carrots

Ground dried garlic chips round out the warming heat of ginger and paprika and the kick of cayenne here. This North African–inspired combination is delicious with couscous.

SPICE BLEND

1 tablespoon dried garlic slices (5 grams)

1 tablespoon plus 2 teaspoons sweet paprika (10 grams)

2½ teaspoons ground ginger (5 grams)

1 teaspoon cayenne pepper (2 grams)

Finely grind the garlic and immediately mix with the paprika, ginger, and cayenne. Or mix 2 teaspoons granulated garlic with the paprika, ginger, and cayenne. Use this spice blend instead of the main spice blend in the rack of lamb recipe on page 206.

Follow the rack of lamb recipe, substituting 3 tablespoons extra-virgin olive oil for the mustard in step 3.

In step 4, substitute 2 large carrots, scrubbed and grated on the large holes of a box grater, for the onions.

curried rack of lamb with butternut squash

Mild yellow curry spices lend an Indian-inspired aroma and flavor to this yogurt-crusted rack of lamb. It tastes great with basmati rice or naan.

SPICE BLEND

1½ teaspoons green cardamom pods (3 grams)

2 teaspoons cumin seeds (6 grams)

1¼ teaspoons fenugreek seeds (6 grams)

1 tablespoon plus 2 teaspoons ground turmeric (5 grams)

Finely grind the cardamom, cumin, and fenugreek together and immediately mix with the turmeric. Use this spice blend instead of the main spice blend in the rack of lamb recipe on page 206.

Follow the rack of lamb recipe, substituting ½ cup labne or plain Greek yogurt for the mustard in step 3.

Peel, halve, and thinly slice the neck of 1 small butternut squash, substituting it for the onions in step 4.

sweet-and-sour pomegranate-glazed rack of lamb

Both sumac and Urfa pepper have tangy citrus notes that are accentuated by the syrupy tartness of pomegranate molasses. Allspice balances the sweet and sour with its warming aroma.

SPICE BLEND

2½ teaspoons allspice berries (10 grams)

1 tablespoon plus 2 teaspoons sumac (15 grams)

1 tablespoon plus 2 teaspoons Urfa pepper (10 grams)

Finely grind the allspice and immediately mix with the sumac and Urfa. Or mix 2 teaspoons pre-ground allspice with the sumac and Urfa. Use this spice blend instead of the main spice blend in the rack of lamb recipe on page 206.

Follow the rack of lamb recipe, substituting ⅓ cup pomegranate molasses for the mustard in step 3.

tarragon, mint, and dill buttered rack of lamb with shallots

Whole dill seeds add a slightly sweet and pleasantly bitter pop to this herb rub that's fragrant with mint and tarragon. As the lamb roasts, the butter melts into the meat, basting it with zero effort on your part and delivering a luxuriously rich, showstopping dish.

SPICE BLEND

¼ cup dried onion slices (16 grams)

¼ cup dried tarragon (4 grams)

1 tablespoon plus 2 teaspoons dried mint (5 grams)

1 tablespoon plus 2 teaspoons dill seeds (10 grams)

Coarsely grind the onion, tarragon, and mint and mix with the whole dill seeds. Or mix 3 tablespoons onion powder with the tarragon, mint, and dill. Use this spice blend instead of the main spice blend in the rack of lamb recipe on page 206.

Follow the rack of lamb recipe, substituting 4 tablespoons softened salted butter for the mustard in step 3.

In step 4, substitute 6 shallots, halved and thinly sliced, for the onions.

ROASTED ROLLED LEG OF LAMB

rosemary and mint roasted leg of lamb

The classic mix of fresh garlic, rosemary, and mint tastes even more intense when the herbs are used in their dried forms. Fennel seeds bring a pop of licorice and peperoncini provides a little heat.

SERVES 12

MAIN SPICE BLEND

2 tablespoons dried garlic slices (10 grams)

3 tablespoons dried rosemary (3 grams)

1 tablespoon dried mint (3 grams)

2½ teaspoons fennel seeds (5 grams)

1 teaspoon peperoncini (dried Calabrian chile) or red pepper flakes (2 grams)

Finely grind the garlic, rosemary, mint, and fennel together and immediately mix with the peperoncini.

LAMB

1 whole boneless leg of lamb (4 to 5 pounds), butterflied

1 cup green olives, preferably Castelvetrano, pitted

1 lemon, scrubbed, quartered, and seeded

3 medium yellow onions, halved and thinly sliced

Extra-virgin olive oil

Kosher salt

MAKE AHEAD

The spice-rubbed and tied lamb can be covered and refrigerated for up 1 day. If prepared ahead, don't let the lamb sit at room temperature before seasoning and don't salt the exterior of the lamb before refrigerating. Instead, let the seasoned and tied lamb sit out at room temperature for 30 minutes before roasting and then rub it with olive oil and salt it as directed in step 4.

This impressive roast is made for entertaining. Not only does it easily serve a crowd, but it tastes as good hot as it does warm or at room temperature. Rolling the spice-rubbed leg of lamb infuses so much flavor in the meat that it's okay if it goes past medium-rare.

1. Remove the lamb from the refrigerator, untie it if needed, and let it sit out at room temperature for 30 minutes.

2. Preheat the oven to 350°F. Put the olives, lemon, and onions in a medium roasting pan, drizzle with oil, sprinkle with 1 tablespoon of the spice blend, and season with salt. Toss until well coated and then spread in an even layer.

3. Open the lamb on a large cutting board. If needed, cut deeper slits in the lamb at intervals so that it will lie flat when opened. Season the inside of the lamb generously with salt, rub the remaining spice blend all over both sides, and roll back to its original shape with the seam side down. To truss the lamb, cut about 4 feet of twine and tightly wrap it once along the length of the lamb down its center, leaving a few inches of twine at one end. Tie that short end to the long piece in a knot. Wrap the long piece tightly around the lamb crosswise and loop it under the tied length of twine to secure it. Move the long piece 1 inch up and wrap it around again, holding it in place with your fingers before you loop it to the central line. Continue tying in 1-inch intervals until the end, then knot the last loop. Tie the end to the first knot to secure it.

4. Put the lamb on top of the onion mixture and scrape any spices and juices from the cutting board on top of it. Rub the lamb all over with olive oil (2 to 3 tablespoons) and generously season it all over with salt. Place it seam-side down in the center of the pan.

5. Roast, rotating the pan halfway through and basting every 20 minutes, for 1 hour. Add ½ cup water to the pan and roast, basting occasionally, until a meat thermometer inserted into the thickest part registers 125°F, about 30 minutes longer.

6. Let the lamb rest at room temperature for 30 minutes before untying and carving it into thin slices. Serve with the onions and pan juices.

*tomato and olive salad with lamb, herbs, and crunchy pita

ROASTED ROLLED LEG OF LAMB
FIVE MORE RECIPES

walnut-and-date-stuffed leg of lamb with pomegranate glaze

Blending port with walnuts and dates creates a sweet stuffing for this Moroccan-inspired lamb roast that is crusted with coriander and cumin. Pomegranate juice reduces in the onion-olive base for a salty-sweet sauce.

SPICE BLEND

2½ teaspoons coriander seeds (5 grams)

1½ teaspoons cumin seeds (5 grams)

1 teaspoon anise (3 grams)

1 teaspoon whole cloves (2 grams)

1½ teaspoons ground cinnamon, preferably Vietnamese (5 grams)

Finely grind the coriander, cumin, anise, and cloves together and immediately mix with the cinnamon. Use this spice blend instead of the main spice blend in the leg of lamb recipe on page 210.

In a food processor, pulse ½ cup chopped walnuts, 8 pitted Medjool dates, and ½ cup port to form a paste.

Follow the leg of lamb recipe, spreading the walnut-date paste all over the inside of the lamb after rubbing with the spice blend and before rolling and tying in step 3.

In step 5, substitute 1 cup pomegranate juice for the water.

cocoa-chile roasted leg of lamb

Chocolate may sound like an odd ingredient for lamb, but its bitterness balances the meat's richness beautifully. Mexican chocolate, in particular, works well with meat since it's infused with spices such as cinnamon, nutmeg, allspice, and chiles. To complement those spices, I add smoky hot ancho and chipotle chiles along with sesame seeds and fragrant oranges.

SPICE BLEND

1 teaspoon unsweetened cocoa powder (5 grams)

1 teaspoon ground ancho chile (2 grams)

1 teaspoon ground chipotle chile (2 grams)

1 teaspoon ground coffee (3 grams)

1 teaspoon ground ginger (2 grams)

Mix together the cocoa, ancho, chipotle, coffee, and ginger. Use this spice blend instead of the main spice blend in the leg of lamb recipe on page 210.

Zest 2 oranges into a small bowl and add ⅓ cup white sesame seeds, preferably unhulled, and ¼ cup grated Mexican chocolate and mix well. Cut the zested oranges into wedges.

Follow the leg of lamb recipe, substituting the orange wedges for the lemon in step 2 and omitting the olives.

In step 3, spread the sesame mixture all over the inside of the lamb after rubbing with the spice blend and before rolling and tying.

goat cheese, almond, and caper–stuffed roasted leg of lamb

Creamy goat cheese, studded with crunchy almonds and briny capers, makes this stuffed leg of lamb taste extra luxurious.

SPICE BLEND

2 teaspoons dried sage (2 grams)

¾ teaspoon black peppercorns, preferably Tellicherry (3 grams)

1 tablespoon freshly grated nutmeg (3 grams)

1 tablespoon plus 1 teaspoon dried oregano (2 grams)

Finely grind the sage and peppercorns together and immediately mix with the nutmeg and oregano. Use this spice blend instead of the main spice blend in the leg of lamb recipe on page 210.

Mix 8 ounces softened goat cheese, ¼ cup chopped capers, ⅓ cup finely chopped yellow onion, and ⅓ cup chopped roasted and salted almonds in a small bowl.

Follow the leg of lamb recipe, spreading the goat cheese mixture all over the inside of the lamb after rubbing with the spice blend in step 3.

tomato and olive salad with lamb, herbs, and crunchy pita*

Leftover lamb tastes great when chopped and served over a tossed salad with juicy tomatoes, salty olives, crisp red onion, and lots of herbs in a creamy yogurt dressing. Of course, crunchy pita croutons don't hurt, either, and add lots of great texture. If you're starting with cooked lamb

straight from the fridge, warm it up a bit to take the chill off before adding to the salad.

Follow the leg of lamb recipe on page 210.

Coat a small skillet with extra-virgin olive oil (2 to 3 teaspoons) and heat over medium-high heat until hot and shimmering. Add 1 diced pita bread and cook, stirring occasionally, until golden brown and crisp, about 3 minutes. Transfer to a paper-towel-lined plate, sprinkle with kosher salt, and set aside to cool and crisp.

In a large bowl, whisk ⅓ cup plain Greek yogurt and the juice of 1 lemon until smooth. Add ½ cup pitted black kalamata olives, 2 cups halved grape tomatoes, 1 halved and thinly sliced red onion, ½ cup fresh cilantro leaves, ½ cup fresh mint leaves, 2 tablespoons nigella seeds (18 grams), and 1 pound of warmed lamb cut into bite-size pieces. Toss until evenly coated and season to taste with salt. Divide among serving plates and top with the pita.

Serves 4 to 6

lamb panini with muenster, scallions, and pickles

Slices of leftover lamb make for amazing sandwiches. This is one of my favorite combinations, with mild melted Muenster cheese, bright scallions, and pickles.

Follow the leg of lamb recipe on page 210.

Split 4 small (5-inch-square) ciabatta breads in half. Spread 4 of the bread halves with 4 tablespoons Dijon mustard and the remaining 4 halves with 4 tablespoons mayonnaise. Divide 1 pound of lamb slices among the bottom halves and top each with a slice of Muenster cheese; top with ¼ cup thinly sliced scallions (white and green parts) and 16 thin slices of dill pickle. Cover with the bread tops.

Heat a panini press, grill pan, or griddle to medium-high heat. Brush the outsides of the sandwiches with some olive oil and place on the hot surface, working in batches if needed. Close the panini press or balance a heavy cast-iron skillet on top of the sandwiches if you're using a grill pan or griddle. Cook until the bread is crisp and the cheese melted, about 5 minutes with a press and about 3 minutes per side for a pan or griddle.

Serves 4

DESSERT-ING

BAKED GOODS

What do you mean, you're not a baker? If you can mix three things in a bowl, then you can bake. After years of professional training, I can pull sugar into threads and create crazy chocolate sculptures, but that's not really my thing. My desserts come from a savory chef's style of throwing ingredients together to make an easy, delicious dish. The years I spent professionally training in pastry taught me that once you nail a technique, you can use it to create endless varieties of desserts. My goals when I make something sweet are simplicity and enough versatility to switch spices and other ingredients like fruits, nuts, and frostings for a range of flavor variations. I like to call my way of baking "dessert-ing." The recipes here are easy things you can make quickly with stuff you likely already have.

Yes, you do need to measure, preferably by weight. Common baking ingredients such as flour and sugar settle differently into measuring cups, so volume measurements are never as accurate as gram-based ones. But the measuring and the process that follows aren't complicated. I avoid any over-the-top equipment or prep work. The techniques behind baking aren't as forgiving as cooking, which is why I've chosen my favorite tried-and-true formulas here. You just need to read and follow the instructions carefully to end up with foolproof and delicious desserts.

As for the spices, I'm here to show you that cinnamon is not the only one destined for dessert. Sugar takes on a whole range of spices, from sour amchoor to bitter orange peel to savory black mustard seeds and more. Heat from chiles or ginger works especially well in baked goods because it helps offset the sweetness. In most cases, I try to balance everything for nuanced desserts that make everyone happy.

If you're already a dedicated baker looking to expand your repertoire, try one of these blends in your own creations.

MASTER SPICE BLENDS

for sprinkling on homemade cracker dough

1 tablespoon plus 2 teaspoons anise (15 grams), toasted (see page 37)

¾ teaspoon caraway seeds (3 grams), toasted (see page 37)

1 teaspoon yellow mustard seeds (5 grams)

¼ teaspoon black mustard seeds (2 grams)

½ teaspoon poppy seeds (2 grams)

Mix together all the seeds.

for stirring into cookie dough

3 tablespoons plus 2 teaspoons Sichuan peppercorns (15 grams)

2½ teaspoons ground ginger (5 grams)

1½ teaspoons granulated dried orange peel (5 grams)

1½ teaspoons white sesame seeds, preferably unhulled (5 grams)

1 teaspoon pink pepper (2 grams)

Finely grind the Sichuan peppercorns and immediately mix with the ginger, orange peel, sesame, and pink pepper.

for stirring into pound cake batter

24 whole star anise (24 grams)

1 teaspoon coriander seeds (2 grams)

1 teaspoon green peppercorns (2 grams)

1½ teaspoons ground cinnamon, preferably Vietnamese (5 grams)

1½ teaspoons amchoor (dried mango powder; 3 grams)

Finely grind the star anise, coriander, and peppercorns together and immediately mix with the cinnamon and amchoor.

for stirring into fruit that's to be baked

15 whole vanilla beans (15 grams)

2½ teaspoons pink pepper (5 grams)

2½ teaspoons ground ginger (5 grams)

½ teaspoon black peppercorns, preferably Tellicherry (2 grams)

1 tablespoon mace (2 grams)

Grind together the vanilla, pink pepper, ginger, peppercorns, and mace.

OLIVE OIL CAKE

ginger olive oil cake with fennel seeds and black pepper

In this master recipe, the sweet olive oil cake batter benefits from the warming heat of ginger and the piquant heat of black pepper. Both are tempered by the licorice pop of fennel seeds, which are toasted with the peppercorns to draw out an even bolder and more pronounced flavor.

**MAKES 1 LOAF
SERVES 10 TO 12**

MAIN SPICE BLEND

1½ teaspoons fennel seeds (3 grams)

½ teaspoon black peppercorns, preferably Tellicherry (2 grams)

2 teaspoons ground ginger (4 grams)

Toast the fennel and peppercorns in a small skillet over medium heat, shaking the pan occasionally, until fragrant and lightly browned, about 3 minutes. Immediately transfer them to a spice grinder, finely grind them together, and mix with the ginger.

CAKE

Nonstick pan spray, oil, or butter, for the pan

1¾ cups all-purpose flour (240 grams)

1 cup sugar (210 grams)

1½ teaspoons baking powder (8 grams)

1¼ teaspoons baking soda (7 grams)

½ teaspoon kosher salt (3 grams)

¾ cup extra-virgin olive oil (155 grams)

⅔ cup whole milk (150 grams)

2 large eggs (120 grams)

2 tablespoons dark rum (30 grams)

1 orange

MAKE AHEAD

The cake will keep, tightly wrapped, at room temperature for up to 2 weeks or in the freezer for up to 3 months. Thaw before serving.

As much as I love butter, I prefer olive oil in my cake batter. It's a flavorful and interesting fat that's a vehicle for either savory or sweet seasonings. Plus, it keeps this fine-crumbed cake fresh and moist even after sitting out for days. Just be sure to start with a high-quality olive oil that isn't too bitter or aggressively bold. Anyone intimidated by baking will appreciate this no-fail batter that's mixed by hand, and everyone will enjoy the complex flavors that come from such a simple technique. Slices are excellent on their own and taste especially good when toasted and served with fresh butter or honey. I use this technique to make sweet-spiced loafs, savory goat cheese bread, a zucchini loaf, and even a dried fruit Bundt cake (see page 221)—all without having to break out the electric mixer.

1. To make the cake: Preheat the oven to 375°F. Coat an 8 × 4-inch loaf pan with nonstick cooking spray, line the bottom with parchment paper, and grease again. Set the pan in a roasting pan in case any batter spills over (it shouldn't) and to prevent the cake bottom from browning too much.

2. Whisk together the flour, sugar, baking powder, baking soda, salt, and spice blend until well mixed. In another bowl, combine the oil, milk, eggs, and rum. Zest the orange directly into the bowl. Halve the orange, squeeze 2 tablespoons juice (30 grams), and add to the bowl with the liquids. Whisk until smooth.

3. Pour the wet ingredients into the dry. Start whisking slowly from the center of the bowl, gradually drawing in the dry ingredients to prevent them from clumping. Once all the dry ingredients are incorporated, whisk just until smooth. The thick batter should drip off the whisk. Pour into the prepared loaf pan.

4. Bake, rotating the loaf pan 180 degrees once halfway through, until a wooden skewer inserted into the center comes out clean, about 1 hour.

5. Cool in the pan on a wire rack for 10 minutes. Unmold and cool completely on the rack.

*glazed cocoa and orange blossom bundt cake

OLIVE OIL CAKE
FIVE MORE RECIPES

savory goat cheese and herb olive oil loaf

Scented with the classic Italian American pizza pairing of basil and oregano, this savory loaf also gets creamy goat cheese throughout. Toasted slices taste great topped with charcuterie or more cheese.

SPICE BLEND

3 tablespoons dried rosemary (3 grams)

3 tablespoons dried basil (3 grams)

1 tablespoon plus 1 teaspoon dried oregano (2 grams)

Coarsely grind the rosemary and mix immediately with the basil and oregano. Use this spice blend instead of the main spice blend in the olive oil cake recipe on page 218.

Follow the olive oil cake recipe, substituting 1 tablespoon plus 1½ teaspoons honey (30 grams) for the rum in step 2.

In step 3, fold 1 cup crumbled fresh goat cheese (134 grams) into the batter just before pouring it into the pan.

zucchini bread with walnuts and thyme

Sweet enough to be a breakfast treat and savory enough for a cheese board, this fluffy cake combines thyme with the faint anise scent of caraway. Cayenne adds a hint of heat to the lemon-scented batter.

SPICE BLEND

1¼ teaspoons caraway seeds (5 grams)

1 tablespoon plus 1½ teaspoons dried thyme (3 grams)

¼ teaspoon cayenne pepper (½ gram)

Toast the caraway in a small skillet over medium heat, shaking the pan occasionally, until fragrant and lightly browned, about 2 minutes. Immediately transfer to a spice grinder along with the thyme, coarsely grind them together, and mix with the cayenne. Use this spice blend instead of the main spice blend in the olive oil cake recipe on page 218.

Follow the olive oil cake recipe, but prep a 10 × 5-inch loaf pan or eight 4½ × 2½-inch mini loaf pans or line twelve standard muffin cups with paper liners in step 1.

In step 2, substitute 2 tablespoons carrot or orange juice (30 grams) for the rum and substitute a lemon for the orange (zesting the whole fruit and juicing 2 tablespoons).

In step 3, fold 1 cup coarsely grated zucchini (143 grams) and ½ cup chopped toasted walnuts (51 grams) into the batter just before pouring it into the pan.

In step 4, bake until a wooden skewer inserted into the center comes out clean, about 45 minutes for the extra-large loaf pan, about 30 minutes for the mini loaf pans, or about 20 minutes for the muffin cups.

cardamom olive oil bundt cake with dried fruit and mixed nuts

The warming trio of clove, nutmeg, and cardamom scent this festive Bundt cake. Plummy port makes this warming on winter nights.

SPICE BLEND

2½ teaspoons green cardamom pods (5 grams)

1½ teaspoons whole cloves (3 grams)

1 whole nutmeg (5 grams), grated

Finely grind the cardamom and cloves and immediately mix with the nutmeg. Use this spice blend instead of the main spice blend in the olive oil cake recipe on page 218.

Follow the olive oil cake recipe, but use a small greased (10-cup) Bundt pan in step 1.

In step 2, substitute 2 tablespoons port for the rum.

In step 3, fold ¼ cup chopped pecans (30 grams), ¼ cup chopped almonds (42 grams), ¼ cup raisins (42 grams), and ¼ cup diced dried apricots (42 grams) into the batter just before pouring it into the pan.

In step 4, bake until a wooden skewer inserted into the cake comes out clean (or with a crumb or two attached), about 45 minutes.

glazed cocoa and orange blossom bundt cake*

The chocolate and citrus aroma of Urfa pepper is echoed in both the cocoa powder and orange blossom water added to the cake base.

SPICE BLEND

½ cup plus 1 tablespoon unsweetened cocoa powder (53 grams)

1 tablespoon plus 2 teaspoons ground cinnamon, preferably Vietnamese (15 grams)

1 tablespoon plus 1 teaspoon Urfa pepper (8 grams)

Stir together the cocoa, cinnamon, and Urfa. Use this spice blend instead of the main spice blend in the olive oil cake recipe on page 218. Reserve one-third of the mix (¼ cup; 25 grams) for the glaze.

Follow the olive oil cake recipe, but use a small greased (10-cup) Bundt pan in step 1.

In step 2, substitute 1 tablespoon orange blossom water (10 grams) for the rum and increase the orange juice to ¼ cup (57 grams).

In step 4, bake until a wooden skewer comes out clean, about 45 minutes.

Mix the reserved spice blend with 1 cup confectioners' sugar (127 grams). Add 3 to 6 tablespoons milk to make a thick glaze. Pour the glaze over the cooled unmolded cake and set aside until the glaze sets up, about 45 minutes.

seed and grain olive oil loaf

The pop and crunch of seeds and millet make this loaf hearty. It's wonderful for breakfast, especially spread with labne or cream cheese.

SPICE BLEND

2 tablespoons plus 1½ teaspoons poppy seeds (30 grams)

3 tablespoons white sesame seeds, preferably unhulled (30 grams)

2 tablespoons plus ¼ teaspoon nigella seeds (20 grams)

1 tablespoon plus 1½ teaspoons millet (20 grams)

¼ cup raw shelled sunflower seeds (35 grams)

Stir together all the seeds and grains. Use this spice blend instead of the main spice blend in the olive oil cake recipe on page 218.

Follow the olive oil cake recipe, but don't add the spice blend to the dry ingredients in step 2. Also in step 2, omit the orange juice and instead add 2 tablespoons pomegranate juice (28 grams) to the wet ingredients.

In step 3, stir the spice blend into the batter just before pouring it into the pan.

BROWN SUGAR BANANA BREAD

cardamom and cinnamon banana bread with poppy seeds

Poppy seeds dot this loaf, which combines the classic duo of cinnamon and cardamom. The floral heat of Muntok white pepper brings a subtle complexity to each bite.

MAKES ONE 9 × 5-INCH LOAF

MAIN SPICE BLEND

1 teaspoon green cardamom pods (2 grams)

¼ teaspoon Muntok white peppercorns (1 gram)

1¼ teaspoons poppy seeds (5 grams)

¾ teaspoon ground cinnamon, preferably Vietnamese (2 grams)

Finely grind the cardamom and peppercorns together and immediately mix with the whole poppy seeds and cinnamon.

BANANA BREAD

½ cup (8 tablespoons) salted butter (114 grams), softened, plus more for the pan

1¼ cups all-purpose flour (168 grams)

1½ teaspoons baking soda (7 grams)

1 cup packed light brown sugar (200 grams)

1 cup mashed overripe bananas (from 2 large or 3 medium bananas; 235 grams)

2 large eggs (100 grams), at room temperature

⅓ cup labne or plain whole milk Greek yogurt (80 grams)

½ teaspoon pure vanilla extract (3 grams)

MAKE AHEAD

The banana bread will keep, tightly wrapped with plastic wrap, at room temperature for up to 2 weeks or in the freezer in an airtight freezer bag for up to 3 months. Thaw before serving (I like to toast the slices too).

When I had to create a banana bread recipe for a baking magazine, I realized that banana bread is the perfect vehicle for the heat of pepper or chile. Both add excitement to the comforting loaf, which is flavorful and hearty enough to round out the heat of pepper and chile. I always seem to have a lot of overripe bananas around, so I often find myself doubling the recipe and serving one loaf right away and freezing the other loaf for another day. If you prefer, you can scoop the batter into a well-greased or paper-lined standard muffin tin to make a dozen muffins; bake until a toothpick inserted into the center of one comes out clean, about 25 minutes. Or you can make three dozen mini muffins, which only take about 18 minutes to bake.

1. To make the bread: Preheat the oven to 350°F. Butter a 9 × 5-inch loaf pan. Line the bottom with parchment paper and butter the parchment.

2. Whisk the flour, baking soda, and spice mix in a small bowl. Beat ½ cup butter (114 grams) and the brown sugar in a stand mixer fitted with the paddle attachment on low speed just until well combined and then raise the speed to medium-high and beat until pale and fluffy. Scrape down the bowl and add the bananas, eggs, labne, and vanilla. Beat on medium-low speed until thoroughly mixed. It's okay if the mixture looks broken. Scrape the bottom and sides of the bowl.

3. With the machine running on low speed, gradually add the flour mixture. Beat just until the flour is incorporated, scraping the bowl as needed. Pour the batter into the prepared pan and bake until a wooden skewer inserted into the center comes out clean, 45 to 50 minutes.

4. Cool the loaf in the pan on a wire rack for 15 minutes and then turn it out, discard the parchment, and cool completely on the rack.

*chocolate chip–banana mini muffins

BROWN SUGAR BANANA BREAD
FIVE MORE RECIPES

lavender and hibiscus banana bread with anise

Both lavender and hibiscus bring subtle floral notes to this loaf that is also speckled with anise and chewy sweet raisins. You can swap the raisins for dried currants if you'd like.

SPICE BLEND

1 tablespoon dried lavender (1 gram)

1½ teaspoons dried hibiscus blossoms (2 grams)

¾ teaspoon anise (2 grams)

Finely grind the lavender and hibiscus together and immediately mix with the whole anise. Use this spice blend instead of the main spice blend in the banana bread recipe on page 222.

Follow the banana bread recipe, folding ½ cup raisins (50 grams), chopped if large, into the batter after folding in the flour mixture in step 3.

pecan banana bread with sichuan peppercorns and nigella seeds

Pecans have a natural sweetness that plays nicely with the tingling sensation of Sichuan peppercorns, the earthy aroma of nutmeg, and the nutty crunch of nigella seeds.

SPICE BLEND

1½ teaspoons Sichuan peppercorns (2 grams)

2 teaspoons freshly grated nutmeg (2 grams)

1 tablespoon plus ¼ teaspoon nigella seeds (10 grams)

Finely grind the peppercorns and immediately mix with the nutmeg and whole nigella seeds. Use this spice blend instead of the main spice blend in the banana bread recipe on page 222.

Follow the banana bread recipe, folding ½ cup chopped pecans (80 grams) into the batter after folding in the flour mixture in step 3.

chocolate chip–banana mini muffins*

Banana and chocolate are a natural pairing, made more interesting here with the addition of soothing chamomile and funky, smoky black cardamom. You can use chopped chocolate instead of chips if you prefer. Dried chamomile flowers are sold loose, as well as in chamomile tea bags. You can tear open the bags and use the flowers here.

SPICE BLEND

1 tablespoon dried chamomile flowers (3 grams)

1 teaspoon (2 whole) black cardamom pods (2 grams)

1 teaspoon pink pepper (2 grams)

¼ teaspoon cayenne pepper (½ gram)

Finely grind the chamomile, cardamom, and pepper together and immediately mix with the cayenne. Use this spice blend instead of the main spice blend in the banana bread recipe on page 222.

Follow the banana bread recipe, substituting 3 dozen greased or lined mini muffin cups for the loaf pan in step 1.

In step 3, fold ½ cup bittersweet chocolate chips (88 grams) into the batter after folding in the flour mixture. Bake until a toothpick inserted in the center of a muffin comes out clean, about 18 minutes.

ancho chile banana bread with banana chips

The sugary crunch of banana chips dotting this loaf is tempered by the peppery notes of cubeb, the tangy warmth of amchoor, and the heat of ancho.

SPICE BLEND

1 teaspoon cubeb (2 grams)

2½ teaspoons amchoor (dried mango powder; 5 grams)

1 teaspoon ground ancho chile (2 grams)

Finely grind the cubeb and immediately mix with the amchoor and ancho. Use this spice blend instead of the main spice blend in the banana bread recipe on page 222.

Follow the banana bread recipe, folding ¾ cup chopped banana chips (50 grams) into the batter after folding in the flour in step 3.

rosemary and star anise banana bread with dried apricots

The pine scent of rosemary is echoed here in green peppercorns and complemented by sweet-tart dried apricots. The resulting loaf tastes especially good when spread with cream cheese or softened goat cheese.

SPICE BLEND

2 tablespoons dried rosemary (2 grams)

2 whole star anise (2 grams)

1½ teaspoons green peppercorns (3 grams)

Finely grind together the rosemary, star anise, and peppercorns. Use this spice blend instead of the main spice blend in the banana bread recipe on page 222.

Follow the banana bread recipe, folding ½ cup diced dried apricots (50 grams) into the batter after folding in the flour mixture in step 3.

FRUIT CRISP

mixed berry crisp with sumac-anise almond topping

I add an extra dose of rum into the fruit base. When it combines with warming anise, cinnamon, and Sichuan peppercorns, it creates a kind of magic. Tangy sumac highlights the fruity tartness of berries and dried apricots in the jammy filling.

**MAKES ONE 9-INCH CRISP
SERVES 4 TO 8**

MAIN SPICE BLEND

1 teaspoon anise (3 grams)

2 teaspoons Sichuan peppercorns (3 grams)

1 teaspoon ground cinnamon, preferably Vietnamese (3 grams)

1 teaspoon sumac (3 grams)

Finely grind the anise and peppercorns together and immediately mix with the cinnamon and sumac.

TOPPING

4 tablespoons salted butter (56 grams), diced

½ cup confectioners' sugar (64 grams)

¼ cup packed light brown sugar (50 grams)

¼ cup slivered almonds (29 grams)

½ cup all-purpose flour (67 grams)

FRUIT

3 tablespoons dark rum

2 tablespoons packed light brown sugar (26 grams)

8 ounces blackberries (1¾ cups), halved if large

8 ounces blueberries (1¾ cups)

8 ounces strawberries, hulled and cut into ½-inch pieces (1¾ cups)

4 ounces dried apricots (1 cup), halved

1 tablespoon cornstarch

MAKE AHEAD

The crisp topping can be stored in an airtight container in a cool, dry place for up to 1 week. The fruit can be refrigerated for up to 3 days. Bring back to a simmer before topping and serving, if you'd like.

Sherry Yard, a brilliant pastry chef and dear friend, asked me to create a blend to spice up her signature fruit crisp. In the process of trying different spices with her recipe, I found that her fruit crisp is simply the best because the topping is extra crisp while the seasonal fruit filling is juicy without being mushy. She does this by baking the topping separately from the fruit and by simmering the fruit on the stovetop to control how tender it becomes before marrying the two just before serving. Both components can be prepared far ahead of time, making this crisp ideal for entertaining. And both elements can take a variety of different spices, even unexpected ones like tongue-tingling Sichuan peppercorns. Start by trying out the combinations on the pages that follow and then experiment with other seasonal fruit.

1. To make the topping: Preheat the oven to 375°F. Line a half sheet pan with parchment paper.

2. Combine the butter, confectioners' sugar, and brown sugar in a large bowl. Squeeze and mix with your fingers until well blended and only a few streaks of confectioners' sugar remain. Add the almonds and half the spice blend. Mix and squeeze with your hands until evenly incorporated. Add the flour and keep squeezing and pinching until the flour is incorporated and the mixture forms almond-size chunks with coarse crumbs.

3. Spread the mixture evenly in the prepared pan, scraping every last bit from your hands. Bake, stirring occasionally, until golden brown and crisp, 22 to 25 minutes. Cool completely on a wire rack.

4. While the topping bakes, prepare the fruit: Place the rum and brown sugar in a deep 9-inch skillet set over medium heat. Cook, stirring occasionally, until the sugar dissolves, about 1 minute.

5. Add the blackberries, blueberries, strawberries, apricots, and remaining spice blend. Cook, stirring gently once or twice, until the fruit is soft, about 3 minutes.

6. Stir the cornstarch with 2 tablespoons cold water in a small bowl. Drizzle over the fruit while stirring. Cook, stirring occasionally, until the mixture is jammy, 6 to 8 minutes. Remove from the heat.

7. You can keep the fruit in the pan if you'd like to serve from it, or transfer to a 9-inch baking dish or individual bowls. Evenly scatter the crisp mixture on top right before serving the crisp hot.

*dutch apple pie

FRUIT CRISP
FIVE MORE RECIPES

dutch apple pie*

If you've ever been too intimidated to make a pie from scratch, start with this one. Crisp topping also acts as the pie dough, which is simply pressed into the pie plate—so easy. The rest of the topping is scattered over the pie before serving.

Follow the crisp recipe on page 226, using the main spice blend and substituting a generously buttered 9-inch pie dish for the parchment-lined half sheet pan in step 1.

In step 3, use your fingers to press three-quarters of the crisp mixture into the bottom and up the sides of the pie dish to the rim. Reserve the remaining quarter of the crisp mixture in a small bowl and cover. Refrigerate both until ready to use.

In steps 4 through 7, substitute the following for the fruit filling:

Combine 2 tablespoons honey (43 grams) and the remaining main spice blend (what you didn't use in the topping) in a deep 9-inch skillet. Bring to a simmer over medium heat, stirring, and add 4 large Honeycrisp or Fuji apples, peeled and cut into 1-inch wedges. Stir until the apples are evenly coated with the honey mixture. Add 1 tablespoon salted butter (15 grams) and stir until melted. Cook, stirring occasionally, until the apples are golden brown, about 5 minutes. Add ⅓ cup Calvados (75 grams), raise the heat to high, and boil, stirring, until all the liquid has evaporated, about 2 minutes (or flambé the Calvados instead: just tilt the skillet toward the flame so that the alcohol catches fire and let it burn until the flames subside). Cool completely.

Preheat the oven to 375°F.

Scatter ¼ cup raisins (42 grams) over the chilled crust. Arrange the apples over the raisins in an even layer and top with another ¼ cup raisins (42 grams). Scatter the reserved crisp mixture over the apple mixture.

Bake until the crust and topping are golden brown and the apples are tender, about 35 minutes. Cool completely and serve.

Makes one 9-inch pie

cardamom and ginger peach crisp

Ginger's heat accentuates peach's sweetness, especially when combined with heady cardamom and cloves. You can make this with nectarines as well. I like the fruit's skin in the filling, but peel it off if you prefer.

SPICE BLEND

1½ teaspoons green cardamom pods (3 grams)

½ teaspoon whole cloves (1 gram)

1 teaspoon ground ginger (2 grams)

½ teaspoon Aleppo pepper (1 gram)

1 teaspoon freshly grated mace or nutmeg (1 gram)

Finely grind the cardamom and cloves together and immediately mix with the ginger, Aleppo, and mace. Use this spice blend instead of the main spice blend in the fruit crisp recipe on page 226.

Follow the fruit crisp recipe, substituting 1½ pounds diced peaches (5¼ cups; 696 grams) for the berries in step 5.

berry jam bars

Here the master berry filling is baked in a crust made from the pressed crisp mixture. After chilling, the filling turns into a luscious jam thick enough to slice. The generous proportion of fruit to crust makes these taste extra special.

Follow the crisp recipe on page 226, substituting a 9-inch-square cake pan for the half sheet pan, lining the bottom and sides with parchment paper in step 1.

In step 2, substitute ¼ cup sliced almonds (29 grams) for the slivered almonds.

In step 3, spread the crisp mixture evenly over the bottom of the pan, using your fingers to press it firmly into an even layer. Bake until the top is dry to the touch, about 10 minutes.

Meanwhile, prepare the fruit as instructed in steps 4 through 6. Spread the hot fruit filling evenly over the hot crust. Return to the oven and bake until the top is bubbling and the fruit is very thick, about 15 minutes.

Cool completely on a wire rack and then refrigerate until cold, at least 2 hours. Cut into bars and serve.

berry yogurt parfait with almond crispies

For a refreshing and light dessert, simply layer the crisp topping with creamy, tangy yogurt and fresh berries. You can swap in other fruit according to the season. For a more indulgent dessert, you can swap the yogurt for ice cream, whipped cream, custard, or crème fraîche.

Follow the fruit crisp recipe on page 226 through step 3, using the main spice blend and omitting the rum. Toss the brown sugar with the berries and the remaining spice blend until evenly coated.

Omit steps 5 through 7. Instead, divide the berries among 8 cups and spoon ½ cup plain Greek yogurt (117 grams) into each one. Top evenly with the crisp mixture and serve.

ice cream sundaes with pineapple topping and spiced almond crunch

Classic pineapple topping for ice cream gets a hit of tangy amchoor, warming nutmeg, and the surprising heat of yellow mustard and peppery cubeb.

SPICE BLEND

1 teaspoon yellow mustard seeds (5 grams)

½ teaspoon cubeb (1 gram)

2 teaspoons freshly grated nutmeg (2 grams)

1½ teaspoons amchoor (dried mango powder; 3 grams)

Finely grind the mustard seeds and cubeb together and immediately mix with the nutmeg and amchoor. Use this spice blend instead of the main spice blend in the fruit crisp recipe on page 226.

Follow the fruit crisp recipe, substituting 1 pound diced fresh pineapple (4 cups; 464 grams) for the berries and ½ cup unsweetened shredded coconut (50 grams) for the apricots in step 5.

At the end of step 6, cool the mixture completely then fold in 8 ounces diced fresh mango (2 cups; 242 grams).

Omit step 7. Instead, scoop ice cream, such as vanilla or coconut, into 8 sundae dishes. Divide the fruit topping and then the crisp among the dishes. Top with whipped cream, if you'd like.

Makes 8 sundaes

SHORTBREAD

poppy seed shortbread with ginger and nutmeg

The combination of ginger, amchoor, and nutmeg offer a hint of gingerbread's warmth, but the poppy seeds keep the cookies a little nutty.

MAKES ABOUT 6½ DOZEN

MAIN SPICE BLEND

1¾ teaspoons poppy seeds (7 grams)

1 teaspoon ground ginger (2 grams)

½ teaspoon amchoor (dried mango powder; 1 gram)

1 teaspoon freshly grated mace or nutmeg (1 gram)

Mix together the poppy seeds, ginger, amchoor, and nutmeg.

COOKIES

1¾ cups all-purpose flour (235 grams)

½ teaspoon baking powder (2 grams)

¼ teaspoon kosher salt (2 grams)

½ cup (8 tablespoons) salted butter (114 grams), preferably European (85% fat), cold and diced

¾ cup sugar (144 grams)

½ teaspoon pure vanilla extract (3 grams)

3 tablespoons extra-virgin olive oil (25 grams)

1 large egg (51 grams)

MAKE AHEAD

The cookies will keep in a tin at room temperature for up to 2 weeks or in an airtight container in the freezer for up to 1 month.

I make cookies so I have cookies to eat—and not just any cookie, but a French sablé, my favorite buttery shortbread that I enhance with olive oil and spices. I was taught to make sablé Breton in Cancale, France, by chef Olivier Roellinger; it became my weekly task, one I loved. Decades later, I returned to the sablé to sell at La Boîte. For years, I tinkered with formulas to hit the right balance of butter, sugar, and spice (we still change our selections each season), so they snap at first, then crumble, and finally melt in your mouth. When sandwiched, they stay crunchy with drier fillings and meld into tenderness with others. To achieve that magical texture, there's a high proportion of fat and sugar to flour. That can make the dough a little sticky and soft, so just keep popping it back in the fridge or freezer if it's difficult to work with. The dough's still easy to roll and bake, and the cookies are especially satisfying to eat when they come out of your own oven.

1. To make the cookies: Whisk the flour, baking powder, salt, and spice blend together in a medium bowl.

2. Cream the butter and sugar together in a large bowl with an electric mixer on medium-low speed until well blended but not fluffy. With the machine running, add the vanilla first and then the olive oil, beating until smooth and scraping the bowl occasionally. Add the egg and beat just until incorporated. Reduce the speed to low and gradually add the flour mixture. Mix just until incorporated.

3. Turn the dough out onto a very large sheet of parchment paper. Pat into a rectangle and cover with another very large sheet of parchment. Roll the dough into a 12 × 7-inch rectangle that's a scant ¼ inch thick, lifting and replacing the top sheet as needed to smooth out any wrinkles in the paper. Use a bench scraper or spatula to press in all four edges to keep them even and straight, and roll lightly again to achieve an even thickness. Refrigerate until firm, about 1 hour. If you're in a rush, you can freeze the dough until stiff, about 15 minutes.

4. Remove the top sheet of parchment. Using a pizza wheel or sharp knife, cut the dough into 1-inch squares. Chill again if the dough has softened. Transfer the squares to two parchment-paper-lined cookie sheets, spacing them 1 inch apart. Chill again while the oven heats. You want them to be firm if they have softened.

5. Preheat the oven to 375°F.

6. Bake one sheet at a time until the shortbread is golden brown, 12 to 15 minutes. Cool completely on the sheets on wire racks.

BROWNIES

cardamom and pink pepper brownies

Pink pepper brings a floral piquancy that cuts through the richness of chocolate and complements the aroma of cardamom. Urfa pepper heightens the chocolate flavor with its natural cocoa notes.

MAKES ONE 9 X 13-INCH PAN (ABOUT 2 DOZEN)

MAIN SPICE BLEND

1 teaspoon green cardamom pods (2 grams)

1½ teaspoons pink pepper (3 grams)

1 teaspoon Urfa pepper (2 grams)

¾ teaspoon ground cinnamon, preferably Vietnamese (2 grams)

Finely grind the cardamom and pink pepper together and immediately mix with the Urfa and ground cinnamon.

BROWNIES

1 cup salted butter (226 grams), cut into tablespoons

1 cup semisweet chocolate chips (173 grams)

1¾ cups all-purpose flour (242 grams)

⅔ cup natural unsweetened cocoa powder (64 grams)

½ teaspoon kosher salt (5 grams)

6 large eggs (360 grams)

2½ cups sugar (500 grams)

MAKE AHEAD

The brownies will keep in an airtight container at room temperature for up to 1 week or in the freezer for up to 3 months.

Chocolate is one of my favorite vehicles for spices. Its sweetness and fat hold flavors nicely, especially when baked into brownies rich with butter. The shortcut to success here is melting the butter and chocolate in the microwave. It's a trick I learned from a pastry chef in France who swore by it because, with the traditional bain-marie method of melting chocolate in a heatproof bowl over simmering water, there's a risk of water splashing into the mix and seizing the chocolate. Besides, brownies don't require perfectly tempered chocolate to come out delicious, so the microwave works just fine. If you don't have one, simply place the butter and chocolate together in a heavy saucepan over very low heat and stir just until melted. The rest of the batter is straightforward and foolproof and can turn into mini cakes or even ice cream treats (see page 237). Just don't overbake it, and you'll be guaranteed fudgy brownies.

1. To make the brownies: Preheat the oven to 375°F. Line the bottom and all four sides of a 9 × 13-inch baking pan with parchment paper. If the paper won't stay down, you can wet the pan a little before pressing in the paper.

2. Combine the butter and chocolate chips in a large microwave-safe bowl. Microwave for 1 minute and stir until smooth. If the chocolate and butter don't melt completely, microwave for another 15 seconds and stir. Repeat, heating in 15-second intervals, until smooth. Let stand to cool slightly.

3. Sift the flour, cocoa powder, and salt into a medium bowl and whisk in the spice blend. Whisk the eggs in a large bowl until foamy. While whisking the eggs, add the sugar in a steady stream and whisk until the sugar dissolves. Add the butter-chocolate mixture and stir rapidly with a silicone spatula until fully incorporated. Add the dry ingredients and fold gently with the spatula until no traces of flour remain.

4. Scrape the batter into the prepared pan, spread it in an even layer, and bake until a toothpick inserted 1 inch from the edge comes out clean, 25 to 30 minutes. Cool completely in the pan on a wire rack.

5. To serve, lift the brownies out of the pan using the parchment paper and cut into 2-inch squares.

*ice cream brownie bites

BROWNIES
FIVE MORE RECIPES

bittersweet chocolate frosted brownies

To add an extra layer of spiced richness to your brownies, swirl this easy two-ingredient frosting all over the top. It's as smooth and luscious as a chocolate truffle.

Follow the brownie recipe on page 234 through step 4.

Meanwhile, make another half batch of the main spice blend. Place it in a large microwave-safe bowl with 1½ cups bittersweet chocolate chips (270 grams) and 4 tablespoons salted butter (57 grams). Microwave for 30 seconds and stir. Repeat, microwaving in 30-second intervals, until the mixture is melted. Immediately pour it over the cooled brownies and spread evenly. Let stand until set. The brownies will keep in an airtight container in the refrigerator for up to 1 week or in the freezer for up to 3 months.

mocha black pepper brownies with pecans and walnuts

Nut lovers will appreciate these chunky brownies that get extra depth from freshly ground coffee beans and black pepper. Dried apricots add a surprising tang that complements the anise and allspice.

SPICE BLEND

¾ teaspoon anise (2 grams)

½ teaspoon allspice berries (2 grams)

2 teaspoons whole coffee beans (4 grams)

¼ teaspoon black peppercorns, preferably Tellicherry (1 gram)

Finely grind the anise, allspice, coffee, and peppercorns together. Use this spice blend instead of the main spice blend in the brownie recipe on page 234.

Follow the brownie recipe, folding ¼ cup diced dry apricots (46 grams), ½ cup chopped walnuts (59 grams), and ½ cup chopped pecans (59 grams) into the batter at the end of step 3.

minted brownies with candied ginger

Chewy bits of candied ginger are a welcome surprise in these brownies that also have a hint of mint and tangy sumac.

SPICE BLEND

1 teaspoon dried mint (1 gram)

½ teaspoon whole cloves (1 gram)

¾ teaspoon sumac (2 grams)

1½ teaspoons ground ginger (3 grams)

Finely grind the mint, cloves, and sumac together and immediately mix with the ginger. Use this spice blend instead of the main spice blend in the brownie recipe on page 234.

Follow the brownie recipe, folding ⅓ cup diced candied ginger (57 grams) into the batter at the end of step 3.

glazed mini coconut brownies

Shredded coconut lightens the texture of these two-bite brownies, while coconut extract in the glaze highlights their nutty flavor. These can be served like petits fours at any party.

Follow the brownie recipe on page 234, substituting 7 dozen mini muffin cups for the cake pan in step 1. Line the cups with paper liners or generously grease them.

At the end of step 3, stir ½ cup unsweetened finely shredded coconut (50 grams) into the batter.

In step 4, divide the batter evenly among the prepared mini muffin cups, filling each two-thirds full.

In step 4, bake until a toothpick inserted into the center of a brownie comes out with a few crumbs attached, 10 to 12 minutes.

In step 5, unmold the brownie bites after cooling completely. Stir together 1 cup confectioners' sugar (127 grams), ½ teaspoon coconut extract, and 1 tablespoon water in a small bowl to form a thick glaze. If the mixture is too stiff to drizzle, stir in more water 1 teaspoon at a time to your desired consistency. Pour the glaze over the brownie bites and sprinkle with more unsweetened shredded coconut.

ice cream brownie bites*

When frozen, these brownies become an extra-chewy, extra-delicious base for ice cream. I prefer vanilla ice cream, but you can use any flavor you like. These are easiest to make in a silicone mini muffin mold: bake the batter in the mold, fill with ice cream, and pop out when frozen. If you're using regular mini muffin tins, run a thin-bladed offset spatula around the edges of each to release.

Follow the brownie recipe on page 234, substituting 4 dozen mini muffin cups, preferably silicone, for the cake pan in step 1. If you're not using silicone, generously grease the mini muffin cups. If you don't have enough mini muffin cups, you can halve the quantities below (which is a half batch of the original recipe) or bake them in batches.

Make the batter with ½ cup salted butter (114 grams), ½ cup semisweet chocolate chips (87 grams), ¾ cup all-purpose flour (104 grams), ⅓ cup unsweetened cocoa powder (32 grams), ¼ teaspoon kosher salt (3 grams), 3 large eggs (180 grams), and 1¼ cups sugar (250 grams). Use only half the main spice blend in the batter.

In step 4, fill the muffin cups one-third of the way with batter and bake until a toothpick inserted into the center of a brownie comes out clean, about 15 minutes. The baked brownie bites should come only halfway up the sides of the muffin cups.

In step 5, cool the brownies completely in the silicone molds or tins. Fill each cup to the rim with slightly softened vanilla ice cream, smoothing the tops. (You'll need about 1 pint of ice cream.) Freeze until firm. If you'd like, you can sprinkle the remaining spice blend on top before serving. Otherwise, reserve the leftover spice blend for another use. The ice cream brownie bites can be frozen in an airtight container for up to 2 weeks.

CRÈME FRAÎCHE CLAFOUTIS

apple and prune crème fraîche clafoutis with nutmeg and allspice

I resisted the impulse to pair apples with cinnamon here, choosing instead to explore all the other options that work with this fall fruit. The heat of black pepper and ginger bring out the apples' sweetness, as do warming allspice and cardamom. Nutmeg delivers all the comfort of apple pie.

MAKES ONE 12-INCH SKILLET
SERVES 6 TO 8

MAIN SPICE BLEND

¼ teaspoon black peppercorns, preferably Tellicherry (1 gram)

¼ teaspoon allspice berries (1 gram)

¾ teaspoon green cardamom pods (1½ grams)

¼ teaspoon ground ginger (½ gram)

½ teaspoon freshly grated nutmeg (½ gram)

Finely grind the peppercorns, allspice, and cardamom together and immediately mix with the ginger and nutmeg.

CLAFOUTIS

2 tablespoons salted butter (29 grams), plus more for the pan

2 medium sweet-tart apples (340 grams), such as Honeycrisp or Fuji, peeled, cored, and cut into ¾-inch-thick slices

1 tablespoon packed brown sugar (13 grams)

1 cup pitted prunes (184 grams)

½ cup rum (113 grams)

1 cup whole milk (224 grams)

1 cup crème fraîche or sour cream (284 grams)

½ teaspoon pure vanilla extract (3 grams)

1¼ cups granulated sugar (125 grams), plus more for the pan

½ cup all-purpose flour (71 grams)

3 large eggs (180 grams), at room temperature

Confectioners' sugar, for dusting

Clafoutis is a French dessert that falls somewhere between soufflé and flan, with a light texture that's sturdy enough to slice. I learned the classic version—with fruit at the base and caramelized sugar around the edges of the pan—while cooking in France. To make my custard taste more complex, I use tangy crème fraîche instead of cream and add dried fruit for its natural sweetness. Throughout the year, I like to switch the fruit and spices with the seasons and play around with the baking vessels (see page 241). You can too.

1. To make the clafoutis: Preheat the oven to 350°F.

2. Melt the butter in a 12-inch skillet over medium-high heat. Swirl to coat the bottom of the pan and then add the apples and brown sugar. Stir until the apples are evenly coated. Add one-third of the spice blend, stir to evenly coat the apples, and reduce the heat to medium. Cook, turning the apples occasionally, until softened a bit and evenly browned, about 5 minutes.

3. Add the prunes and stir well. Add the rum and simmer, stirring occasionally, until all the liquid evaporates and glazes the fruit, about 3 minutes. Remove from the heat and cool to room temperature while making the custard.

4. Whisk the milk, crème fraîche, vanilla, and the remaining spice blend in a medium bowl until smooth. Whisk the granulated sugar and flour together in a large bowl; add the eggs and whisk until well blended. Make sure there are no lumps of flour remaining. While whisking, add the milk mixture in a slow, steady stream.

5. Generously butter the sides and bottom of a 9-inch-round, 2-inch-deep cake pan. Coat with granulated sugar, tapping out the excess. Arrange the apples over the bottom of the pan in concentric circles, spacing the pieces ½ inch apart. Stick the prunes between the apple slices. Put the cake pan on a half sheet pan and carefully pour the custard mixture over the fruit.

6. Bake until just set, 35 to 40 minutes. Dust with confectioners' sugar. Cool slightly and serve warm or room temperature.

*mixed berry mini clafoutis

CRÈME FRAÎCHE CLAFOUTIS

FOUR MORE RECIPES

cherry and pistachio clafoutis with chamomile

Cherries are the most iconic fruit for clafoutis. Here, tangy sumac highlights their tart side, Sichuan peppercorns give them a little zing, and mellow, floral chamomile balances those bold flavors. A cherry pitter comes in handy here, but a chopstick or metal straw can poke out the pits too.

SPICE BLEND

¾ teaspoon Sichuan peppercorns (1 gram)

1 teaspoon sumac (3 grams)

2 teaspoons dried chamomile flowers (2 grams)

¾ teaspoon ground cinnamon, preferably
   Vietnamese (2 grams)

Finely grind the peppercorns, sumac, and chamomile together and immediately mix with the cinnamon. Use this spice blend instead of the main spice blend in the clafoutis recipe on page 238.

Follow the clafoutis recipe, substituting 1 pound cherries (464 grams), pitted, for the apples in step 2. Cook until softened, 3 to 4 minutes.

In step 3, add ¾ cup shelled roasted unsalted pistachios (96 grams) along with the prunes.

apple custard pie

Baking claufoutis in a crust makes for an elegant apple pie. You can, of course, start with homemade pie dough, but you'll need to parbake it before filling and then baking it again. If you can find a frozen deep-dish crust, you can make just one pie and bake it until set, about 1 hour 15 minutes.

Follow the clafoutis recipe on page 238 through step 4, using the main spice blend.

In step 5, substitute two 9-inch frozen prepared pie shells for the buttered and sugared 9-inch pan. Divide the apples and prunes between the pie shells and then pour half the custard into each.

In step 6, bake the clafoutis in the lower third of the oven until the crust is golden brown and the filling is set and browned, 50 to 55 minutes. Cool completely before cutting into wedges to serve.

pear and chocolate clafoutis with rose-scented custard

Pear and chocolate work well together, especially when bound with a rose-scented custard. The trio tastes restaurant-worthy, especially with the intriguing heat from Urfa pepper and clove.

SPICE BLEND

2 tablespoons dried rose petals (1 gram)

½ teaspoon whole cloves (1 gram)

1 teaspoon Urfa pepper (2 grams)

¾ teaspoon sumac (2 grams)

Finely grind the rose and cloves together and immediately mix with the Urfa and sumac. Use this spice blend instead of the main spice blend in the clafoutis recipe on page 238.

Follow the clafoutis recipe, substituting 2 ripe but firm Bosc pears (340 grams), peeled, cored, and each cut into 8 wedges, for the apples in step 2, and cooking them for only 3 minutes.

In step 4, add 1 tablespoon plus 1 teaspoon unsweetened cocoa powder (10 grams) to the flour-sugar mixture.

At the end of step 5, scatter ½ cup bittersweet chocolate chips (90 grams) over the custard before baking.

mixed berry mini clafoutis*

Individual clafoutis feel like a special treat for a dinner party. This version is especially easy, since the berries don't even need to be cooked before baking.

Follow the clafoutis recipe on page 238 through step 1, using the main spice blend.

Omit steps 2 and 3 and their accompanying ingredients.

In step 4, add all the spice blend to the custard.

In step 5, substitute eight (8-ounce) ramekins for the 9-inch cake pan. After buttering and sugaring the ramekins, place them on a half sheet pan. Divide 8 ounces blackberries (242 grams), 8 ounces blueberries (232 grams), and 8 ounces raspberries (232 grams) among the ramekins and pour the custard over the berries, filling each two-thirds full.

In step 6, bake on the half sheet pan until just set and golden brown on top, 30 to 35 minutes. Dust with confectioners' sugar and serve.

Condiments and More Master Spice Blends

At La Boîte, I sell spice blends without describing how to use them because I want people to experiment with them however they like. Despite my attempt to give cooks freedom, customers always ask for guidance, so I'm happy to offer that here. These are spice blends you can make anytime and store in jars or airtight containers. To determine how much to use, start with a pinch, taste, and add more if you want. Sprinkle on bits at a time until you're happy with the taste. If you're trying the spices on meat or other ingredients that shouldn't be eaten raw, you can sprinkle a bit on a sliver and quickly fry it to see how much you want on the rest of it.

Keep in mind that the matches I make between categories and blends are just my suggestions—you can apply the blends to whichever dishes you like. The same is true for condiments. I like keeping them in the fridge to incorporate into spiced mustard or mayonnaise by the spoonful. I encourage you to think outside the box and try them on whatever you're cooking!

MASTER BLENDS FOR FOUNDATIONS

FOR BLANCHING WATER FOR VEGETABLES

2 tablespoons plus 1½ teaspoons fennel seeds (15 grams)

1 tablespoon dried garlic slices (5 grams)

1 tablespoon plus ¾ teaspoon dried onion slices (5 grams)

1 tablespoon plus 1½ teaspoons dried thyme (3 grams)

Finely grind together the fennel, garlic, onion, and thyme.

FOR STIRRING INTO SALT

¾ cup plus 3 tablespoons dried rosemary (15 grams)

1¼ teaspoons black peppercorns, preferably Tellicherry (5 grams)

1 teaspoon yellow mustard seeds (5 grams)

¾ teaspoon sumac (2 grams)

Finely grind the rosemary, peppercorns, and mustard seeds together and immediately mix with the whole sumac.

FOR MIXING WITH SOFTENED BUTTER FOR COMPOUND BUTTER

1½ teaspoons saffron (½ gram)

2½ teaspoons fennel seeds (5 grams)

1 teaspoon ajowan (1 gram)

1 teaspoon sweet paprika (2 grams)

½ teaspoon ground ginger (1 gram)

Finely grind the saffron, fennel, and ajowan together and immediately mix with the paprika and ginger.

FOR STIRRING INTO OLIVE OIL FOR DRIZZLING

1½ teaspoons fennel seeds (3 grams)

1 teaspoon cumin seeds (3 grams)

2 tablespoons dried rosemary (2 grams)

1 tablespoon plus 2 teaspoons sumac (15 grams)

½ teaspoon Aleppo pepper (1 gram)

Finely grind the fennel, cumin, and rosemary together and immediately mix with the whole sumac and Aleppo.

FOR STIRRING INTO OR TOASTING ON BREAD CRUMBS

3 tablespoons dried garlic slices (15 grams)

1 tablespoon plus 2 teaspoons dried savory (5 grams)

2 tablespoons plus 1½ teaspoons dried thyme (5 grams)

1½ teaspoons green peppercorns (3 grams)

Finely grind together the garlic, savory, thyme, and peppercorns.

FOR MIXING INTO SUGAR

1½ teaspoons green cardamom pods (3 grams)

¼ teaspoon anise (1 gram)

1 teaspoon freshly grated mace (1 gram)

¼ teaspoon ground cinnamon, preferably Vietnamese (1 gram)

Finely grind together the cardamom and anise and immediately mix with the mace and cinnamon.

MASTER BLENDS FOR SAUCES

FOR SIMMERING WITH TOMATO SAUCE

1 tablespoon dried garlic slices (5 grams)

1 tablespoon plus ¾ teaspoon dried onion slices (5 grams)

¾ teaspoon cumin seeds (2 grams)

¼ teaspoon fenugreek seeds (1 gram)

Finely grind together the garlic, onion, cumin, and fenugreek.

FOR SIMMERING WITH CREAM SAUCE

2 teaspoons dried onion slices (3 grams)

1 tablespoon dried tarragon (1 gram)

1 teaspoon ajowan (1 gram)

¾ cup plus 3 tablespoons dried basil (15 grams)

2 tablespoons dried dill weed (5 grams)

Finely grind the onion, tarragon, and ajowan together and immediately mix with the basil and dill.

MASTER BLENDS FOR CONDIMENTS

FOR STIRRING INTO MAYONNAISE

1 tablespoon plus 2 teaspoons dried savory (5 grams)

1 teaspoon dried mint (1 gram)

1 tablespoon fennel pollen (1 gram)

1 tablespoon plus 2 teaspoons nigella seeds (15 grams)

Finely grind the savory and mint together and immediately mix with the fennel pollen and nigella.

FOR STIRRING INTO KETCHUP

1 teaspoon amchoor (dried mango powder; 2 grams)

½ teaspoon Aleppo pepper (1 gram)

¼ teaspoon ground cinnamon, preferably Vietnamese (1 gram)

Mix together the amchoor, Aleppo, and cinnamon.

FOR STIRRING INTO MUSTARD

1 tablespoon yellow mustard seeds (15 grams)

2 teaspoons black mustard seeds (10 grams)

1¼ teaspoons caraway seeds (5 grams)

¾ teaspoon poppy seeds (3 grams)

½ teaspoon Aleppo pepper (1 gram)

Mix together both mustard seeds, the caraway seeds, poppy seeds, and Aleppo.

SPICE GLOSSARY

You can find everything you want to know about most spices in my reference book, *The Spice Companion.* Here I've distilled the details into an easy-to-use chart, broken it down into several categories.

Family. Each spice belongs to a flavor family. Savory is slightly salty, sweet mimics sweetness, bitter is bitter, heat is spicy, sour has acidic notes, and warm evokes a feeling that's not quite sweet and not quite heat. Knowing which family each spice belongs to will help you create balanced blends. Some spices, such as pimentón (smoked paprika), cumin, garlic, and cinnamon also have umami, that elusive sixth taste that's a sort of savory depth.

Form. This describes from which part of the plant the spice comes.

Look. Color, shape, size, and texture are outlined here.

Smell. This gives you a sense of the aroma and fragrance to expect.

Taste. While batches and varieties vary, spices have general tastes that are depicted in this category.

Origin. This gives you the country of origin (not necessarily the current country of production, which varies with different purveyors).

Friends. These are the spices that will play well with the specific spice in blends. Don't feel limited by these suggestions. They're just a starting point for blending.

Notes. Anything unique to a spice will be explained here.

Also known as. This identifies other names that spices are sometimes sold under.

Substitutions. You can swap spices that are very similar too. For example, if you don't have peperoncini, which are dried Calabrian chile flakes, you can use red pepper flakes instead. If you don't have Tellicherry black peppercorns, other peppercorns will work as well. Nutmeg and mace are interchangeable. Ginger can replace amchoor in a pinch.

SPICE	FAMILY	FORM	LOOK	SMELL	TASTE
Ajowan	bitter	seeds	gray-and-green-striped seeds; shorter and fatter than cumin	perfumy	complex herbaceous blend with hints of thyme, oregano, fennel, cumin, and celery seeds
Aleppo Pepper	heat	flakes whole	thin, delicate, brick-red flakes	chile, citrus, tomatoey	mild heat with sweet-tart citrus and tomato fruitiness, plus earthy cumin and salt undertones
Allspice	warm	berries finely ground	dusty-brown spheres the size of capers	piney with hints of clove	a blend of cinnamon, clove, nutmeg, juniper, and pepper
Amchoor	sour	dried unripe mango slices finely ground	golden-brown slices or powder	fresh citrus, like dried orange peel	sour, slightly sweet, herbaceous notes with hint of tamarind
Ancho Chile	heat	dried whole peppers finely ground	brown or brick-red wrinkled dried chiles or powder	plummy chiles, a little smoky	mild chile with notes of plums and raisins
Anise	sweet	seeds	brown-and-cream-striped seeds; smaller than cumin	licorice	natural sweetness with a little acidity and fennel, caraway, licorice, and/or camphor notes
Basil	sweet	seeds dried leaves	tiny black seeds (like chia); dark khaki-green leaves are small and flaky when dried	sweet like fresh basil with a perfumy aroma	peppery, clove-like
Bay Leaves	bitter	dried leaves	matte olive-green leaves	eucalyptus	piney resin notes
Black Cardamom	savory	pods seeds	large, wrinkled black pods	smoky camphor	savory and smoky with floral ginger notes
Black Tellicherry Peppercorns	heat	dried whole peppercorns finely ground	small, wrinkled black balls	peppery	peppery with a bit of sweetness and citrus
Caraway	sweet	seeds	black-and-brown-striped seeds	rye bread	cross between fresh and sweet; between cumin and fennel with hints of anise
Cardamom (Green)	warm	pods seeds	smooth green-yellow pods	floral with resin notes	slightly sweet, spicy, resinous, floral, citrus, peppery, herbal bitterness, warm
Cayenne	heat	dried whole chiles finely ground	dark red chiles; orange-red fine powder when ground	pleasant dusty chile	hot with sweet and sour notes
Celery Seed	savory	seeds	tiny brown-and-cream-striped seeds; a little bigger than poppy seeds	celery	very savory with fresh, earthy, herbaceous notes
Chamomile	sweet	flowers	yellow buds and fluffy light brown powder	floral, like the tea	sweet like honeysuckle, with fruity apple and herbaceous qualities
Chipotle Chile	heat	dried whole chiles finely ground	wrinkled maroon chiles; brick-red powder when ground	fruity and bright chile	medium heat with smoky-sweet notes

ORIGIN	FRIENDS	NOTES	ALSO KNOWN AS	SUBSTITUTIONS
South India	caraway, chile, cumin, fennel, turmeric	Mellows to nutty when toasted dry or in fat; adds texture when left whole.	ajwain carum	none
South and Central America North Syrian town of Aleppo	cumin, oregano, rose, sesame, sumac	Increasingly hard to find because of Syria's geopolitical state.	Halaby pepper	chile flakes
West Indies Central America	black pepper, cardamom, cinnamon, clove, vanilla	Crush the berries for added texture in a slow-cooked dish.	Jamaican pepper poivre de la Jamaique bois d'inde pimento	none
India	basil, garlic, ginger, orange peel, turmeric	Its enzymes can tenderize meat.	mango powder	none
Mexico	cumin, garlic, orange peel, oregano, paprika	Anchos are fully ripened poblano peppers that are sun-dried.		chipotle
Eastern Mediterranean Egypt Middle East	caraway, clove, mace, pink pepper, tarragon	Chewing on whole seeds releases a cooling sensation, which is why they're often used for coughs.	green anise	fennel
Asia Africa	cilantro, fennel, pink pepper, rosemary, white pepper	It's best in dressings and marinades.		none
Eastern Mediterranean	anise, lemon peel, onion, oregano, white pepper	Their scent and taste are much more pronounced when ground.	bay laurel	none
Eastern Himalayas	basil, cumin, garlic, fennel, lemongrass	Pair with dark chocolate and fruit desserts.		none
India	basil, cinnamon, juniper berries, orange peel, tarragon	Pre-ground is often adulterated, so start with whole and grind before use.		any black pepper
Central Europe Asia	clove, dill, juniper berries, orange peel	The seeds are small enough to keep whole in baked goods.		none
South India	caraway, cinnamon, cumin, dill, juniper berries	Grind the whole pods, including the seeds, before use.		none
South and Central America	coriander, garlic, ginger, lemon peel, sumac	This is the most versatile form of heat and works in anything.	cayenne pepper	chile powder
Mediterranean	cubeb, fennel, mustard, onion, rosemary	They contain natural sodium and can replace some salt.		none
Western Europe North Africa	cardamom, clove, orange peel, sage, vanilla	Whole flowers work with savory and sweet applications.		none
Central America Mexico	annatto, cumin, ginger, oregano	These are dried and smoked fully ripe jalapeños.	morita chile	ancho chile

SPICE	FAMILY	FORM	LOOK	SMELL	TASTE
Cilantro	savory	dried leaves	thin khaki-green flakes	fresh, grassy, and green	peppery, citrusy, fresh herbaceous, floral
Cinnamon	sweet	sticks finely ground	sticks are brown spirals of dried bark; ground is dark brown	clove-like and warm	heady sweetness with a savory edge
Cloves	warm	dried flower buds	tiny light brown balls attached to dark brown stems	warm sharpness with hints of citrus	sweet, bitter, peppery
Coriander	warm	seeds	very small golden-brown striated balls	sweet, woodsy, and spicy	warm and nutty with citrus notes
Cubeb	heat	dried fruits	like extra-large black peppercorns with stems	piney resin with peppery notes	cross between black pepper and clove with warm mild heat and camphorous citrus bitterness
Cumin	savory	seeds finely ground	tan-and-dark-brown-striped seeds	nearly meaty with a hint of sweat	nutty, peppery, leathery, savory
Dill	savory	dried leaves seeds	fine dark-green threads for weed; flat black seeds edged with tan	sweet with an herbaceous freshness	savory, sweet, and slightly bitter with grassy notes
Fennel	sweet	seeds	large, curved yellow-and-green-striped seeds	stronger licorice scent than anise	sweet and delicate licorice qualities with piney bitter notes
Fenugreek	savory bitter	dried leaves seeds	leaves are slender and dark green with thread-thin stems; seeds are mustard yellow and irregularly shaped like tiny pieces of gravel	sweet caramelized onion	pungent maple syrup, burnt sugar; nutty seeds and bitter leaves
Galangal	heat	finely ground	pink-orange powder	mild peppery	sharp spicy-sweet heat less potent than ginger
Garlic	savory	dried slices	golden-brown chips	garlicky	intense, warm spicy-sweet garlic flavor without the sharpness of raw or the dusty taste of garlic powder
Ginger	heat	finely ground	golden powder that clumps slightly when fresh	warm floral sharpness	peppery warmth that's bright with floral notes
Green Peppercorns	heat	dried whole peppercorns	small, wrinkled olive-green balls	herbaceous and sharp	mild heat with a green freshness
Hibiscus blossom	sweet	leaves flowers	wavy burgundy rose petals	floral and tangy	sour, tart, and floral sweet
Jalapeño	heat	finely ground	golden-green-tinted powder	fresh and green heat	a lot of heat with some acidic notes and complex chile tastes
Juniper	savory	berries	small, round balls	pine	piney resin with a touch of sweetness, brightness, and sharpness
Kaffir Lime Leaves	sour	leaves	large, curved olive-green leaves	grassy citrus	floral citrus with a little acidity and bitterness

ORIGIN	FRIENDS	NOTES	ALSO KNOWN AS	SUBSTITUTIONS
Mediterranean North Africa Western Asia	caraway, clove, garlic, green chiles, onion	Some taste cilantro as bitter and soapy because of its aldehydes.	coriander Chinese parsley	none
Southeast Asia	caraway, cardamom, clove, cumin, ginger	The Vietnamese variety is especially pungent and complex.	canela cassia	none
Indonesia	cardamom, cinnamon, cumin, fennel, rose	It's very strong, so use sparingly.		none
Mediterranean North Africa Western Asia	cumin, fennel, mint, rose, tarragon	Dhania is a variety from India that's pale green, sweeter than coriander, and more oval in shape.		none
Indonesia	clove, lemongrass, nutmeg, orange peel, pink pepper	It has a mild numbing effect that's refreshing on the palate.		none
Egypt	caraway, cardamom, cinnamon, coriander, fennel	Black cumin from India is mellower than regular with smoky and fresh floral notes.		none
Russia Eastern Mediterranean Western Asia	fennel, onion, oregano, pomegranate, tarragon	Dill weed is especially tasty when charred, making it ideal for grilling or searing fish.		none
Mediterranean	caraway, cumin, mustard, nigella, oregano	Fennel pollen is another form of the dried plant that can be used in cooking.		anise
Southeastern Europe Western Asia	cumin, mace, orange peel, pimenton, star anise	These are a common ingredient in curry powder mixes.	Greek hay Greek clover bird's foot	none
Indonesia	chiles, cilantro, lemongrass, pink pepper, turmeric	It's similar to ginger, but not interchangeable because it's milder.		ginger
Central Asia	Aleppo pepper, basil, fennel, ginger, thyme	Compared to fresh, it doesn't burn as easily, doesn't go bad, and gives a more concentrated flavor.		granulated garlic (although not the same)
China	cardamom, cinnamon, clove, lemongrass, turmeric	It should have a strong scent, stick to the jar, and feel almost oily when rubbed.		galangal
Malabar, southwest India	dill, ginger, lemon peel, onion, rosemary	Harvested before they're ripe, these grind very easily.		none
West Africa	anise, ginger, juniper berries, mint, pink pepper	Its flavor transforms when cooked or steeped in hot liquid.		sumac
Mexico	cilantro, cumin, garlic, oregano, pimenton	Unlike chipotle, which is ground smoked ripe jalapeños, this is ground from green chiles.		chile powder
British Isles	bay leaf, cinnamon, nutmeg, sage, star anise			none
Southeast Asia	basil, galangal, garlic, lemongrass, turmeric	Fresh can be used interchangeably with dried.	makrut	none

SPICE	FAMILY	FORM	LOOK	SMELL	TASTE
Lavender	sweet	flowers	lavender-colored seed-shaped buds	floral, like perfume	floral with hints of mint and citrus
Lemongrass	sour	dried stalks finely ground	stalks are pale yellow and stiff; ground is an olive-green powder	peppery citrus with rose notes	sweet, rounded, fresh lemon, and clean citrus
Licorice	sweet	finely ground	dark brown powder	sweet and floral with hints of tobacco	sweet anise with floral notes
Limon Omani	sour	dried fruit	wrinkled white, cream, brown, or black dried Ping-Pong-size balls	concentrated lime with sweet fermented notes	citrus, sour, and musky, with a slight bitterness
Mahleb	bitter	dried kernels	hay-colored drop-shaped seeds	nutty, almond-like	fruity and bitter nuttiness with hints of vanilla
Marjoram	bitter	leaves	crumbled khaki-green dried leaves	dry grass	fresh and sharp; more delicate than oregano with spicy-sweet notes and a slight bitterness
Mint	savory	leaves	crumbled brown leaves	minty	fresh sharp somewhat peppery
Muntok White Peppercorns	heat	peppercorns	small, smooth, cream-colored balls	pleasantly funky, sharp, and peppery	earthy and herbaceous with a mild heat and elegant delicacy
Mustard Seeds	heat	seeds	tiny, round black, brown, or yellow seeds	mild and earthy	mellow heat with a slight bitterness
Nigella	bitter	seeds	matte black seeds the size of sesame seeds	hint of savory	oregano-like herbaceousness with a slight bitterness and warm, toasted onion flavor
Nutmeg and Mace	warm	whole kernels arils (mace) ground	brown to dark brown ¾-inch-long ovals or rounds; or medium brown powder (mace)	warm and pungent	citrus and light floral notes
Onion	savory	dried slices	creamy white chips in half-moons and rings	oniony	like fresh onion soup mix
Orange Peel	bitter	granulated dried peel	orange-colored bits like coarse cornmeal	citrusy and sweet	bitter with a hint of citrus sweetness
Oregano	bitter	leaves	pale green bits of leaves	piney and peppery, like a pizza parlor	warm and slightly bitter herbaceousness
Paprika	heat	finely ground	brilliant red powder	sweet like fresh bell peppers	mild to hot deep vegetal chile flavor
Parsley	savory	leaves	little curved forest-green leaves	herbaceous with a hint of cannabis	mild peppery notes with a hint of sweetness
Peperoncini	heat	flakes	thin bright- and dark-red flakes and cream-colored seeds	sweet chile with mild smokiness	mild to medium heat with sweet and sour notes and bright citrus and acid

ORIGIN	FRIENDS	NOTES	ALSO KNOWN AS	SUBSTITUTIONS
Mediterranean	basil, fennel, pink pepper, rosemary, sumac	It's very potent, so use it sparingly or your food will taste like hand lotion.		none
South India Ceylon Indonesia	basil, coriander, garlic, ginger, turmeric	Dried tastes less intense than fresh but with a stronger aroma.		none
Southeastern Europe Middle East	ginger, orange peel, star anise, vanilla, white pepper	The powder doesn't taste like black licorice candy; it's much more subtle and versatile.		none
Oman	basil, cardamom, dill, garlic, tarragon	Press down against a hard surface to crack these or crush before grinding.	Persian lime black lime Omani lime noomi Basra limon amoni	lemon peel
Middle East Southern Europe	anise, caraway, cinnamon, clove, ginger	These bitter ground sour-cherry pits work best in sweet baked goods.	mahlab mahaleb mahlepi	none
Mediterranean Western Asia	cumin, paprika, sumac, Urfa pepper, yellow mustard			oregano
Southern Europe Mediterranean	basil, caraway, cardamom, green peppercorns, lavender			none
Indonesia	anise, cinnamon, clove, galangal, lemongrass	Look for plump cream-colored balls.		none
Southern Europe Western Asia India	allspice, bay leaves, caraway, cumin, ginger	Yellow is the mildest; brown and black are more pungent. All are more intense when ground and mixed with liquid.		none
Mediterranean	caraway, lemon peel, mustard seeds, paprika, thyme	They're a great replacement for sesame seeds when you want something more savory.	kalonji onion seeds black cumin black caraway fennel flower	black sesame
Indonesia	allspice, cardamom, clove, ginger, vanilla	Mace is more pungent in scent than nutmeg, but more delicate in taste. Both should be freshly grated just before use.		none
Chive	caraway, chile, cumin, paprika	Look for slices, not powder.		granulated onion
North India China	Aleppo pepper, basil, caraway, fennel, pink pepper	It works as well in savory as in sweet dishes.		none
Mexico Central and South America	basil, garlic, orange peel, sumac, thyme	It often smells and tastes better than fresh.		marjoram
Americas	caraway, cumin, garlic, ginger, thyme	Its dense powdery texture helps thicken sauces too.		none
Mediterranean	cayenne, garlic, green peppercorns mustard, tomato powder	Its flavor and scent diminish over time, so smell before using.		none
South and Central America	cumin, garlic, orange peel, oregano	The best varieties come from Calabria in Italy.	Calabrian chile	red pepper flakes

INDEX

Skillet-Braised Fennel pages 50–53
Skillet-Braised Fennel with Citrus, Caraway, and Celery Seeds
Caramelized Fennel Salad with Pecorino, Green Olives, and Almonds
White Wine–Braised Fennel with Dried Cranberries
Coconut Milk–Glazed Fennel with Turmeric and Mint
Braised Fennel with Gremolata
Vegan Fennel "Aioli"

Roasted Mixed Vegetables pages 54–57
Sumac Roasted Vegetables with Fennel Seeds
Tarragon Roasted Vegetables with Citrus and Mustard Seeds
Pink-Pepper Roasted Vegetable Salad with Feta and Olives
Juniper-Rosemary Roasted Vegetables with Dried Fruits and Almonds
Roasted Vegetable and Parmesan Frittata
Sesame and Prosciutto Roasted Vegetables with Fenugreek

Pan-Roasted Potatoes pages 58–61
Crispy Herbed Skillet-Fried Potatoes
Spicy Saffron and Coriander Crusted Potatoes
Creamy Herbed Mashed Potatoes
Crispy Duck Fat Potatoes
Crushed Roasted Potatoes with Pistachios
Potato Salad with Bacon, Nigella, and Lime

Potato Gratin pages 62–65
Rosemary and Thyme Potato Gratin with Bay Leaves
Tomato Sauce Potato Gratin with Marjoram and Mozzarella
Sweet Potato and Goat Cheese Gratin
Dijon-Gruyère Potato Gratin with Basil and Tarragon
Crunchy Fried Potato Gratin Cubes

Sweet Potato Puree pages 66–69
Cumin and Caraway Sweet Potato Puree
Sweet Potato Dip with Pepitas and Jalapeños
Gingery Double Apple Sweet Potato Puree
Sweet Potato and Walnut Casserole with Melted Cheddar
Pomegranate Sweet Potato Puree with Anise, Cardamom, and Mustard Seeds
Sweet Potato Croquettes

Cabbage and Apple Slaw with Carrots pages 70–73
Spicy Slaw with Poppy and Mustard Seeds
Sesame-Lime Slaw with Ginger
Slaw with Anise Seeds and Tangy Tamarind Dressing
Cabbage, Carrot, and Apple Sauté with Mustard Seeds
Creamy Slaw with Labne-Tahini Dressing

Creamy Carrot Soup pages 74–77
Smoky Cumin and Chipotle Carrot Soup
Smoky Carrot Soup with Cinnamon and Crispy Chorizo
Carrot Pasta with Poppy Seeds
Curried Coconut Carrot Soup with Green Peppercorns
Creamy Tomato-Carrot Soup with Basil, Fennel, and Oregano
Chunky Turmeric Carrot Soup with Lime Leaves

Chunky Vegetable Soup pages 78–81
French Country Vegetable Soup with Sage and Thyme
Turmeric Coconut Vegetable Soup with Ginger and Cardamom
Creamy Vegetable Soup
Green Lentil and Jasmine Rice Soup with Sautéed Vegetables
Black Bean and Tomato Tortilla Soup
Comforting and Quick Chicken Soup

Baked Penne pages 86–89
Garlic and Tomato Baked Penne with Rosemary and Oregano
Baked Penne with Sautéed Italian Sausage
Spicy and Smoky Baked Penne with Olive Oil–Packed Tuna
Eggplant and Olive Baked Penne with Feta
Creamy Baked Penne with Halloumi

Stovetop Paella pages 90–93
Summer Harvest Paella with Saffron and Coriander
Savory Pan-Fried Paella Cake
Paella Fried Rice with Scallions and Eggs
Chorizo and Seafood Paella with Saffron and Fennel
Chicken Paella with Red and Green Peppers
Lemon and Artichoke Paella with Pumpkin

Risotto pages 94–97
Rosemary and Garlic Risotto with Mascarpone and Parmesan
Farrotto with Feta
Tomato-Saffron Risotto with Turmeric
Red Wine Mushroom Risotto with Marjoram and Mint
Pea and Asparagus Herb Risotto with Green Peppercorns
Arancini (Crunchy Fried Risotto Balls)

Farro with Toasted Noodles pages 98–101
Savory Minted Farro
Savory Pan-Fried Farro Cakes with Goat Cheese and Cilantro
Tomato Basil Farro with Oregano
Bacon and Onion Farro with Ajowan
Wheat Berry Pilaf with Raisins and Almonds
Farro Salad with Tomatoes, Olives, and Feta

Chickpea Flatbreads pages 102–105
Sesame Sumac Flatbreads with Nigella Seeds
Cinnamon Toast Flatbreads
Zucchini Flatbreads with Caraway Seeds
Hummus Rosemary Flatbreads
Fennel and Marjoram Flatbreads with Labne and Onion
Grated Tomato Flatbreads with Poppy Seeds

Yogurt Challah pages 106–109
Golden Turmeric Challah with Nigella Seeds
Smoky Cheddar Challah with Pepitas
Raisin Walnut Challah with Cinnamon
Hazelnut Chocolate Babka with Nutmeg
Garlic Knots
Challah Sandwich Loaves

Chickpeas pages 114–117
Smoky Chickpeas with Garlic and Ginger
Chickpea Salad with Raisins, Orange, and Celery
Cumin and Garlic Hummus
Crisp Fried Chickpeas with Ajowan and Amchoor
Chickpea Fritters with Mint and Cilantro
Lemon and Turmeric Chickpea Soup

Braised White Beans with Charred Spinach pages 118–121
Tunisian Braised White Beans with Charred Spinach, Fennel, and Cumin
Mushroom and Rosemary Braised White Beans with Charred Spinach
Bacon-and-Cider-Braised Beans
Tomato-and-Spinach-Braised Beans with Aleppo and Ginger
Baked White Beans with Feta and Spiced Panko Bread Crumbs
White Bean Spread with Walnuts and Yogurt

Lentils pages 122–125
Garlicky Le Puy Lentils with Mustard Seeds
Lentil Veggie Burgers with Scallions and Cilantro
Lentil Salad with Cornichons and Mustard Vinaigrette
Lentil and Carrot Coconut Curry
Carrot and Tomato Lentil Soup with Lemon Yogurt
Smoky Lentils with Garlic, Bacon, and Cinnamon

Baked Frittata pages 126–129
Zucchini and Arugula Frittata with Feta and Oregano
Vegetable and Feta Cheese Quiche
Bacon, Cremini Mushroom, and Spinach Frittata
Asparagus and Artichoke Frittata with Fennel Seeds
Tuna and Arugula Frittata with Fresh Lemon Juice
Mini Potato, Olive, and Bell Pepper Frittatas

Shakshuka pages 130–133
Tomato and Pepper Shakshuka with Coriander and Paprika
Shakshuka with Halloumi and Pistachios
Italian Sausage Shakshuka with Pimentón and Cinnamon
Squashuka
Tomato and Pepper Pizzas with Sunny-Side-Up Eggs
Green Shakshuka with Cumin and Caraway

Olive Oil Deviled Eggs pages 134–137
Labne Deviled Eggs with Paprika and Ginger
Tahini and Olive Deviled Eggs with Mint and Sumac
Walnut-Scallion Deviled Eggs with Coriander and Turmeric
Deviled Egg Salad
Goat Cheese Deviled Eggs with Sesame Seeds
Tuna and Caper Deviled Eggs

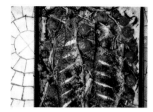

Sugar-and-Salt-Cured Salmon pages 142–145
Dilled Cured Salmon with Mustard and Caraway Seeds
Sumac-and-Pernod-Cured Salmon with Cilantro, Cumin, and Fennel
Salmon and Scallion Labne Spread
Juniper-and-Orange-Cured Salmon
Seed-Crusted Cured Salmon
Scrambled Eggs with Cured Salmon

Poached Salmon pages 146–149
Basil and Garlic Poached Salmon
Tomato-Poached Salmon with Rosemary and Aleppo Pepper
Flaked Salmon Salad with Cornichons
Butter-Poached Salmon with Capers and Green Peppercorns
Cream-Poached Salmon with Fennel Seeds
Soy-Poached Salmon with Coconut Broth and Shiitakes

Seared Salmon pages 150–153
Coriander-and-Fennel-Crusted Seared Salmon
Cornmeal-Crusted Seared Salmon with Fenugreek and Sumac
Chickpea Flour–Crusted Seared Salmon with Savory and Nutmeg
Arugula Salad with Salmon and Sesame and Nigella Seeds
Salmon Potato Patties
Soy-Garlic Seared Salmon with Limon Omani

Roasted Whole Fish pages 154–157
Savory and Aleppo Pepper Roasted Fish with Fennel and Cherry Tomatoes
Chimichurri Roasted Fish
Buttered and Roasted Fish with Leeks, Capers, and Tarragon
Tomato-Roasted Fish with Sweet and Hot Peppers
Honey-Vinegar-Glazed Roasted Fish with Star Anise
Sesame-Roasted Whole Fish with Olives and Preserved Lemon

Chraime: Seafood in Tomato Sauce pages 158–161
Cod Simmered in Turmeric-Coriander Tomato Sauce
Stuffed Squid in Tomato Sauce
Chraime with Clams, Mussels, and Shrimp
Shrimp, Olive, and Tomato Penne
Grilled Tomato Toasts with Anchovies and Sardines
Cod Chraime with Orange, Apple, Ginger, and Thyme

Seared Seafood with Pan Sauce pages 162–165
Thyme-Seared Scallops with Capers and Lemon
Za'atar Shrimp in Tomato-Caper Sauce
Seared Scallops with Pancetta and Apple
Seared Calamari with Vermouth Sauce
Seared Oregano-Turmeric Shrimp with Olives
Seared Swordfish with Orange-Soy Glaze

Steamed Mussels pages 166–169
Steamed Mussels with Limon Omani and Bay Leaves
Vermouth-Steamed Mussels with Lemon Verbena, Sage, and Ginger
Steamed Mussels with Bacon and Cabbage
Spanish-Style Pickled Mussels with Coriander and Pimentón
Coconut Milk–Steamed Mussels with Thai Chiles and Lemongrass
Beer-Steamed Mussels with Thyme and Caraway

Crab Cakes pages 170–173
Crab Cakes with Sesame Seeds and Aleppo Pepper
Chipotle Corn and Crab Cakes
Chorizo Crab Cakes with Cumin and Turmeric
Fish Cakes with Fennel Seeds
Zucchini Crab Cakes with Corn Bread Crust

Glazed Seared Chicken Breasts pages 178–181
Coriander and Black Pepper Chicken Breasts with Balsamic Glaze
Soy-and-Orange-Glazed Chicken Breasts
Honey-Dijon-Glazed Chicken Breasts
Chicken Salad with Black Beans and Cilantro
Balsamic Chicken with Sautéed Cherry Tomatoes
Chicken Breasts with Shiitake Mushroom Cream Sauce

Braised Chicken Thighs pages 182–185
Herb-Braised Chicken with Dried Apricots
Cumin and Cardamom Chicken Tajine with Preserved Lemon
Red Wine and Mushroom Braised Chicken with Caraway and Allspice
Braised Tarragon Chicken in Creamy Leek Sauce
Chicken Braised with Carrots, Grapes, and Rosé Wine
Beer-Braised Chicken with Bacon and Cabbage

Roasted Butterflied Chicken pages 186–189
Bay Leaf and Garlic Roasted Chicken with Savory and Paprika
Chicken Tacos with Hummus and Sesame-Mint Salsa
Za'atar Roasted Chicken with Lemons and Olives
Chicken and White Bean Soup with Turmeric and Amchoor
Pomegranate-Glazed Roasted Chicken with Figs
Sautéed Spinach and Arugula with Chicken and Feta

Oven-Roasted Chicken Soup pages 190–193
Limon Omani Roasted Chicken Soup with Celery Seeds
Tomato-Basil Chicken Soup with Ancho and Cumin
Two-Bean Soup with Chicken and Cilantro
Sesame-Shiitake Chicken Soup with Galangal
Coconut-Cilantro Chicken Soup with Lemongrass
Creamy Labne Chicken Soup with Dill Seeds

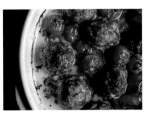

Quick-Seared Pork Chops pages 194–197
Brown Sugar–Seared Pork Chops with Orange Glaze
Dijon Mustard–Crusted Pork Chops with Rosemary
Crumb-Crusted Smoky Pork Chops with Apple Glaze
Pork Chops with Peanut Satay Sauce
Pork and Pineapple Salad with Honey-Lime Dressing
Cider Vinegar–Glazed Pork Chops with Apples and Raisins

Oven-Roasted Meatballs pages 198–201
Spicy Garlic and Oregano Meatballs with Blistered Grape Tomatoes
Tahini-Parsley Meatballs with Paprika
Feta-Stuffed Meatballs with Green Olives
Rose and Ginger Lamb Meatballs with Black Olives
Crunchy Parmesan Meatballs
Quick Tomato Meat Sauce

Braised Short Ribs pages 202–205
Citrus-Braised Short Ribs with Star Anise and Cocoa
Red Wine–Braised Short Ribs with Black Pepper and Yellow Mustard
Chili-and-Tomato-Braised Short Ribs with Cinnamon
Vermouth-Braised Short Ribs with Warm Spices and Dried Fruit
Carrot Juice–Braised Short Ribs with Sweet Potatoes
Short Rib and Potato Hash Cakes

Roasted Rack of Lamb pages 206–209
Fennel-and-Coriander-Crusted Rack of Lamb with Caramelized Onions
Tomato-Glazed Rack of Lamb with Eggplant
Paprika and Ginger Rack of Lamb with Caramelized Carrots
Curried Rack of Lamb with Butternut Squash
Sweet-and-Sour Pomegranate-Glazed Rack of Lamb
Tarragon, Mint, and Dill Buttered Rack of Lamb with Shallots

Roasted Rolled Leg of Lamb pages 210–213
Rosemary and Mint Roasted Leg of Lamb
Walnut-and-Date-Stuffed Leg of Lamb with Pomegranate Glaze
Cocoa-Chile Roasted Leg of Lamb
Goat Cheese, Almond, and Caper–Stuffed Roasted Leg of Lamb
Tomato and Olive Salad with Lamb, Herbs, and Crunchy Pita
Lamb Panini with Muenster, Scallions, and Pickles

Olive Oil Cake pages 218–221
Ginger Olive Oil Cake with Fennel Seeds and Black Pepper
Savory Goat Cheese and Herb Olive Oil Loaf
Zucchini Bread with Walnuts and Thyme
Cardamom Olive Oil Bundt Cake with Dried Fruit and Mixed Nuts
Glazed Cocoa and Orange Blossom Bundt Cake
Seed and Grain Olive Oil Loaf

Brown Sugar Banana Bread pages 222–225
Cardamom and Cinnamon Banana Bread with Poppy Seeds
Lavender and Hibiscus Banana Bread with Anise
Pecan Banana Bread with Sichuan Peppercorns and Nigella Seeds
Chocolate Chip–Banana Mini Muffins
Ancho Chile Banana Bread with Banana Chips
Rosemary and Star Anise Banana Bread with Dried Apricots

Fruit Crisp pages 226–229
Mixed Berry Crisp with Sumac-Anise Almond Topping
Dutch Apple Pie
Cardamom and Ginger Peach Crisp
Berry Jam Bars
Berry Yogurt Parfait with Almond Crispies
Ice Cream Sundaes with Pineapple Topping and Spiced Almond Crunch

Shortbread pages 230–233
Poppy Seed Shortbread with Ginger and Nutmeg
Bittersweet Chocolate Shortbread Sandwiches
Alfajores (Dulce de Leche Sandwich Cookies)
Coconut Cookies with Coriander and Lemongrass
Cocoa-Sesame Cookies with Urfa and Allspice
Peanut Butter and Jelly Sandwich Cookies

Brownies pages 234–237
Cardamom and Pink Pepper Brownies
Bittersweet Chocolate Frosted Brownies
Mocha Black Pepper Brownies with Pecans and Walnuts
Minted Brownies with Candied Ginger
Glazed Mini Coconut Brownies
Ice Cream Brownie Bites

Crème Fraîche Clafoutis pages 238–241
Apple and Prune Crème Fraîche Clafoutis with Nutmeg and Allspice
Cherry and Pistachio Clafoutis with Chamomile
Apple Custard Pie
Pear and Chocolate Clafoutis with Rose-Scented Custard
Mixed Berry Mini Clafoutis

Aioli:
    fennel, vegan, 53
    garlic, with cumin and ginger, 246
Alfajores (dulce de leche sandwich cookies), 233
Almond(s):
    caramelized fennel salad with pecorino, green olives, and, 53
    crispies, berry yogurt parfait with, 229
    crunch, spiced, ice cream sundaes with pineapple topping and, 229
    juniper-rosemary roasted vegetables with dried fruits and, 57
    wheat berry pilaf with raisins and, 101
Anchovies and sardines, grilled tomato toasts with, 161
Apple(s):
    and prune crème fraîche clafoutis with nutmeg and allspice, 238
    apple custard pie, 241
    cabbage and apple slaw with carrots, 70–73
        with anise seeds and tangy tamarind dressing, 73
    cabbage, carrot, and apple sauté with mustard seeds, 73
    creamy, with labne-tahini dressing, 73
    sesame-lime, with ginger, 73
    spicy, with poppy and mustard seeds, 70
    Dutch apple pie, 229
    gingery double apple sweet potato puree, 69
    glaze, crumb-crusted smoky pork chops with, 197
    limon omani roasted chicken soup with celery seeds, 190
    and pancetta, seared scallops with, 165
    and raisins, cider vinegar–glazed pork chops with, 197
Apricots, dried. See Dried fruit
Arancini (crunchy fried risotto balls), 97
Artichoke:
    and asparagus frittata with fennel seeds, 129
    and lemon paella with pumpkin, 93
Arugula:
    and zucchini frittata with feta and oregano, 126
    salad, with salmon and sesame and nigella seeds, 153
    and spinach, sautéed, with chicken and feta, 189
    and tuna frittata with fresh lemon juice, 129
Asparagus:
    and artichoke frittata with fennel seeds, 129
    pea, asparagus, and herb risotto with green peppercorns, 97

Babka, hazelnut chocolate, with nutmeg, 109
Bacon:
    bacon-and-cider-braised beans, 121
    bacon and onion farro with ajowan, 101
    bacon, cremini mushroom, and spinach frittata, 129
    beer-braised chicken with cabbage and, 185
    potato salad with nigella, lime, and, 61
    smoky lentils with garlic, cinnamon, and, 125
    steamed mussels with cabbage and, 169
Banana bread, brown sugar, 222–25
    ancho chile, with banana chips, 225
    cardamom and cinnamon, with poppy seeds, 222
    chocolate chip–banana mini muffins, 225
    lavender and hibiscus, with anise, 225
    pecan, with Sichuan peppercorns and nigella seeds, 225
    rosemary and star anise, with dried apricots, 225

Barley, master spice blend for cooking water, 85
Beans:
    about, 31, 113
    black bean and tomato tortilla soup, 81
    black, chicken salad with cilantro and, 181
    chicken and white bean soup with turmeric and amchoor, 189
    two-bean soup with chicken and cilantro, 193
    white, braised, with charred spinach, 118–21
        bacon-and-cider-braised, 121
        baked white beans with feta and spiced panko bread crumbs, 121
        mushroom and rosemary braised, 121
        tomato-and-spinach-braised, with Aleppo and ginger, 121
        Tunisian, with fennel and cumin, 118
        white bean spread with walnuts and yogurt, 121
Beef:
    braised short ribs, 202–5
        carrot juice–braised, with sweet potatoes, 205
        chili-and-tomato-braised, with cinnamon, 205
        citrus-braised, with star anise and cocoa, 202
        red wine–braised, with black pepper and yellow mustard, 205
        short rib and potato hash cakes, 205
        vermouth-braised, with warm spices and dried fruit, 205
    master spice blends for, 177
    oven-roasted meatballs, 198–201
        crunchy Parmesan meatballs, 201
        feta-stuffed, with green olives, 201
        garlic and oregano, spicy, with blistered grape tomatoes, 198
        quick tomato meat sauce, 201
        tahini-parsley, with paprika, 201
Bell peppers. See Peppers
Berries:
    berry jam bars, 229
    berry yogurt parfait with almond crispies, 229
    mixed berry crisp with sumac-anise almond topping, 226
    mixed berry mini clafoutis, 241
Bread crumbs, 31
    master spice blend for, 250
    spiced, baked white beans with feta and, 121
Breads:
    brown sugar banana bread, 222–25
        ancho chile, with banana chips, 225
        cardamom and cinnamon, with poppy seeds, 222
        chocolate chip–banana mini muffins, 225
        lavender and hibiscus, with anise, 225
        pecan, with Sichuan peppercorns and nigella seeds, 225
        rosemary and star anise, with dried apricots, 225
    chickpea flatbreads, 102–5
        cinnamon toast flatbreads, 105
        fennel and marjoram, with labne and onion, 105
        grated tomato, with poppy seeds, 105
        hummus rosemary, 105
        sesame sumac, with nigella seeds, 102
        zucchini, with caraway seeds, 105
    master spice blends for, 249
    olive oil loaves:
        savory goat cheese and herb, 221
        seed and grain, 221
        zucchini bread with walnuts and thyme, 221
    yogurt challah, 106–9
        garlic knots, 109
        golden turmeric, with nigella seeds, 106

hazelnut chocolate babka with nutmeg, 109
        raisin walnut, with cinnamon, 109
        sandwich loaves, 109
        smoky Cheddar, with pepitas, 109
Breakfast, master spice blends for, 249
Brownies, 234–37
    bittersweet chocolate frosted, 237
    cardamom and pink pepper, 234
    ice cream brownie bites, 237
    mini coconut, glazed, 237
    minted, with candied ginger, 237
    mocha black pepper, with pecans and walnuts, 237
Brown sugar banana bread, 222–25
    ancho chile, with banana chips, 225
    cardamom and cinnamon, with poppy seeds, 222
    chocolate chip–banana mini muffins, 225
    lavender and hibiscus, with anise, 225
    pecan, with Sichuan peppercorns and nigella seeds, 225
    rosemary and star anise, with dried apricots, 225
Bundt cake:
    cardamom olive oil, with dried fruit and mixed nuts, 221
    cocoa and orange blossom, glazed, 221
Butter, 31
    master spice blend for, 250
Butternut squash:
    curried rack of lamb with, 209
    squashuka, 133

Cabbage:
    beer-braised chicken with bacon and, 185
    cabbage and apple slaw with carrots, 70–73
        with anise seeds and tangy tamarind dressing, 73
        cabbage, carrot, and apple sauté with mustard seeds, 73
        creamy, with labne-tahini dressing, 73
        sesame-lime, with ginger, 73
        spicy, with poppy and mustard seeds, 70
    chunky vegetable soup, 78–81
    steamed mussels with bacon and, 169
Cake:
    master spice blend for pound cake, 217
    olive oil, 218–21
        cardamom olive oil Bundt cake with dried fruit and mixed nuts, 221
        ginger, with fennel seeds and black pepper, 218
        glazed cocoa and orange blossom Bundt cake, 221
        savory goat cheese and herb olive oil loaf, 221
        seed and grain olive oil loaf, 221
        zucchini bread with walnuts and thyme, 221
Calamari:
    seared, with vermouth sauce, 165
    stuffed squid in tomato sauce, 161
Carrot juice–braised short ribs with sweet potatoes, 205
Carrots:
    cabbage and apple slaw with, 70–73
        with anise seeds and tangy tamarind dressing, 73
        cabbage, carrot, and apple sauté with mustard seeds, 73
        creamy, with labne-tahini dressing, 73
        sesame-lime, with ginger, 73
        spicy, with poppy and mustard seeds, 70
    caramelized, paprika and ginger rack of lamb with, 209
    carrot and tomato lentil soup with lemon yogurt, 125
    chicken braised with grapes, rosé wine, and, 185
    chunky vegetable soup, 78–81

creamy carrot soup, 74–77
    carrot pasta with poppy seeds, 77
    chunky turmeric carrot soup with lime leaves, 77
    creamy tomato-carrot soup with basil, fennel, and oregano, 77
    curried coconut carrot soup with green peppercorns, 77
    smoky, with cinnamon and crispy chorizo, 77
    smoky, with cumin and chipotle, 74
    lentil and carrot coconut curry, 125
    roasted mixed vegetables, 54–57
Challah, yogurt, 106–9
    garlic knots, 109
    golden turmeric, with nigella seeds, 106
    hazelnut chocolate babka with nutmeg, 109
    raisin walnut, with cinnamon, 109
    sandwich loaves, 109
    smoky Cheddar, with pepitas, 109
Cheddar:
    challah, smoky, with pepitas, 109
    melted, sweet potato and walnut gratin with, 69
Cherry and pistachio clafoutis with chamomile, 241
Chicken:
    breasts, glazed seared, 178–81
        balsamic chicken with sautéed cherry tomatoes, 181
        chicken salad with black beans and cilantro, 181
        honey-Dijon glazed, 181
        with shiitake mushroom cream sauce, 181
        soy-and-orange-glazed, 181
        with coriander, black pepper, and balsamic glaze, 178
    oven-roasted chicken soup, 190–93
        coconut-cilantro, with lemongrass, 193
        creamy labne chicken soup with dill seeds, 193
        limon omani roasted, with celery seeds, 190
        sesame-shiitake, with galangal, 193
        tomato-basil, with ancho and cumin, 193
        two-bean soup with chicken and cilantro, 193
    paella, with red and green peppers, 93
    roasted butterflied chicken, 186–89
        bay leaf and garlic roasted, with savory and paprika, 186
        chicken and white bean soup with turmeric and amchoor, 189
        chicken tacos with hummus and sesame-mint salsa, 189
        pomegranate-glazed, with figs, 189
        sautéed spinach and arugula with chicken and feta, 189
        za'atar roasted, with lemons and olives, 189
    soup, comforting and quick, 81
    thighs, braised, 182–85
        beer-braised, with bacon and cabbage, 185
        with carrots, grapes, and rosé wine, 185
        cumin and cardamom chicken tajine with preserved lemon, 185
        herb-braised, with dried apricots, 182
        red wine and mushroom braised, with caraway and allspice, 185
        with tarragon and creamy leek sauce, 185
    wings, master spice blend for, 177
Chickpea(s), 114–17. See also Hummus
    crisp fried, with ajowan and amchoor, 117
    cumin and garlic hummus, 117
    fritters, with mint and cilantro, 117
    lemon and turmeric chickpea soup, 117
    salad, with raisins, orange, and celery, 117
    smoky, with garlic and ginger, 114
    summer harvest paella with saffron and coriander, 90

Chickpea flour:
  chickpea flatbreads, 102–5
    cinnamon toast flatbreads, 105
    fennel and marjoram, with labne and onion, 105
    grated tomato, with poppy seeds, 105
    hummus rosemary, 105
    sesame sumac, with nigella seeds, 102
    zucchini, with caraway seeds, 105
  chickpea flour–crusted seared salmon with savory and nutmeg, 153
Chimichurri roasted fish, 157
Chipotle corn and crab cakes, 173
Chocolate and cocoa:
  bittersweet chocolate shortbread sandwiches, 233
  brownies, 234–37
    bittersweet chocolate frosted, 237
    cardamom and pink pepper, 234
    ice cream brownie bites, 237
    mini coconut, glazed, 237
    minted, with candied ginger, 237
    mocha black pepper, with pecans and walnuts, 237
  chocolate chip–banana mini muffins, 225
  cocoa-chile roasted leg of lamb, 213
  cocoa-sesame cookies with Urfa and allspice, 233
  glazed cocoa and orange blossom Bundt cake, 221
  hazelnut chocolate babka with nutmeg, 109
  master spice blend for hot chocolate, 248
  pear and chocolate clafoutis with rose-scented custard, 241
Chorizo:
  chorizo crab cakes with cumin and turmeric, 173
  crispy, smoky carrot soup with cinnamon and, 77
  and seafood paella with saffron and fennel, 93
Chraime: seafood in tomato sauce, 158–61
  with clams, mussels, and shrimp, 161
  cod simmered in turmeric-coriander tomato sauce, 158
  grilled tomato toasts with anchovies and sardines, 161
  shrimp, olive, and tomato penne, 161
  stuffed squid in tomato sauce, 161
Cinnamon toast flatbreads, 105
Clafoutis, crème fraîche, 238–41
  apple and prune, with nutmeg and allspice, 238
  apple custard pie, 241
  cherry and pistachio, with chamomile, 241
  mixed berry mini clafoutis, 241
  pear and chocolate, with rose-scented custard, 241
Clams:
  chorizo and seafood paella with saffron and fennel, 93
  chraime with mussels, shrimp, and, 161
Cocoa. See Chocolate and cocoa
Coconut:
  broth, soy-poached salmon with shiitakes and, 149
  coconut-cilantro chicken soup with lemongrass, 193
  coconut milk–braised fennel with turmeric and mint, 53
  coconut milk–steamed mussels with Thai chiles and lemongrass, 169
  cookies, with coriander and lemongrass, 233
  curried coconut carrot soup with green peppercorns, 77
  glazed mini coconut brownies, 237
  lentil and carrot coconut curry, 125
  turmeric and coconut vegetable soup with ginger and cardamom, 81

Cod:
  fish cakes with fennel seeds, 173
  simmered in turmeric-coriander tomato sauce, 158
Condiments, 244–47
  about, 244
  coriander and fennel pickled raisins, 247
  garlic aioli with cumin and ginger, 246
  limon omani quick pickles, 247
  master spice blends for, 250
  mustard vinaigrette, 246
  poppy seed labne dressing with caraway, 246
  tahini sauce, 247
Cookies:
  berry jam bars, 229
  master spice blend for, 217
  shortbread, 230–33
    alfajores (dulce de leche sandwich cookies), 233
    bittersweet chocolate shortbread sandwiches, 233
    cocoa-sesame, with Urfa and allspice, 233
    coconut, with coriander and lemongrass, 233
    peanut butter and jelly sandwich cookies, 233
    poppy seed, with ginger and nutmeg, 230
Corn and crab cakes, chipotle, 173
Corn bread crust, zucchini crab cakes with, 173
Crab:
  crab cakes, 170–73
    chipotle corn and crab cakes, 173
    chorizo, with cumin and turmeric, 173
    with sesame seeds and Aleppo pepper, 170
    zucchini, with corn bread crust, 173
  master spice blend for, 141
Crackers, master spice blend for, 217
Crème fraîche clafoutis, 238–41
  apple and prune, with nutmeg and allspice, 238
  apple custard pie, 241
  cherry and pistachio, with chamomile, 241
  mixed berry mini clafoutis, 241
  pear and chocolate, with rose-scented custard, 241
Crisp, fruit, 226–29
  berry jam bars, 229
  berry yogurt parfait with almond crispies, 229
  cardamom and ginger peach, 229
  Dutch apple pie, 229
  ice cream sundaes with pineapple topping and spiced almond crunch, 229
  mixed berry, with sumac-anise almond topping, 226
Croquettes, sweet potato, 69
Curry:
  curried coconut carrot soup with green peppercorns, 77
  curried rack of lamb with butternut squash, 209
  lentil and carrot coconut curry, 125

Date- and walnut-stuffed leg of lamb with pomegranate glaze, 213
Desserts, 214–41
  about, 217
  brownies, 234–37
    bittersweet chocolate frosted, 237
    cardamom and pink pepper, 234
    ice cream brownie bites, 237
    mini coconut, glazed, 237
    minted, with candied ginger, 237
    mocha black pepper, with pecans and walnuts, 237
  brown sugar banana bread, 222–25
    ancho chile, with banana chips, 225
    cardamom and cinnamon, with poppy seeds, 222

chocolate chip–banana mini muffins, 225
    lavender and hibiscus, with anise, 225
    pecan, with Sichuan peppercorns and nigella seeds, 225
    rosemary and star anise, with dried apricots, 225
  crème fraîche clafoutis, 238–41
    apple and prune, with nutmeg and allspice, 238
    apple custard pie, 241
    cherry and pistachio, with chamomile, 241
    mixed berry mini clafoutis, 241
    pear and chocolate, with rose-scented custard, 241
  fruit crisp, 226–29
    berry jam bars, 229
    berry yogurt parfait with almond crispies, 229
    cardamom and ginger peach crisp, 229
    Dutch apple pie, 229
    ice cream sundaes with pineapple topping and spiced almond crunch, 229
    mixed berry, with sumac-anise almond topping, 226
  master spice blends for, 217
  olive oil cake, 218–21
    cardamom olive oil Bundt cake with dried fruit and mixed nuts, 221
    ginger, with fennel seeds and black pepper, 218
    glazed cocoa and orange blossom Bundt cake, 221
    seed and grain olive oil loaf, 221
    zucchini bread with walnuts and thyme, 221
  shortbread, 230–33
    alfajores (dulce de leche sandwich cookies), 233
    bittersweet chocolate shortbread sandwiches, 233
    cocoa-sesame, with Urfa and allspice, 233
    coconut, with coriander and lemongrass, 233
    peanut butter and jelly sandwich cookies, 233
    poppy seed, with ginger and nutmeg, 230
Deviled eggs, 134–37
  deviled egg salad, 137
  goat cheese, with sesame seeds, 137
  labne, with paprika and ginger, 134
  tahini and olive, with mint and sumac, 137
  tuna and caper, 137
  walnut-scallion, with coriander and turmeric, 137
Dips and spreads:
  master spice blend for, 49
  salmon and scallion labne spread, 145
  sweet potato dip with pepitas and jalapeños, 69
  white bean spread with walnuts and yogurt, 121
Dried fruit, 31. See also Raisins
  apple and prune crème fraîche clafoutis with nutmeg and allspice, 238
  cardamom olive oil Bundt cake with mixed nuts and, 221
  herb-braised chicken with dried apricots, 182
  juniper-rosemary roasted vegetables with almond and, 57
  pomegranate-glazed roasted chicken with figs, 189
  rosemary and star anise banana bread with dried apricots, 225
  vermouth-braised short ribs with warm spices and, 205
  walnut- and date-stuffed leg of lamb with pomegranate glaze, 213
  white wine–braised fennel with dried cranberries, 53

Drinks, master spice blends for, 248
Duck fat potatoes, crispy, 61
Dulce de leche sandwich cookies (alfajores), 233
Dutch apple pie, 229

Eggplant:
  eggplant and olive baked penne with feta, 89
  summer harvest paella with saffron and coriander, 90
  tomato-glazed rack of lamb with, 209
Eggs:
  about, 113
  frittata, baked, 126–29
    asparagus and artichoke, with fennel seeds, 129
    bacon, cremini mushroom, and spinach, 129
    mini potato, olive, and bell pepper frittatas, 129
    roasted vegetable and Parmesan, 57
    tuna and arugula, with fresh lemon juice, 129
    vegetable and feta cheese quiche, 129
    zucchini and arugula, with feta and oregano, 126
  master spice blends for, 113
  olive oil deviled eggs, 134–37
    deviled egg salad, 137
    goat cheese, with sesame seeds, 137
    labne, with paprika and ginger, 134
    tahini and olive, with mint and sumac, 137
    tuna and caper, 137
    walnut-scallion, with coriander and turmeric, 137
  paella fried rice with scallions and, 93
  scrambled, with cured salmon, 145
  shakshuka, 130–33
    green, with cumin and caraway, 133
    with halloumi and pistachios, 133
    Italian sausage, with pimentón and cinnamon, 133
    squashuka, 133
    tomato and pepper pizzas with sunny-side-up eggs, 133
    tomato and pepper, with coriander and paprika, 130

Farro:
  farrotto with feta, 97
  master spice blend for cooking water, 85
  with toasted noodles, 98–101
    bacon and onion, with ajowan, 101
    farro salad with tomatoes, olives, and feta, 101
    savory minted farro, 98
    savory pan-fried farro cakes with goat cheese and cilantro, 101
    tomato basil, with oregano, 101
Fennel (bulb):
  savory and Aleppo pepper roasted fish with cherry tomatoes and, 154
  skillet-braised, 50–53
    caramelized fennel salad with pecorino, green olives, and almonds, 53
    coconut milk–glazed, with turmeric and mint, 53
    with gremolata, 53
    vegan fennel "aioli," 53
    white wine–braised, with dried cranberries, 53
    with citrus, caraway, and celery seeds, 50
Feta:
  baked white beans with spiced panko bread crumbs and, 121
  eggplant and olive baked penne with, 89
  farro salad with tomatoes, olives, and, 101
  farrotto with, 97
  feta-stuffed meatballs with green olives, 201

(Feta, continued)
 pink pepper roasted vegetable salad with olives and, 57
 sautéed spinach and arugula with chicken and, 153
 vegetable and feta cheese quiche, 129
 zucchini and arugula frittata with oregano and, 126
Figs, pomegranate-glazed roasted chicken with, 189
Fish:
 about, 141
 chraime (seafood in tomato sauce), 158–61
 cod simmered in turmeric-coriander tomato sauce, 158
 grilled tomato toasts with anchovies and sardines, 161
 fish cakes with fennel seeds, 173
 master spice blends for, 141
 poached salmon, 146–49
 basil and garlic poached, 146
 butter-poached, with capers and green peppercorns, 149
 cream-poached, with fennel seeds, 149
 flaked salmon salad with cornichons, 149
 soy-poached, with coconut broth and shiitakes, 149
 tomato-poached, with rosemary and Aleppo pepper, 149
 roasted whole, 154–57
 butter, with leeks, capers, and tarragon, 157
 with chimichurri, 157
 honey-vinegar-glazed, with star anise, 157
 savory and Aleppo pepper roasted, with fennel and cherry tomatoes, 154
 sesame-roasted, with olives and preserved lemon, 157
 tomato-roasted, with sweet and hot peppers, 157
 seared salmon, 150–53
 arugula salad with salmon and sesame and nigella seeds, 153
 chickpea flour–crusted, with savory and nutmeg, 153
 coriander-and-fennel-crusted, 150
 cornmeal-crusted, with fenugreek and sumac, 153
 salmon potato patties, 153
 soy-garlic, with limon omani, 153
 seared swordfish with orange-soy glaze, 165
 sugar-and-salt-cured salmon, 142–45
 dilled, with mustard and caraway seeds, 142
 juniper-and-orange-cured, 145
 salmon and scallion labne spread, 145
 scrambled eggs with, 145
 seed-crusted, 145
 sumac-and-Pernod-cured, with cilantro, cumin, and fennel, 145
 tuna:
 and arugula frittata with fresh lemon juice, 129
 and caper deviled eggs, 137
 olive oil–packed, spicy and smoky baked penne with, 89
Flatbreads, chickpea, 102–5
 cinnamon toast flatbreads, 105
 fennel and marjoram, with labne and onion, 105
 grated tomato, with poppy seeds, 105
 hummus rosemary, 105
 sesame sumac, with nigella seeds, 102
 zucchini, with caraway seeds, 105
French country vegetable soup with sage and thyme, 78
Frittata, baked, 126–29
 asparagus and artichoke, with fennel seeds, 129
 bacon, cremini mushroom, and spinach, 129

mini potato, olive, and bell pepper frittatas, 129
 roasted vegetable and Parmesan, 57
 tuna and arugula, with fresh lemon juice, 129
 vegetable and feta cheese quiche, 129
 zucchini and arugula, with feta and oregano, 126
Fritters, chickpea, with mint and cilantro, 117
Fruit, baked. See also Clafoutis; Specific fruits
 fruit crisp, 226–29
 berry jam bars, 229
 berry yogurt parfait with almond crispies, 229
 cardamom and ginger peach crisp, 229
 Dutch apple pie, 229
 ice cream sundaes with pineapple topping and spiced almond crunch, 229
 mixed berry, with sumac-anise almond topping, 226
 master spice blend for, 217

Garlic aioli with cumin and ginger, 246
Garlic knots, 109
Goat cheese:
 goat cheese, almond, and caper-stuffed roasted leg of lamb, 213
 goat cheese deviled eggs with sesame seeds, 137
 and herb olive oil loaf, savory, 221
 savory pan-fried farro cakes with cilantro and, 101
 and sweet potato gratin, 65
Grains, 31. See also Breads; Farro; Pasta; Rice
 farro with toasted noodles, 98–101
 master spice blend for cooking water, 85
 risotto, 94–97
 stovetop paella, 90–93
 wheat berry pilaf with raisins and almonds, 101
Grapes, chicken braised with carrots, rosé wine, and, 185
Gratin:
 potato, 62–65
 crunchy fried potato gratin cubes, 65
 Dijon-Gruyère, with basil and tarragon, 65
 rosemary and thyme, with bay leaves, 62
 tomato sauce gratin with marjoram and mozzarella, 65
 sweet potato and goat cheese, 65
 sweet potato and walnut, with melted Cheddar, 69
Greens. See also Arugula; Spinach
 green shakshuka with cumin and caraway, 133
 sautéed, master spice blend for, 49
Gremolata, braised fennel with, 53

Halloumi:
 creamy baked penne with, 89
 shakshuka with pistachios and, 133
Hazelnut chocolate babka with nutmeg, 109
Hummus:
 chicken tacos and sesame-mint salsa with, 189
 cumin and garlic, 117
 hummus rosemary flatbreads, 105

Ice cream brownie bites, 237
Ice cream sundaes with pineapple topping and spiced almond crunch, 229

Ketchup, master spice blend for, 250

Labne, 31
 creamy labne chicken soup with dill seeds, 193

fennel and marjoram flatbreads with onion and, 105
 labne deviled eggs with paprika and ginger, 134
 labne-tahini dressing, creamy slaw with, 73
 poppy seed labne dressing with caraway, 246
 salmon and scallion labne spread, 145
Lamb:
 leg of, roasted rolled, 210–13
 cocoa-chile roasted, 213
 goat cheese, almond, and caper-stuffed, 213
 lamb panini with Muenster, scallions, and pickles, 213
 rosemary and mint roasted, 210
 tomato and olive salad with lamb, herbs, and crunchy pita, 213
 walnut- and date-stuffed, with pomegranate glaze, 213
 rack of, roasted, 206–9
 curried, with butternut squash, 209
 fennel-and-coriander-crusted, with caramelized onions, 206
 with paprika, ginger, and caramelized carrots, 209
 sweet-and-sour pomegranate-glazed, 209
 tarragon, mint, and dill buttered, with shallots, 209
 tomato-glazed, with eggplant, 209
 rose and ginger lamb meatballs with black olives, 201
Leeks:
 butter roasted fish with capers, tarragon, and, 157
 chunky vegetable soup, 78–81
 creamy leek sauce, braised tarragon chicken in, 185
Legumes. See Beans; Chickpea(s); Lentil(s)
Lemon:
 and artichoke paella with pumpkin, 93
 preserved, cumin and cardamom chicken tajine with, 185
 preserved, sesame-roasted fish with olives and, 157
 and turmeric chickpea soup, 117
Lentil(s), 122–25
 carrot and tomato lentil soup with lemon yogurt, 125
 garlicky Le Puy lentils with mustard seeds, 122
 green lentil and jasmine rice soup with sautéed vegetables, 81
 lentil and carrot coconut curry, 125
 lentil veggie burgers with scallions and cilantro, 125
 salad, with cornichons and mustard vinaigrette, 125
 smoky, with garlic, bacon, and cinnamon, 125
Limon omani quick pickles, 247

Master spice blends:
 about, 37–38, 244
 for baked goods and desserts, 217, 249
 for breakfast, 249
 for condiments, 250
 for drinks, 248
 for eggs, 113
 for foundations, 250
 for grain and pasta cooking water, 85
 for meat and poultry, 177
 for sauces, 250
 for seafood, 141
 for snacks, 249
 for vegetables, 49
Mayonnaise, master spice blend for, 250
Meat and poultry, 174–213. See also Beef; Chicken; Lamb; Pork; Sausage
 about, 177

braised chicken thighs, 182–85
 braised short ribs, 202–5
 glazed seared chicken breasts, 178–81
 master spice blends for, 177
 oven-roasted chicken breasts, 190–93
 oven-roasted meatballs, 198–201
 quick-seared pork chops, 194–97
 roasted butterflied chicken, 186–89
 roasted rack of lamb, 206–9
 roasted rolled leg of lamb, 210–13
Meatballs, oven-roasted, 198–201
 crunchy Parmesan meatballs, 201
 feta-stuffed, with green olives, 201
 garlic and oregano, spicy, with blistered grape tomatoes, 198
 quick tomato meat sauce, 201
 rose and ginger lamb meatballs with black olives, 201
 tahini-parsley, with paprika, 201
Mocha black pepper brownies with pecans and walnuts, 237
Muffins:
 chocolate chip–banana mini muffins, 225
 master spice blend for, 217
Mushrooms:
 bacon, cremini mushroom, and spinach frittata, 129
 mushroom and rosemary braised white beans with charred spinach, 121
 red wine and mushroom braised chicken with caraway and allspice, 185
 red wine and mushroom risotto with marjoram and mint, 97
 sesame-shiitake chicken soup with galangal, 193
 shiitake cream sauce, chicken breasts with, 181
 soy-poached salmon with coconut broth and shiitakes, 149
Mussels:
 chorizo and seafood paella with saffron and fennel, 93
 chraime with clams, shrimp, and, 161
 steamed, 166–69
 with bacon and cabbage, 169
 beer-steamed, with thyme and caraway, 169
 coconut milk–steamed, with Thai chiles and lemongrass, 169
 with limon omani and bay leaves, 166
 Spanish-style pickled mussels with coriander and pimentón, 169
 vermouth-steamed, with lemon verbena, sage, and ginger, 169
Mustard:
 Dijon-Gruyère potato gratin with basil and tarragon, 65
 Dijon mustard–crusted pork chops with rosemary, 197
 honey-Dijon glazed chicken breasts, 181
 master spice blend for, 250
 mustard vinaigrette, 246
 lentil salad with cornichons and, 125

Noodles. See also Pasta
 toasted, farro with, 98–101
Nuts, 31. See also Specific types
 master spice blend for, 249
 mixed, cardamom olive oil Bundt cake with dried fruit and, 221

Olive oil, 30
 master spice blend for, 250
 olive oil cake, 218–21
 cardamom olive oil Bundt cake with dried fruit and mixed nuts, 221
 ginger, with fennel seeds and black pepper, 218
 glazed cocoa and orange blossom Bundt cake, 221
 savory goat cheese and herb olive oil loaf, 221

seed and grain olive oil loaf, 221
zucchini bread with walnuts and thyme, 221
olive oil deviled eggs, 134–37
deviled egg salad, 137
goat cheese, with sesame seeds, 137
labne, with paprika and ginger, 134
tahini and olive, with mint and sumac, 137
tuna and caper, 137
walnut-scallion, with coriander and turmeric, 137
Olives, 30–31
black, rose and ginger lamb meatballs with, 201
eggplant and olive baked penne with feta, 89
farro salad with tomatoes, feta, and, 101
green, caramelized fennel salad with pecorino, almonds, and, 53
green, feta-stuffed meatballs with, 201
mini potato, olive, and bell pepper frittatas, 129
pink pepper roasted vegetable salad with feta and, 57
seared oregano-turmeric shrimp with, 165
sesame-roasted fish with preserved lemon and, 157
shrimp, olive, and tomato penne, 161
tahini and olive deviled eggs with mint and sumac, 137
tomato and olive salad with lamb, herbs, and crunchy pita, 213
Onions, caramelized, fennel-and-coriander-crusted rack of lamb with, 206

Paella, stovetop, 90–93
chicken, with red and green peppers, 93
chorizo and seafood, with saffron and fennel, 93
lemon and artichoke, with pumpkin, 93
paella fried rice with scallions and eggs, 93
savory pan-fried paella cake, 93
summer harvest, with saffron and coriander, 90
Pancetta and apple, seared scallops with, 165
Panini, lamb, with Muenster, scallions, and pickles, 213
Parmesan and roasted vegetable frittata, 57
Pasta, 85
baked penne, 86–89
creamy, with halloumi, 89
eggplant and olive, with feta, 89
garlic and tomato, with rosemary and oregano, 86
with sautéed Italian sausage, 89
spicy and smoky, with olive oil–packed tuna, 89
carrot pasta with poppy seeds, 77
master spice blend for cooking water, 85
shrimp, olive, and tomato penne, 161
Pea, asparagus, and herb risotto with green peppercorns, 97
Peach crisp, with cardamom and ginger, 229
Peanut butter and jelly sandwich cookies, 233
Peanut satay sauce, pork chops with, 197
Pear and chocolate clafoutis with rose-scented custard, 241
Pecans:
mocha black pepper brownies with pecans and, 237
pecan banana bread with Sichuan peppercorns and nigella seeds, 225
Pecorino, caramelized fennel salad with green olives, almonds, and, 53
Penne:
baked, 86–89
creamy, with halloumi, 89
eggplant and olive, with feta, 89

garlic and tomato, with rosemary and oregano, 86
with sautéed Italian sausage, 89
spicy and smoky, with olive oil–packed tuna, 89
shrimp, olive, and tomato, 161
Peppers:
mini potato, olive, and bell pepper frittatas, 129
red and green, chicken paella with, 93
shakshuka:
green, with cumin and caraway, 133
with halloumi and pistachios, 133
Italian sausage, with pimentón and cinnamon, 133
squashuka, 133
tomato and pepper pizzas with sunny-side-up eggs, 133
tomato and pepper, with coriander and paprika, 130
summer harvest paella with saffron and coriander, 90
sweet and hot, tomato-roasted fish with, 157
Pickles:
coriander and fennel pickled raisins, 247
limon omani quick pickles, 247
Spanish-style pickled mussels with coriander and pimentón, 169
Pie:
apple custard, 241
Dutch apple, 229
Pilaf, wheat berry, with raisins and almonds, 101
Pineapple:
pork and pineapple salad with honey-lime dressing, 197
topping, ice cream sundaes with spiced almond crunch and, 229
Pistachio(s):
and cherry clafoutis with chamomile, 241
crushed roasted potatoes with, 61
shakshuka with halloumi and, 133
Pizzas, tomato and pepper, with sunny-side-up eggs, 133
Pork:
quick-seared pork chops, 194–97
brown sugar–seared, with orange glaze, 194
cider vinegar–glazed, with apples and raisins, 197
crumb-crusted smoky pork chops with apple glaze, 197
Dijon mustard–crusted, with rosemary, 197
with peanut satay sauce, 197
pork and pineapple salad with honey-lime dressing, 197
Potato(es):
gratin, 62–65
crunchy fried potato gratin cubes, 65
Dijon-Gruyère, with basil and tarragon, 65
rosemary and thyme, with bay leaves, 62
sweet potato and cheese, 65
tomato sauce gratin with marjoram and mozzarella, 65
mini potato, olive, and bell pepper frittatas, 129
pan-roasted, 58–61
creamy herbed mashed potatoes, 61
crispy duck fat potatoes, 61
crispy herbed skillet-fried potatoes, 58
crushed roasted potatoes with pistachios, 61
potato salad with bacon, nigella, and lime, 61
saffron and coriander crusted, spicy, 61
salmon potato patties, 153
short rib and potato hash cakes, 205
Pound cake, master spice blend for, 217
Prosciutto and sesame roasted vegetables with fenugreek, 57

Prune and apple crème fraîche clafoutis with nutmeg and allspice, 238
Pumpkin, lemon and artichoke paella with, 93

Quiche, vegetable and feta cheese, 129

Raisins:
and apples, cider vinegar–glazed pork chops with, 197
chickpea salad with orange, celery, and, 117
coriander and fennel pickled, 247
raisin walnut challah with cinnamon, 109
wheat berry pilaf with almonds and, 101
Rice:
green lentil and jasmine rice soup with sautéed vegetables, 81
master spice blend for cooking water, 85
risotto, 94–97
stovetop paella, 90–93
chicken, with red and green peppers, 93
chorizo and seafood, with saffron and fennel, 93
lemon and artichoke, with pumpkin, 93
paella fried rice with scallions and eggs, 93
savory pan-fried paella cake, 93
summer harvest, with saffron and coriander, 90
Risotto, 94–97
arancini (crunchy fried risotto balls), 97
farrotto with feta, 97
pea, asparagus, and herb risotto with green peppercorns, 97
red wine and mushroom, with marjoram and mint, 97
rosemary and garlic, with mascarpone and Parmesan, 94
tomato-saffron, with turmeric, 97

Salad(s):
arugula, with salmon and sesame and nigella seeds, 153
cabbage and apple slaw with carrots, 70–73
with anise seeds and tangy tamarind dressing, 73
cabbage, carrot, and apple sauté with mustard seeds, 73
creamy, with labne-tahini dressing, 73
sesame-lime, with ginger, 73
spicy, with poppy and mustard seeds, 70
caramelized fennel, with pecorino, green olives, and almonds, 53
chicken, with black beans and cilantro, 181
chickpea, with raisins, orange, and celery, 117
deviled egg salad, 137
farro, with tomatoes, olives, and feta, 101
flaked salmon salad with cornichons, 149
lentil, with cornichons and mustard vinaigrette, 125
pink pepper roasted vegetable salad with feta and olives, 57
pork and pineapple, with honey-lime dressing, 197
potato, with bacon, nigella, and lime, 61
tomato and olive, with lamb, herbs, and crunchy pita, 213
Salad dressings. See also Salad(s)
master spice blend for, 49
mustard vinaigrette, 246
poppy seed labne dressing with caraway, 246
Salmon:
master spice blends for, 141
poached, 146–49
basil and garlic poached, 146
butter-poached, with capers and green peppercorns, 149
cream-poached, with fennel seeds, 149

flaked salmon salad with cornichons, 149
soy-poached, with coconut broth and shiitakes, 149
tomato-poached, with rosemary and Aleppo pepper, 149
seared, 150–53
arugula salad with sesame, nigella seeds, and, 153
chickpea flour–crusted, with savory and nutmeg, 153
coriander-and-fennel crusted, 150
cornmeal-crusted, with fenugreek and sumac, 153
salmon potato patties, 153
soy-garlic, with limon omani, 153
sugar-and-salt-cured, 142–45
dilled, with mustard and caraway seeds, 142
juniper-and-orange-cured, 145
salmon and scallion labne spread, 145
scrambled eggs with, 145
seed-crusted, 145
sumac-and-Pernod-cured, with cilantro, cumin, and fennel, 145
Salt, 30
master spice blend for, 250
Sandwich cookies:
bittersweet chocolate, 233
dulce de leche (alfajores), 233
peanut butter and jelly, 233
Sardines and anchovies, grilled tomato toasts with, 161
Sauces:
master spice blends for, 250
quick tomato meat sauce, 201
tahini sauce, 247
vegan fennel "aioli," 53
Sausage:
chorizo and seafood paella with saffron and fennel, 93
chorizo crab cakes with cumin and turmeric, 173
crispy chorizo, smoky carrot soup with cinnamon and, 77
Italian sausage shakshuka with pimentón and cinnamon, 133
Italian, sautéed, baked penne with, 89
Scallops:
seared, with pancetta and apple, 165
thyme-seared, with capers and lemon, 162
Seafood, 138–73. See also Fish; Shellfish; specific types
about, 141
chorizo and seafood paella with saffron and fennel, 93
chraime: seafood in tomato sauce, 158–61
crab cakes, 170–73
master spice blends for, 141
poached salmon, 146–49
roasted whole fish, 154–57
seared salmon, 150–53
seared, with pan sauce, 162–65
steamed mussels, 166–69
sugar-and-salt-cured salmon, 142–45
Seed and grain olive oil loaf, 221
Shakshuka, 130–33
green, with cumin and caraway, 133
with halloumi and pistachios, 133
Italian sausage, with pimentón and cinnamon, 133
squashuka, 133
tomato and pepper pizzas with sunny-side-up eggs, 133
tomato and pepper, with coriander and paprika, 130
Shellfish:
about, 141
chorizo and seafood paella with saffron and fennel, 93
chraime: seafood in tomato sauce:
with clams, mussels, and shrimp, 161
shrimp, olive, and tomato penne, 161

(Shellfish, continued)
crab cakes, 170–73
chipotle corn and crab cakes, 173
chorizo, with cumin and turmeric, 173
with sesame seeds and Aleppo pepper, 170
zucchini, with corn bread crust, 173
master spice blend for, 141
seared, with pan sauce, 162–65
oregano-turmeric shrimp with olives, 165
scallops with pancetta and apple, 165
thyme-seared scallops with capers and lemon, 162
za'atar shrimp in tomato-caper sauce, 165
steamed mussels, 166–69
with bacon and cabbage, 169
beer-steamed, with thyme and caraway, 169
coconut milk–steamed, with Thai chiles and lemongrass, 169
Spanish-style pickled mussels with coriander and pimentón, 169
vermouth-steamed, with lemon verbena, sage, and ginger, 169
with limon omani and bay leaves, 166
Shiitake mushrooms. See Mushrooms
Shortbread, 230–33
alfajores (dulce de leche sandwich cookies), 233
bittersweet chocolate shortbread sandwiches, 233
cocoa-sesame, with Urfa and allspice, 233
coconut, with coriander and lemongrass, 233
peanut butter and jelly sandwich cookies, 233
poppy seed, with ginger and nutmeg, 230
Short ribs, braised, 202–5
carrot juice–braised, with sweet potatoes, 205
chili-and-tomato-braised, with cinnamon, 205
citrus-braised, with star anise and cocoa, 202
red wine–braised, with black pepper and yellow mustard, 205
short rib and potato hash cakes, 205
vermouth-braised, with warm spices and dried fruit, 205
Shrimp:
chorizo and seafood paella with saffron and fennel, 93
chraime with clams, mussels, and, 161
master spice blend for, 141
oregano-turmeric shrimp with olives, 165
shrimp, olive, and tomato penne, 161
za'atar shrimp in tomato-caper sauce, 165
Slaw, cabbage and apple, with carrots, 70–73
with anise seeds and tangy tamarind dressing, 73
cabbage, carrot, and apple sauté with mustard seeds, 73
creamy, with labne-tahini dressing, 73
sesame-lime, with ginger, 73
spicy, with poppy and mustard seeds, 70
Snacks, master spice blends for, 249
Soup:
carrot and tomato lentil soup with lemon yogurt, 125
carrot, creamy, 74–77
carrot pasta with poppy seeds, 77
chunky turmeric carrot soup with lime leaves, 77
creamy tomato-carrot soup with basil, fennel, and oregano, 77
curried coconut carrot soup with green peppercorns, 77
smoky, with cinnamon and crispy chorizo, 77
smoky, with cumin and chipotle, 74

chicken and white bean, with turmeric and amchoor, 189
lemon and turmeric chickpea soup, 117
oven-roasted chicken soup, 190–93
coconut-cilantro, with lemongrass, 193
labne chicken, creamy, with dill seeds, 193
limon omani roasted, with celery seeds, 190
sesame-shiitake, with galangal, 193
tomato-basil, with ancho and cumin, 193
two-bean, with chicken and cilantro, 193
vegetable, chunky, 78–81
black bean and tomato tortilla soup, 81
comforting and quick chicken soup, 81
creamy vegetable soup, 81
French country, with sage and thyme, 78
green lentil and jasmine rice soup with sautéed vegetables, 81
turmeric and coconut, with ginger and cardamom, 81
Spanish-style pickled mussels with coriander and pimentón, 169
Spice basics, 16–17, 37–38. See also Master spice blends
Spinach:
and arugula, sautéed, with chicken and feta, 189
bacon, cremini mushroom, and spinach frittata, 129
charred, braised white beans with, 118–21
bacon-and-cider-braised beans, 121
baked white beans with feta and spiced panko bread crumbs, 121
mushroom and rosemary braised white beans with charred spinach, 121
tomato-and-spinach-braised beans with Aleppo and ginger, 121
Tunisian braised white beans with charred spinach, fennel, and cumin, 118
white bean spread with walnuts and yogurt, 121
green shakshuka with cumin and caraway, 133
Squash. See Winter squash; Zucchini
Squashuka, 133
Squid:
seared calamari with vermouth sauce, 165
stuffed, in tomato sauce, 161
Sugar, master spice blend for, 250
Sweet potato(es):
carrot juice–braised short ribs with, 205
and goat cheese gratin, 65
puree, 66–69
with cumin and caraway, 66
gingery double apple sweet potato puree, 69
pomegranate, with anise, cardamom, and mustard seeds, 69
sweet potato and walnut gratin with melted Cheddar, 69
sweet potato croquettes, 69
sweet potato dip with pepitas and jalapeños, 69
roasted mixed vegetables, 54–57
Swordfish, seared, with orange-soy glaze, 165

Tacos, chicken, with hummus and sesame-mint salsa, 189
Tahini. See also Hummus
labne-tahini dressing, creamy slaw with, 73
and olive deviled eggs with mint and sumac, 137
tahini-parsley meatballs with paprika, 201
tahini sauce, 247
Tajine, cumin and cardamom chicken, with preserved lemon, 185
Thai chiles, coconut milk–steamed mussels with lemongrass and, 169

Toasts, grilled tomato, with anchovies and sardines, 161
Tomato(es), 30
balsamic chicken with sautéed cherry tomatoes, 181
and black bean tortilla soup, 81
blistered grape tomatoes, spicy garlic and oregano meatballs with, 198
carrot and tomato lentil soup with lemon yogurt, 125
cherry tomatoes, savory and Aleppo pepper roasted fish with fennel and, 154
chili-and-tomato-braised ribs with cinnamon, 205
farro salad with olives, feta, and, 101
garlic and tomato baked penne with rosemary and oregano, 86
grated tomato flatbreads with poppy seeds, 105
and olive salad with lamb, herbs, and crunchy pita, 213
quick tomato meat sauce, 201
sauce, master spice blend for, 250
sauce, seafood in (chraime), 158–61
with clams, mussels, and shrimp, 161
cod simmered in turmeric-coriander tomato sauce, 158
grilled tomato toasts with anchovies and sardines, 161
shrimp, olive, and tomato penne, 161
stuffed squid in tomato sauce, 161
shakshuka, 130–33
green, with cumin and caraway, 133
with halloumi and pistachios, 133
Italian sausage, with pimentón and cinnamon, 133
tomato and pepper pizzas with sunny-side-up eggs, 133
tomato and pepper, with coriander and paprika, 130
and spinach braised beans with Aleppo and ginger, 121
tomato-basil chicken soup with ancho and cumin, 193
tomato and basil farro with oregano, 101
tomato-caper sauce, za'atar shrimp in, 165
tomato-carrot soup, creamy, with basil, fennel, and oregano, 77
tomato-glazed rack of lamb with eggplant, 209
tomato-poached salmon with rosemary and Aleppo pepper, 149
tomato-roasted fish with sweet and hot peppers, 157
tomato-saffron risotto with turmeric, 97
tomato sauce potato gratin with marjoram and mozzarella, 65
Tortilla soup, black bean and tomato, 81
Tuna:
and arugula frittata with fresh lemon juice, 129
and caper deviled eggs, 137
olive oil–packed, spicy and smoky baked penne with, 89
Tunisian braised white beans with charred spinach, fennel, and cumin, 118

Vegetables, 46–81. See also specific vegetables
about, 49
cabbage and apple slaw with carrots, 70–73
chunky vegetable soup, 78–81
creamy carrot soup, 74–77
master spice blends for, 49, 250
pan-roasted potatoes, 58–61
roasted mixed vegetables, 54–57
juniper-rosemary, with dried fruits and almond, 57
pink pepper roasted vegetable salad with feta and olives, 57

roasted vegetable and Parmesan frittata, 57
sesame and prosciutto roasted, with fenugreek, 57
sumac roasted, with fennel seeds, 54
tarragon roasted, with citrus and mustard seeds, 57
skillet-braised fennel, 50–53
sweet potato puree, 66–69
vegetable and feta cheese quiche, 129
Veggie burgers, lentil, with scallions and cilantro, 125
Vinaigrette:
master spice blend for, 49
mustard vinaigrette, 246

Walnuts:
mocha black pepper brownies with walnuts and, 237
raisin walnut challah with cinnamon, 109
sweet potato and walnut gratin with melted Cheddar, 69
walnut- and date-stuffed leg of lamb with pomegranate glaze, 213
walnut-scallion deviled eggs with coriander and turmeric, 137
white bean spread with yogurt and, 121
zucchini bread with thyme and, 221
Wheat berry pilaf with raisins and almonds, 101
Winter squash:
curried rack of lamb with butternut squash, 209
lemon and artichoke paella with pumpkin, 93
squashuka, 133

Yogurt:
berry yogurt parfait with almond crispies, 229
lemon, carrot and tomato lentil soup with, 125
master spice blend for, 249
white bean spread with walnuts and, 121
yogurt challah, 106–9
garlic knots, 109
golden turmeric, with nigella seeds, 106
hazelnut chocolate babka with nutmeg, 109
raisin walnut, with cinnamon, 109
sandwich loaves, 109
smoky Cheddar, with pepitas, 109

Zucchini:
and arugula frittata with feta and oregano, 126
bread, with walnuts and thyme, 221
flatbreads, with caraway seeds, 105
summer harvest paella with saffron and coriander, 90
zucchini crab cakes with corn bread crust, 173

ACKNOWLEDGMENTS

Cooking is an act of sharing love with others. I have been and still am fortunate to share many tasty memories with so many people around the world. This book would not have been possible without the huge love and support that I have received over the years. It is a result of many hours, days, and years of fun (and less fun) moments behind the stove and in markets, and endless spicy and tasty moments.

I would like to thank all those who helped me and believed in me (and those who did not). This book is one chapter of an ongoing culinary journey that I hope will never end.

Thank you to my wife, Lisa, for being part of this amazing life; my boys, Luca and Lennon (aka the spice brothers), for making me smile every single moment; my parents, Ayala and Moshe, for never saying no to my ideas and wishes; my sisters, Shelly and Iris, and their families; my in-laws, Susan and Gary Fisher, for their support; the incredible team at La Boîte, without whom nothing happens; Amanda and Joe from The Villa at Saugerties for hosting us every time; Thomas Schauer and Sahinaz Agamola Schauer for the fantastic photography; Genevieve Ko for her magical writing; thoughtmatter for the design; Raquel Pelzel for getting me to do this book and for her editing; and Aaron Wehner, Doris Cooper, and the whole Clarkson Potter team. Also, to Gil Franck and Oded Sroka, who took a chance on me and put me on the right track; Eric Ripert for his friendship and inspiration; Daniel Boulud and Olivier Roellinger for mentoring me; Apollonia Poìlâne for sharing many gourmand moments; Jeremy Flowers, David Malbequi, Helen Park, Julie and Fredrick Rosenberg, Ronit Vered, Russell Robinson, Efi Naon, Michael Solomonov, Jennifer Carroll, Paul Kahan, Michelle Bernstein, Brad Farmerie, Robert Fedorko and the Nestlé culinary team; David Chang; Justin Smilie; and Bertrand Chemel. I owe a debt of gratitude to all those who have made food a global language.

To all those I forgot but wanted to mention, thank you.

For the love of spices,

Lior Lev Sercarz

I am so grateful to Lior for bringing me on this spice journey. Thank you for sharing your spice knowledge and life. I'm grateful to Lisa, Luca, and Lennon for welcoming me into your home. Christian was a great partner at La Boîte. The photo team was incomparable, as was the hospitality of Amanda and Joe for letting us shoot at their stunning Villa at Saugerties. A big thank-you to Mitchell Barr for help with recipe testing. Thank you to Raquel for being a wonderful editor and to every partner at Clarkson Potter and the design studio.

Genevieve Ko

CONTRIBUTORS

Joe Moseley and Amanda Zaslow are the creators and owners of The Villa at Saugerties, a luxury bed-and-breakfast in New York's Hudson Valley. Inspired by the hospitality they experienced while honeymooning in Spain, Joe left his job at Food Network and Amanda resigned from her Manhattan interior design firm to fulfill their dream of opening their own property. With their combined talents in cooking and design, they've built a modern, Mediterranean-inspired oasis where they serve their guests handmade meals in the idyllic countryside.

Thomas Schauer is a world-renowned food photographer and commercial director with over twenty years in the business. Born and raised in Austria, Thomas completed his master's certificate in photography at the most prestigious photography school in the country. He now runs photography and film studios in both Vienna and New York City. He has shot cookbooks for some of the best chefs in the world, including Dominique Ansel and Daniel Boulud, and has created the visual campaigns for leading multinational food companies.

Genevieve Ko is a food writer, recipe developer, and culinary consultant, and the cooking editor for the *Los Angeles Times*. She is the author of *Better Baking* and has collaborated on more than a dozen books with renowned chefs. A native Californian, Genevieve went east to attend Yale University and moved on to New York City to work as a food editor, contributing to national media outlets, including the *New York Times, Better Homes & Gardens,* and *Food & Wine*.

FOR THE LOVE OF SPICES